Finance with a Purpose

FinTech, Development and Financial Inclusion in the Global Economy

Transformations in Banking, Finance and Regulation

Print ISSN: 2752-5821
Online ISSN: 2752-583X

Series Editors: Sabri Boubaker
(*EM Normandie Business School, France & Swansea University, UK*)
Duc Khuong Nguyen
(*IPAG Business School, France*)

Presently, the banking and finance sectors evolve within a globalized and highly uncertain environment. Each business and financial decision requires careful consideration of country-specific and international factors due to high levels of shock transmission and volatility spillovers. Furthermore, it would be remiss to omit the COVID-19 health crisis, which caused harmful effects to all areas of the real economy and made profound changes in the way our firms, economies, and markets used to function.

Many other already well-known aspects, including the repercussions of quantitative easing policies, disruptive technologies in finance (e.g., FinTech, Big Data, Data Analytics, Artificial Intelligence, and Blockchains), as well as innovative financing instruments for startups (e.g., ICOs and crowdfunding) are currently revolutionizing banking and finance and posing numerous challenges to regulatory bodies and policymakers. Climate change emergencies also put pressure on governments and firms worldwide to improve policy on governance, corporate social responsibility, and sustainability practices.

This book series "Transformations in Banking, Finance, and Regulation" attempts to address these issues by focusing on transformative perspectives in banking and finance. Accordingly, it provides evidence-based guidance, recommendations, and pathways to assist businesses and policy decision-makers through an interdisciplinary and in-depth understanding of ongoing changes in the behavior of economic agents.

Published

Transformations in Banking, Finance and Regulation

Volume 3

Finance with a Purpose

FinTech, Development and Financial Inclusion in the Global Economy

FREDERIC DE MARIZ

Columbia University, USA

World Scientific

NEW JERSEY · LONDON · SINGAPORE · BEIJING · SHANGHAI · HONG KONG · TAIPEI · CHENNAI · TOKYO

Published by

World Scientific Publishing Europe Ltd.

57 Shelton Street, Covent Garden, London WC2H 9HE

Head office: 5 Toh Tuck Link, Singapore 596224

USA office: 27 Warren Street, Suite 401-402, Hackensack, NJ 07601

Library of Congress Cataloging-in-Publication Data

Names: De Mariz, Frederic, author.
Title: Finance with a purpose : fintech, development and financial inclusion in the
    global economy / Frederic de Mariz, Columbia University, USA.
Description: New Jersey : World Scientific, [2022] | Series: Transformations in banking,
    finance and regulation, 2752-5821 ; vol. 3 | Includes bibliographical references and index.
Identifiers: LCCN 2022008147 | ISBN 9781800612198 (hardcover) |
    ISBN 9781800612204 (ebook) | ISBN 9781800612211 (ebook other)
Subjects: LCSH: Finance--Technological innovations. | Financial services industry.
Classification: LCC HG173 .D386 2022 | DDC 332--dc23/eng/20220223
LC record available at https://lccn.loc.gov/2022008147

British Library Cataloguing-in-Publication Data
A catalogue record for this book is available from the British Library.

The views expressed in this book by the author do not represent in any way views of UBS.

First published 2022 (hardcover)
Reprinted 2025 (in paperback edition)
ISBN 9781800618442 (pbk)

For any available supplementary material, please visit
https://www.worldscientific.com/worldscibooks/10.1142/Q0359#t=suppl

Desk Editors: Balasubramanian Shanmugam/Adam Binnie/Shi Ying Koe

Typeset by Stallion Press
Email: enquiries@stallionpress.com

About the Author

Frederic de Mariz is Adjunct Professor at Columbia University in Innovative Finance and Impact Investing, Lecturer at Sciences Po in Sustainable Finance, and Head of FinTech and ESG for Latin America at UBS Investment Bank. He is a member of the Brazilian banking association and a former advisor to microfinance institutions. Prior to his role in investment banking, he was a senior equity research analyst and received numerous awards from independent organizations, such as Institutional Investors or Starmine. He has published a number of academic papers in renowned peer-reviewed journals (*Journal of Private Equity, Journal of Risk and Financial Management, French Politics, Culture & Society,* etc.) and co-authored several books on sustainable finance. He won a Farsight Award for his research on microfinance in 2011. Frederic graduated from Sorbonne with a Master's in History, Columbia University, with a Master's in Economic Policy, Sciences Po, with a Master's in Public Policy, ESSEC, with an MBA, and completed his PhD in Finance at University of São Paulo with a thesis on payments and financial inclusion.

Contents

Introduction: Financial Disruption with a Purpose

From vehicles to music, from power generation to retail, every aspect of our daily routine has experienced drastic changes in the recent past, driven by secular forces such as digitization, a growing focus on sustainability, regulatory changes and evolving consumer behavior, further accelerated by the Great Lockdown. Financial services are no exception. A change in paradigm is at play in the financial sector, with a surge in competition from non-traditional actors, a revolution in customer experience evidenced by rising transparency and customer-centric strategies. FinTech is defined as "technologically-enabled financial innovation that could result in new business models, applications, processes, or products, with an associated material effect on financial markets and institutions and the provision of financial services."[1]

Offering extra convenience and lower prices is of course welcome, but it is only one side of the story. The ongoing disruption bears the unique promise to include more citizens in a sustainable way by giving them quality access to financial services, including payments and transfers, credit, savings, asset management and insurance.

This book is the result of close to 20 years of observation of financial services and financial inclusion, mostly in emerging markets.

---

[1]Financial Stability Board (2017). Artificial intelligence and machine learning in financial services: Market developments and financial stability implications. 1 November 2017, p. 35.

Financial services in emerging markets are marked by low — albeit improving — levels of inclusion, high prices for customers and an overall dismal customer experience. The flip side for banks includes record volatility in political and macroeconomic conditions, high informality, ingenious frauds schemes and physical violence. To paraphrase Brazilian singer and composer Tom Jobim, emerging markets are not for beginners. But it would be a mistake to think that the disruption is only taking place in developing countries. Financial inclusion has become a central policy consideration in richer countries also, with a meaningful number of households excluded from formal financial tracks following the Great Financial Crisis of 2008.

This book tells the story of entrepreneurs, capitalists, researchers and regulators who are building the financial services of tomorrow and the mechanisms that will allow us as a society to fulfill the promise of inclusion. Their experiences complement and illustrate the latest academic knowledge on the matter. This work combines the theory in the fields of economics, finance and law with the practice of financial institutions, corporates, households and investors. When FinTech enables the purpose of inclusion, it can have the largest impact, simplify the financial journey of citizens and offer access for the largest number so that they can reach their potential. Financial services can be a powerful driver of prosperity and security for all.

The book tries to answer one simple question: how can the financial industry globally be better programmed to allow economic agents to get access to the right financial opportunities and fulfill their potential, and therefore unlock development?

About 1.7 billion adults globally remain left out of the financial sector, without an account at a financial institution or through a mobile money provider. 300 million adults have been included since 2014, when the figure was 2 billion. Globally, 69% of adults have an account, up from 62% in 2014 and 51% in 2011. Account ownership varies among economies and by individual characteristics like gender, age, education and income.[2]

The challenge is huge for policymakers and businesses, mirroring an equally large opportunity to improve well-being and lift

---

[2]Demirgüç-Kunt *et al.* (2018). *The Global Findex Database 2017: Measuring Financial Inclusion and the FinTech Revolution.* World Bank, April.

development levels. This book is not a report on the end of banks, but rather a careful analysis of the historic transformation of financial services within and outside of the changing boundaries of traditional banks. The power of creative destruction — especially in financial services — can transform capitalism and be a formidable source of sustainable and inclusive prosperity.[3]

We embark on a journey to make financial services more inclusive and accessible through technology. The benefits of inclusion are considerable and a link between inclusion and development has long been demonstrated. That said, this relationship is not linear and can bear risks, especially in case of excess growth, poor oversight and limited financial education.

Microcredit – the provision of small amounts of credit — is especially dedicated to the bottom of the pyramid and micro- and small-sized enterprises. The segment met with global fame in 2006 when the Nobel Peace Prize was awarded to Professor Yunus for his leading work in group microcredit at Grameen Bank in Bangladesh. 15 years later, microcredit has gone through cycles, experiencing crises and maturing to incorporate other products along with credit. Microcredit has shed the light on the social role of finance and the creditworthiness of previously excluded citizens.

While microcredit has gained global fame, electronic payments represent the entry point of financial inclusion. Regulators have coordinated efforts to reduce the reliance on cash in order to reduce friction in payments, fight money laundering, and enhance the effectiveness of the monetary policy. Cashless economies are not quite in sight yet, despite the tremendous growth in electronic payments, boosted in particular by the Great Lockdown. Electronic payments have morphed from the plastic card to include virtual cards, quick response (QR) codes and peer-to-peer transfers.

The sector of payments illustrates the rapid evolution experienced by finance in the past few years, impacting simple acts such as payments, or unquestioned aspects of our routine like currencies. The distributed ledger technology, also improperly referred to as blockchain, has led to innovations in financial services, mostly in registration,

---

[3]Aghion *et al.* (2021). *The Power of Creative Destruction*. Belknap Harvard, pages 58 and 73.

trading, and cryptocurrencies. We revisit the classic role of currencies, in light of those changes and the use case for blockchain in Central Bank Digital Currency.

While blockchain leads us to question the role of currencies, platform banking also triggers a reinvention of the provision of financial services. With payments being the first step for inclusion and disruption, financial institutions have offered a growing set of services, sometimes exceeding the traditional boundaries of financial services. The rise of "super apps" and the idea that customers can rely on platforms for most of their needs — from e-commerce to food delivery to financial services — has met particular interest in China and Latin America.

Those disruptions have been based on the wider exchange of customer data. Open banking best symbolizes the new customer-centric approach experienced by several industries. While open banking was first idealized in 2013, it has expanded to the majority of large economies and allows customers to be known from day one by financial providers and reduce asymmetries of information. Open banking is an essential tool to modernize banks and increase competition, but it bears the challenge of interoperability. Information sharing puts the spotlight on financial market infrastructure, which allows an exchange that is both safe and transparent.

Digitization has allowed to simplify access and reduce cost, leading to drastic cuts in physical network of bank branches and staff reduction. While banks have relied on non-branch channels to offer their services for decades, such as banking correspondents, this time creates a disruption for branches, leading to the reinvention of their role, with a corollary of branch closures impacting employment, commercial real estate and the relationship with customers.

With the reinvention of client services without branches, digitization also elevates data as the most valuable asset for financial institutions. Data — properly assessed — play a key role to reduce asymmetries of information between users and providers of financial services, and better understand the profile of customers, especially via credit bureaus. On the flip side, data bring the question of the neutrality of scoring systems, their accountability, privacy protection and the emergence of surveillance capitalism. Digitization also increases the risk of frauds and data leakage, with banks being the target of choice for cybercrime.

In this context, regulators have played a key role in accelerating and keeping up with changes with the concept of sandboxes. Changes in regulations were accelerated by the 2008 Global Financial Crisis, and the 2020 Great Lockdown led to a strong policy response. Regulators have maintained their focus on traditional policies including customer protection, financial stability and financial inclusion. FinTech brings new types of challenges to regulators and redefines their relationship with banks.

This book would not be complete without a reflection on the role of banks in a technology-enabled, customer-centric future. Financial services have become omnipresent yet invisible, simple and accessible, so much so that incumbent banks, with their legacy systems and mindsets, may look unprepared. Capital markets, including venture capital and private equity funds, have been better positioned to finance innovation and disintermediate banks. In other cases, platforms offering peer-to-peer lending or equity have tried to bridge the supply and demand of capital, with limited success so far.

As we witness the revolution in financial services, from digital banks in Latin America to mobile payments in Kenya, from open banking in the UK to microfinance in Cambodia, financial market infrastructure in Brazil and superapps in China, we inquire into the best path to ensure that this disruption serves true inclusion.

Chapter 1

The Promise of Open Banking

Open Banking: Toward a Customer-Centric System

Customers, businesses and regulators globally have embraced the challenge of FinTech, favoring new business models in the financial sector, which can increase contestability and improve both the access to and the quality of financial services. In fact, regulators have moved from a traditional focus on system stability to a goal of increased contestability. However, if innovation is only meant to generate new business opportunities, we may be missing a unique opportunity. FinTech offers the promise of more inclusion, more efficient macroeconomic policies, and a better allocation of capital to unlock development.

The case studies of the UK and continental Europe shed light on one key principle that is guiding regulators nowadays: open banking. Recent directives have shifted the focus to the customer under the principle that banking data should belong to the user and not to corporates. Regulations in the UK and directives from the European Commission on transparency, portability and interoperability are putting more emphasis on customers' rights and protection. By contrast, the previous consensus implied that data belonged to financial intermediaries in exchange for the classic functions they performed such as deposit-taking. This principle is influencing policymakers globally.

The Bank for International Settlements defines open banking as the "sharing and leveraging of customer-permissioned data from banks with third-party developers and firms to build applications and services to provide more efficient and transparent options in banking."[1] Open banking creates huge opportunities but also challenges for firms and regulators. The main advantage is that open banking allows financial institutions to "know" their customers from day one based on past information gathered by other firms on behalf of customers. At the same time, it enables customers to know and compare banks' offerings. While customer-centricity is demystifying financial services, it also raises some technological challenges related to data exchange and analysis. As a result, this disruption magnifies the role of financial market infrastructures (FMI). Open banking raises the question of how customers permission the exchange of data, the technological challenges of that exchange and connectivity between firms.

Open banking originated from a European piece of regulation known as Payment Service Directive (PSD) and its subsequent evolution (PSD2), but its background includes 20 years of progress around innovation.[2]. The Lisbon Council of 2000 set the goal for Europe to become a more dynamic and competitive economic zone, which included a focus on innovation, competition and efficiency. As part of the implementation of the Euro, a group of 42 financial institutions created the European Payments Council (EPC) in 2002 with a view of simplifying cross-border payments and in the end remove friction for transactions in the zone. The European Commission prepared the Payment Services Directive (PSD), which went into force on December 25, 2007, and provided the legal framework for the Single Euro Payments Area (SEPA).[3] While the Directive was proposed by the Directorate-General for Internal Market of the European Commission in 2007, it was transposed into national legislation by all member states two years later, by November 1, 2009, as is the rule for EU Directives. SEPA covers 36 countries, including the

---

[1]Bank for International Settlements (2019). Report on open banking and application programming interfaces (APIs). Available at https://www.bis.org/bcbs/publ/d486.htm. Last accessed October 6, 2021.
[2]European Parliament and Council (2015). Directive 2015/2366.
[3]European Parliament and Council (2007). Directive 2007/64/EC.

27 members of the European Union, the European Free Trade Association (Iceland, Liechstentein, Norway, Switzerland), the United Kingdom and four additional participants (Andorra, Monaco, Vatican City, San Marino).

PSD regulated and harmonized two mechanisms: Payment Initiation Services (PIS) and Account Information Services (AIS). Account Information Services, as the name suggests, include the collection and storage of information from customers' bank accounts in a single place, permitting a consolidated view of their current financial situation, past revenues and expenses and potential financial needs. PIS facilitate the use of online banking for online payments. They also enable payments to be initiated from the customer's account to a merchant's account, for example, by creating an automated and safe interface. While AIS can be thought of as a static view, PIS offer the dynamic angle of payments.

PSD's objectives were to make European payments easier and cheaper, facilitating the growth of the single market. The regulation created a level playing field by harmonizing consumer protection and the rights and obligations of payment providers, while fostering the competition from non-banks. PSD was successful at guaranteeing faster payments (no later than next day since January 1, 2012) and describing refund rights. The PSD contained two main sections: a "market rules" section listed the type of organizations that could provide payment services. The "business conduct rules" required payment services to disclose information such as charges, exchange rates, transaction references and maximum execution time.

In 2013, the European Commission proposed an amendment to PSD, improving consumer protection, data harmonization and reinforcing security in the payments market. On 8 October 2015, the European Parliament adopted the Commission's proposal for PSD2, which explicitly promoted the development and use of innovative online and mobile payments such as through open banking, making cross-border European payments safer. On 16 November 2015, the Council of the European Union passed PSD2, giving member states two years to incorporate the directive into their national laws. PSD2 came into force on 13 January 2018. Due to delays in the implementation, the European Banking Authority allowed for an extension of the strong customer authentication (SCA) until 31 December 2020.

Therefore, the new directive PSD2, also called Open Banking and implemented in 2020, is the result of 20 years of discussions and regulations in the industry, leading banks in Europe to release their data in a secure and standardized form, so that it could be shared easily. While the full consequences of PSD2 are still unfolding, it is clear that the mindset of an open economy and open banking has been extraordinarily impactful with regulators and businesses globally.

In this overall context, the UK decided to innovate and take the concept of open banking a few steps further. In August 2016, the United Kingdom Competition and Markets Authority (CMA) issued a ruling that required the nine biggest UK banks — HSBC, Barclays, RBS, Santander, Bank of Ireland, Allied Irish Bank, Lloyds and Nationwide — to allow licensed startups direct access to their clients' data down to the level of transactions. Open Banking Limited, a non-profit, was created especially for this task. The CMA ruling applied to those nine banks, while the broader PSD2 applied to all payments providers.

CMA defended open banking with the goal to increase competition, innovation and make financial services cheaper in the UK. In particular, regulators noted the high cost of current accounts and overdrafts and the difficult access by small and medium-sized enterprises (SMEs) to loans. The UK government commissioned the Open Data Institute to explore "how competition and consumer outcomes in UK banking could be affected by banks giving customers the ability to share their transaction data with third parties."[4] The Open Data Institute noted that UK banks made GBP1.2 billion a year from unarranged overdraft charges. The report also noted that only 3% of personal and 4% of business customers switch to a different bank in any year, in a highly concentrated market. A study from the CMA also concluded that "older and larger banks do not have to

---

[4]Open Data Institute and Fingleton Associates (2014). Data sharing and open data for banks, a report for HM treasury and cabinet office. Available at https://assets.publishing.service.gov.uk/government/uploads/system/upload s/attachment_data/file/382273/141202_API_Report_FINAL.PDF. Last accessed October 6, 2021.

compete hard enough for customers' business, and smaller and newer banks find it difficult to grow."[5]

The conclusions of the UK authorities were clear and included strong wording. It was time for banks to work harder for their clients, compete on a level playing field with newcomers and for fees to come down. The plan proposed by CMA and the Open Banking Institute was bold and favored banks' Application Program Interfaces (APIs) with a universal standard. In 2016, CMA mandated banks to implement Open Banking by early 2018. To this end, Open Banking Limited, the non-profit set up to deliver open banking, started to build APIs and be a repository for APIs built by third parties. APIs are protocols that transfer data automatically from one institution to another. We will come back to APIs later in this chapter.

Today, more than 40 banks and 250 service providers participate in open banking in the UK. As of 2021, more than 2.5 million consumers and businesses use open banking-enabled products. The first business loan using open banking data was issued in November 2018. Third-party providers now "routinely use open data to help consumers boost their credit scores."[6] The UK pioneered open banking in 2018, inspiring other regulators globally, including Australia (2019) and Brazil (2020).

Brazil is one of the recent adopters. In Brazil, open banking was regulated by Central Bank Circular n° 4.015 of 4 May 2020 and includes four phases, as detailed in Figure 1. This document was complemented by 13 other regulations during 2020 and 2021. The first phase of implementation started in February 2021. Open Banking follows the existing regulations of bank secrecy of 2001 (Complementary Law n° 105/2001) and data protection of 2020.

The first phase of open banking mandated banks to release data about themselves in a standardized manner, including physical

---

[5]Competition and Markets Authority (2016). CMA paves the way for Open Banking revolution. Available at https://www.gov.uk/government/news/cma-paves-the-way-for-open-banking-revolution. Last accessed October 6, 2021.

[6]Open Banking (2021). Three years since PSD2 marked the start of Open Banking, the UK has built a world-leading ecosystem. Available at https://www.ope nbanking.org.uk/about-us/latest-news/three-years-since-psd2-marked-the-sta rt-of-open-banking-the-uk-has-built-a-world-leading-ecosystem/. Last accessed October 6, 2021.

branches and digital channels. Banks were also required to provide information on their products and services, including fees charged for each product.

The second phase started in August 2021 and includes customers' data exchange, with their explicit agreement. This phase includes customers' information and data on transactions, current accounts, savings accounts, pre-paid cards, credit cards and lending operations. Customers can initiate the exchange at the institution of their choice, be it banks, payments institutions or any entity authorized by the Central Bank. The process is entirely digital and free of charge for customers.

Phase three was launched in October 2021 and involved third parties. It allowed users to initiate payments or receive lending proposals without having to access the financial institution where they usually bank.

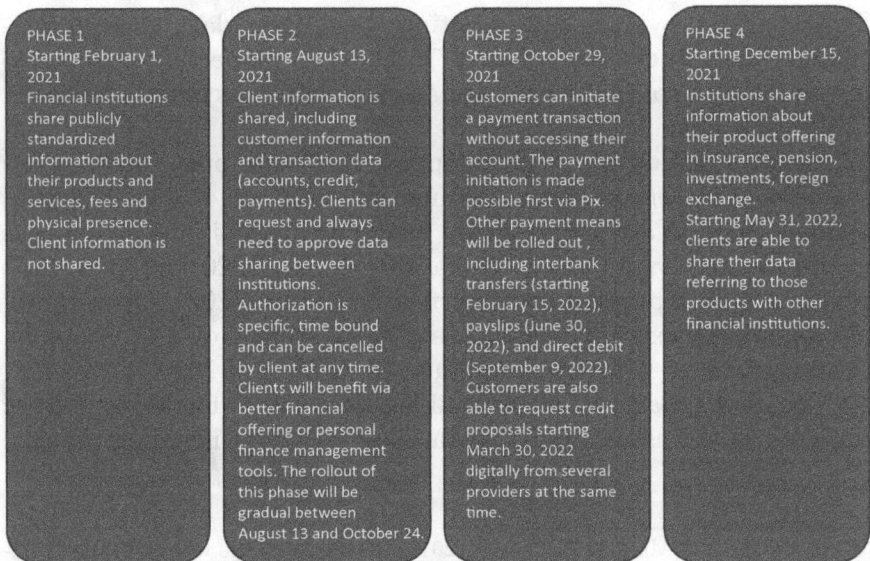

PHASE 1	PHASE 2	PHASE 3	PHASE 4
Starting February 1, 2021	Starting August 13, 2021	Starting October 29, 2021	Starting December 15, 2021
Financial institutions share publicly standardized information about their products and services, fees and physical presence. Client information is not shared.	Client information is shared, including customer information and transaction data (accounts, credit, payments). Clients can request and always need to approve data sharing between institutions. Authorization is specific, time bound and can be cancelled by client at any time. Clients will benefit via better financial offering or personal finance management tools. The rollout of this phase will be gradual between August 13 and October 24.	Customers can initiate a payment transaction without accessing their account. The payment initiation is made possible first via Pix. Other payment means will be rolled out, including interbank transfers (starting February 15, 2022), payslips (June 30, 2022), and direct debit (September 9, 2022). Customers are also able to request credit proposals starting March 30, 2022 digitally from several providers at the same time.	Institutions share information about their product offering in insurance, pension, investments, foreign exchange. Starting May 31, 2022, clients are able to share their data referring to those products with other financial institutions.

Figure 1:   The Four Phases of Open Banking in Brazil
Source: Central Bank of Brazil.[7]

---

[7]Central Bank of Brazil. Available at https://www.bcb.gov.br/estabilidadefinan ceira/openbanking, last accessed October 18, 2021.

Finally, phase four, which started in December 2021, deepens open banking to include other services used by clients, such as foreign exchange, brokerage, insurance and private pension plans.

What does open banking change in concrete terms?

First and foremost, open banking is about sharing data in an easy and transparent way. Open Data requires banks to release data about the location of branches, ATMs, and key features of their products. The release is standardized, which allows to contrast and compare the offerings. This also means that product comparison sites will be able to show different accounts and loans for the first time. Open Data includes simple records, making it easier to compare branch opening hours, find one with disabled access, or find the bank with the best rate on a savings account for example. Open data is about creating a level playing field to empower customers. This first part of Open Banking went live in March 2017 in the UK.

Information asymmetries go both ways. Financial institutions may not have a good enough picture of a customer and might be concerned with his credit risk. On the flip side, customers may not have enough information on their financial providers and therefore be unable to compare service offerings, distribution channels, prices and switch to the best provider.

Marcelo Blay, founder of the Brazilian insurtech Minuto Seguros, now part of FinTech Creditas, underlined that one of the biggest barriers for users was to compare the offerings of insurance carriers. Products were not standardized; customers would not be willing or able to compare fine prints of insurance policies, leading to a lack of trust in the product. Minuto Seguros was created in 2011 as a tool to help customers compare auto insurance products and choose the most suitable offering.[8]

Blay, after a successful career in insurance, decided to launch a solution that would make protection more approachable and affordable to customers. He selected insurance brokerage, as opposed to insurance underwriting, because of the lower capital requirements,

---

[8]Interview with Marcelo Blay, founder and CEO of Brazilian insurtech Minuto Seguros, November 15, 2021.

and because of the potential to enhance insurance distribution. Minuto Seguros is the largest independent online insurance broker in Brazil and derives a fee from every policy it distributes. Blay was backed by several venture capital funds. He notes the challenge for founders to balance the desire to raise large amounts of capital and accelerate client acquisition on the one hand, and the aim not to give up control too fast on the other hand. He also flags that the Brazilian ecosystem for FinTechs has grown tremendously over the past five years, with the emergence of a number of unicorns and much larger capital raises.

Minuto offers an online tool to compare auto insurance policies in a transparent and fair way and choose the most appropriate offering. While one-third of autos in Brazil are insured, the goal of Minuto was to expand the market and reach customers who had never acquired protection for their vehicles before. Seventy percent of customers of Minuto since its inception did not have auto insurance coverage before, representing first-time access. Minuto has sold coverage in every municipality of the country and targets the middle class. Moreover, contrary to other digital players that appeared in Brazil, Minuto early on identified the challenge to be entirely digital in the insurance segment. The company adopted a hybrid model, relying on a call center and human contact to acquire first-time clients and explain the product, while policy renewals rely more on digital channels. In fact, just 2% of sales to new clients are done entirely online, while this number jumps to 13% for "self-service" renewals. The trend is that both figures will rise in the coming years, as clients are more comfortable with online purchases and insurance products gain relevance in Brazil. He flags that the insurance product, within the world of financial inclusion, is still relatively expensive, difficult to understand for customers, and requires clients to define intertemporal priorities.

Minuto has built a business model based on transparency, and Blay expects open finance and open insurance to boost the demand for Minuto's product. Minuto merged with Creditas in 2021, a Brazilian unicorn active in collateralized credit, especially auto and home equity. This strategy to collaborate allows to fast-track time-to-market for players and provide a more complete offering to customers. Blay recognizes there have been a few attempts to modernize and digitize insurance in Brazil with mixed success. Pay-per-use has not gained its market, for example. Within the FinTech space, he sees a trend of convergence between some successful incumbents and challengers and believes there is room for a small number of challengers to firm up their position.

The second step of open banking dives into customer information, including profile and transactions. Open banking shows customer data in a standardized way. Banks morphed from opaque safekeeping to open platforms, making available the wealth of information they gather on behalf of their customers.

One use case is to allow digital apps to provide a consolidated view of customers' finances. Data aggregators allow customers to have a consolidated view of their financial situation and plan ahead. The consolidated view can be useful to better manage cash flows, avoid overdrafts by rebalancing account balances between banks for example. Open Data facilitates the comparison of offerings and creates a favorable backdrop for personal financial management tools. Blomfield, founder of the UK challenger bank Monzo, explains that the functionality pulls in all of the data from different bank accounts and shows an aggregated view of all the user's money in one place. As of 2021, Monzo counted more than 5 million users and provided services such as prepaid card, debit cards, savings and insurance. Aggregators such as Monzo Plus, Emma or Yolt in the UK allow to sort transactions by categories, offering better control to users. Some services already offered those functionalities prior to open banking, but in order to use them, customers had to hand over their login details, raising questions about security, data accuracy and data corruption, while open banking is automated, safe and does not require human intervention, only the user's explicit approval.

In the US, the personal financial management app Yodlee provides customers with a consolidated view of their finance and offers customized planning tools. Brazilian FinTech Guia Bolso, now part of Picpay, has been a reference for financial data aggregation and is the largest personal financial management tool in Brazil with more than three million users. It signed a partnership with Mexico-based Finerio in May 2021, also active in personal finance management in order to strengthen its aggregation tools at the regional level and offer "Open Banking as a Service," which allows institutions to adjust to open banking.

Lenders pointed out that the biggest impact of improved data access would be on loan concession. Incumbents have built their own datasets over time, which provide the basis of their credit risk modelling, but new entrants do not have similar historical data that they can use to calibrate their risk models. As such, the availability of data on loan performance and defaults would likely reduce barriers to entry to this market. Beyond credit, openness creates the opportunity for an institution to offer more adapted, more convenient and cheaper products. Open Banking offers the conditions for the emergence of customer-centric business models. Third-party service providers (TPPs) can analyze a customer cash flow history to assess a credit score and propose the best lending offer in terms of ticket, maturity, repayment profile and interest rate. Open banking enables automation, such as switching to the cheapest insurance provider at the time of policy renewal.

Building a customer-centric organization is not just about technology, and requires organizational design based on open culture and alliances. Studies suggest that sales to existing loyal customers are more profitable than sales to new customers. Therefore, customer loyalty and brand recognition are among the most valuable assets for service companies, and they come with openness. An important part of becoming customer-centric is shifting profitability analysis from transactions or products to customers and incorporating activity over a longer time.[9]

The exchange of information has been a key element behind bank account portability. In Brazil, portability is regulated by the Central Bank Resolution 4639/2018. Despite an easy process, portability remains limited for bank accounts and salaries. Customers tend to bank with the financial institution where they receive their wages, implying a relative stickiness of the market structure. Joao Vitor Menin, CEO and founder of Brazilian platform Inter, which counts more than 15 million customers and is one of the fastest growing FinTechs in Latin America, notes that while account and loan portability has met with limited success in Brazil, open banking reduces the appeal of portability, since customers can simply shop for the best

---

[9]Kilara, T. and Rhyne, E. (2014). Customer-centricity for financial inclusion. CGAP brief; World Bank, Washington, DC. Available at https://openknowledg e.worldbank.org/handle/10986/20260. Last accessed October 6, 2021.

products without the need to change banks. With Open Banking, customer relationship becomes less rigid. Customers may end up switching less from one bank to the other since data will be connected and they will simply consume financial products where they see fit without having to start a relationship from zero.[10]

Banking as a Service: Demystifying Financial Services

In the previous sections, we have discussed how Open Banking brings a seismic impact to financial services by enabling the exchange of data on both the bank's service offering and the client's history. What started as a regulatory innovation led to a number of new business opportunities.

One new business vertical has emerged from this newly acquired openness: banking as a service. As third parties gain access to customer information, their goal is to compete with incumbent banks on financial services either nibbling small fee-generating parts of banks' business or sometimes going for a bolder strategy of offering the full stack of services including credit. Intermediaries have developed offerings to allow third parties to act like a bank.

Banking as a service or "BaaS" is a critical element to demystify financial services and the role of banks. In the race to offer better, cheaper and more tailored services to customers, the traditional alternative to buy or build new capabilities also applies to financial providers. Banking as a service allows third-party providers to offer financial services to their customers by leveraging the existing offering of licensed banks. The client-facing app is connected to a BaaS provider via API.

Demystifying bears huge relevance to weaken the traditional argument that banking is different from other types of services and that customers are loyal to their existing bank brand because of trust. The concept of trust is related to culture, and customers in some countries like Brazil or China tend to be more inclined to use a FinTech than in geographies like Europe, where concerns around customer privacy are stronger. Across emerging markets, the younger age of the bankable population may also explain the success of neobanks such as Nubank or WeBank.

---

[10]Interview with João Vitor Menin, founder and CEO of Brazilian FinTech Inter, December 13, 2021.

Banking as a service allows the third-party provider to focus on its competitive advantage: customer experience, customer service or loyalty, and leave the development of new financial products, day-to-day management of those products and compliance and regulatory requirements to the banks.

FinTechs offering BaaS have emerged; examples include Treasury Prime, Synctera, Unit, and Bond. In Europe, providers include Solarisbank, ClearBank, RailsBank and Starling Bank. In Brazil, names include Dock and BV. Within narrower verticals such as payments, Marqeta, founded in 2010, has focused on debit and prepaid card issuing, for clients such as Instacart, DoorDash or Uber. In Europe, Enfuce offers card issuing services for lending and credit FinTechs. White label solutions also include Ebanx in payments, or Órama in investment brokerage in Brazil.

Embedded finance is a related but distinct concept, whereby finance is part of a broader offering of products and services. For example, online retailers have not only focused on offering the best merchandise to their customers, but also providing simplified online payments, sometimes offering credit or ancillary products like insurance together with the sale of a cell phone, for example. Customers are looking for integrated experiences and companies find a better way to monetize their customer relationships. Walmart announced in January 2021 that it was building a financial services offering, while Ikea announced in February 2021 that it would acquire 49% of its banking arm Ikano Bank that it did not already own. In Latin America, e-commerce giant Mercado Libre has increased its offering to include loans to merchants.

To meet the growing need for embedded finance, financial institutions and FinTech participants are increasingly offering BaaS.[11] BaaS is often sold as a "white label" service where the name of the FinTech or provider does not appear, and only the name of the institution that faces the end customer. BaaS is usually deployed thanks to APIs and requires strong risk and compliance management as well as a clear definition of where customer data sit.

---

[11]McKinsey (2021). What the embedded-finance and banking-as-a-service trends mean for financial services. Available at https://www.mckinsey.com/industries/financial-services/our-insights/banking-matters/what-the-embedded-finance-and-banking-as-a-service-trends-mean-for-financial-services. Last accessed October 6, 2021.

BaaS is distinct from open banking: while BaaS integrates a financial service offering into a third-party's business, open banking allows third parties to leverage data accumulated by another participant at the request of a client. BaaS is business-driven and fosters collaboration. Open banking is customer-driven and emphasizes competition. Both participate in the redefinition of financial services and disrupt the traditional role of banks.

The Technical Challenge of Openness: Interoperability

Although PSD2 never explicitly mentioned Application Programming Interfaces (APIs), industry and experts consider that APIs would be the means to achieve openness and be the technical tool to comply with the regulation. APIs allow different applications to communicate with each other and exchange data directly, without the need for human intervention. Put in other words, an "API is a set of instructions that allows one piece of software to interact with another."[12] APIs have become the de facto standard for exchanging data and are the enabler of open banking.

APIs can be developed by the financial institutions themselves or by third-party developers. Paypal has had a developer program since 2009, other examples include Mastercard, Visa and Google. Crédit Agricole launched its own app store, CA store, in 2012. As described by Bernard Larrivière, then Head of Innovation at Crédit Agricole: "every [piece of] data the customer creates in his relationship with the bank, or any partner, is his own property so he should have access to it, but he should have access to it in apps that are useful to him."[13] Brazilian bank Bradesco adopted an open API strategy and built a set of APIs to integrate with Facebook. The app allows customers to

---

[12]Open Data Institute and Fingleton Associates (2014). Data sharing and open data for banks, a report for HM treasury and cabinet office. Available at https://assets.publishing.service.gov.uk/government/uploads/system/upload s/attachment_data/file/382273/141202_API_Report_FINAL.PDF. Last accessed October 6, 2021, p. 16.

[13]*Ibid.*, p. 19.

check their bank balance and make transactions from within Facebook. With an API integrated with Amazon or Paypal, a merchant can automatically pre-populate a customer's delivery address and run fraud checking. Salesforce.com's API ecosystem has brought scale into the software platform, comprising over 800,000 developers who have built more than four million applications that run on the platform. Another famous example includes Apple's App Store, which has successfully leveraged third-party innovation. Third-party software can connect to hardware and software made by Apple, such as the iPhone camera, GPS, photo library or contact list, via APIs. There are more than 1.2 million apps on the app store, which have been downloaded 75 billion times. Some companies specialize in providing APIs. For example, Uber leverages the API of Twillio, which allows to send an SMS message telling the customer that their Uber driver has arrived. APIs are an attractive method for an organization to provide access to its data.

The ProgrammableWeb, a public directory of web APIs, has grown the size of its records from just one in 2005 to a current count of 24,112.[14] Financial services-related categories have been among the fastest growing API categories. This is a reflection of open banking initiatives, the rise of digital forms of payment, the need for real-time market information and ever-increasing customer demand for connected financial services. For the period between 2017 and 2019, ProgrammableWeb notes an average of more than 600 financial APIs added per year.

Before open banking, organizations such as personal finance managers used to access data using means such as manual downloads, screen scraping, or even manual entry. A common approach was to request the user's login details to the service provider's app, which could then be used on behalf of the client. These methods are hard to use, expensive, and rely on full access.[15] Moreover, scraping can be inaccurate. APIs provide a more secure approach to sharing and allow different software applications to communicate with each other

---

[14]Data available at https://www.programmableweb.com/api-research.

[15]Open Data Institute and Fingleton Associates (2014). Data Sharing and Open Data for Banks, A report for HM Treasury and Cabinet Office. Available at https://assets.publishing.service.gov.uk/government/uploads/system/upload s/attachment_data/file/382273/141202_API_Report_FINAL.PDF. Last accessed October 6, 2021.

and exchange data directly, without the need for human input each time. They have enabled organizations that hold large amounts of data to become platforms for third-party innovation.

Importantly, COVID-19 has accelerated the reliance on digital services and greatly improved the perception of FinTech risk by users. Traditional banks and FinTechs now have similar levels of customer trust, a positive development for FinTechs, while traditional banks are no longer the exclusive guardian of safety and stability.[16]

It may sound audacious to encourage openness when cases of data leakages and hacks frequently make headlines, which explains the importance of best practices in data sharing, as shown in Table 1. One of the major developments of PSD2 in Europe lied in the introduction of new security requirements, known as Strong Customer Authentication (SCA). SCA requires the use of two authentication factors for bank operations and access to bank accounts, which was not previously required. SCA also requires a stricter definition of what banks consider an authentication factor. Moreover, if a bank is following a user's explicit instruction to share their data with a third party, then the bank would have no liability for what happens once the data have been shared. However, the bank must be sufficiently confident that the user has consented to the third party accessing their data, and that the user understands which of their data the third party will be able to access. The user must be informed about what is happening to her data, and consent must be specific, informed, and explicit.

The exchange via APIs is crytpographed to protect data and only happens after three events: customer consent, authentication and confirmation. Those three steps happen via digital channels and the exchange follows standards common to all market participants. Only the relevant data are shared, and a customer can revoke the approval for the exchange at any time. OAuth is a widely used open standard — used by platforms such as Linkedin, Facebook, Twitter — that provides a simple mechanism for users to authenticate themselves and authorize how their data can be shared.

---

[16]McKinsey (2020). How US customers' attitudes to FinTech are shifting during the pandemic. Available at https://www.mckinsey.com/industries/financial-serv ices/our-insights/how-us-customers-attitudes-to-FinTech-are-shifting-during-the-pandemic. Last accessed October 6, 2021.

Table 1:   Principles of Data Sharing

Principle	Relevant Technology and Standards
For data sharing to be useful to users, it should be simple, low friction and scalable.	The API is a technology concept that allows different software applications to communicate with each other and exchange data directly, without the need for human input each time.
Users should provide fully informed consent before their personal data is shared and should remain in control of how it is used.	OAuth is a widely used standard that provides a simple and secure mechanism to authenticate themselves, and authorize how their data can be shared.
To create optimal conditions for innovation, datasets that do not contain personal commercially sensitive information should be made as accessible as possible.	The concept of open date sets out how data can be made available for anyone to use freely, for any purpose.

Source: Open Data Institute and Fingleton Associates (2014).

Users can authorize one application to communicate with another on their behalf, without the need to share their login credentials.

Open banking is also essentially linked to the rise and strengthening of a new actor: financial market infrastructure (FMI). FMIs are a key element of the open economy. Historically, exchanges have been the central counterpart allowing the organized exchange of securities. Other types of FMIs include clearing houses, registries and depositaries. Infrastructure can enable economic agents to extract value from their data.

CERC is a Brazilian FMI created in 2015 dedicated to the registration, listing, monitoring and control of companies' receivables such as credit card receivables or invoices. CERC registers receivables and addresses the three most important problems of the market, "checking the existence of receivables, using artificial intelligence; avoiding the double usage of assets as collateral, providing fully digital formalization of contracts; and confirming that money goes to the correct destination, instructing the payers of receivables with the correct beneficiary of the payments." Eventually, CERC may offer settlement of receivables and even a platform for those instruments to be traded, as Marcelo Maziero, founder and Chairman of CERC, explains.[17]

CERC was born from the vision that, "if trading receivables were as safe and efficient as it happens with traditional stocks, the credit market to SME's would grow exponentially, as the amount of receivables generated yearly corresponds to roughly twice the Brazilian GDP."

CERC's growth has gone hand in hand with a rising goal of the Central Bank of Brazil to push for more competition and transparency in the credit card market and other financial assets. Receivables were recognized as a security by law in 2018, as long as they are registered in a FMI, such as CERC. The growth of the receivables market in Brazil has met with a robust regulatory support. In order to foster competition between FMIs, new rules set forth the interoperability between registration platforms, which initially created technical and operational hurdles. Opening up the credit card receivables' market represented "one of the first implementations of open banking globally, relying on FMIs as third-party providers." In other geographies, such as the UK, invoice trading is growing fast.[18]

On the strategic side, Maziero explains that the triggers that allowed CERC to strive included both technological and cultural aspects. Indeed, cloud capacity lowered barriers to entry for new FinTechs by reducing upfront costs. On the cultural side, Maziero mentions the private equity ecosystem that grew tremendously around FinTechs and started to not only allocate capital to ventures in Brazil, but also the entrepreneurial abilities of Brazilian founders. He notes however that human capital remains a hurdle, especially IT hiring, and while COVID-19 has boosted remote working, global recruiting remains a challenge.

Banking on Platforms Is the New Normal?

The analysis of large amounts of data is the enabler of platform banking. Technology has enabled solutions that offer financial services to

---

[17]Interview with CERC's founder and Chairman Marcelo Maziero, 3 November 2021.

[18]Cambridge Center for Alternative Finance (2016). *Sustaining Momentum*, The 2nd European Alternative Finance Industry Report. University of Cambridge, Judge Business School, September 2016.

more clients and under better terms. Big data analysis can be used to profile the risk of companies, such as SMEs, identify the existence and unicity of receivables, or improve fraud detection. Big data refers to datasets that are too large or complex to be analyzed by traditional data-processing software but can potentially reveal patterns in customer preference and behavior and unlock better products to customers.

Platforms operate in two-sided markets, deriving revenues by facilitating transactions between two groups of agents. The structure of the market evolves from one bank to many customers ("one to many") to many providers to many customers meeting through a platform ("many to many").

Two-sided markets or platforms exist in various industries. Some well-known examples include yellow pages where people can find contact information on other people of companies. Within the financial segments, platform models have existed in asset management for some time, offering funds from different providers. Credit networks, such as Visa or Mastercard, put in contact cardholders and merchants and facilitate payments. Video games platforms, such as the Xbox from Microsoft, or PlayStation by Sony, connect users with video-game developers. Other examples include Facebook, Linkedin, Uber, Amazon, or Mercado Libre, connecting merchants with customers. Platforms inherently benefit from network effects.[19] A network effect exists when an additional user of a good or service increases the value of the product to others. More users will attract financial providers and vice versa. According to Rochet and Tirole, "a market is two-sided if the platform can affect the volume of transactions by charging more to one side of the market and reducing the price paid by the other side by an equal amount; in other words, the price structure matters, and platforms must design it so as to bring both sides on board."[20]

---

[19]Rochet, J. C. and Tirole, J. (2003). Platform competition in two-sided markets. *Journal of the European Economic Association*, 1(4), 990–1029. Notes that Rysman (2000) is the first empirical paper to estimate network effects in a two-sided context, namely the market for Yellow Pages.

[20]Rochet, J. C. and Tirole, J. (2004). Two-sided markets: An overview, *IDEI-CEPR Conference on Two-Sided Markets*, Toulouse, January 23–24, p. 40.

Platform banking is the logical answer from financial institutions to the disruptions caused by open banking or BaaS. Embedded finance and the ubiquity of financial services in everyday life bring the question of the perimeter of banks. What should we expect from a bank today? Where will customers buy financial services from?

Big data analysis can impact the depth of financial services. For example, tech-based lending can meaningfully increase access to credit for underserved companies and people. FinTech lenders, as opposed to universal banks or specialized mortgage banks, increased their market share of the U.S. mortgage lending from 2% to 8% from 2010 to 2016, respectively. Research shows that FinTech lenders process applications 20% faster and are less likely to incur bottlenecks upon demand shocks. Interestingly, the same research shows that those FinTech lenders do not target borrowers with low access to traditional finance, but rather traditional customers, suggesting that they are taking away market share from competitors rather than broadening access.[21]

The sector of investments is a good example of the collaborative strategy adopted by select FinTechs. Digital brokers offer platforms where investors can invest their savings in a number of funds that are often created and managed by third-party providers. Digital brokers, such as XP in Brazil, which reported more than three million clients and close to $150 billion in assets under custody, offer access to a broad range of funds, select the best performing asset managers and complement their offering with educational services to increase client loyalty.

Robo-advisors deepen this logic by offering a low-touch service with limited or no intervention of human investment advisors. Empirical studies analyze whether robo-advisors, also known as automated portfolio optimizers, improve investor performance. Based on a sample of users in India, robo-adopters appear to be similar to non-adopters in their prior interaction with human advisors. The study shows that most users become better diversified and reduce portfolio volatility once they adopt robo-advising, especially as robo-advisors

---

[21]Fuster *et al.* (2019). The role of technology in mortgage lending. *The Review of Financial Studies, 32*(5), 1854–1899. doi:10.1093/rfs/hhz018.

help mitigate the most prominent behavioral biases, such as the disposition effect and momentum chasing.[22]

Lending and brokerage have benefited from the open logic to distribute third-party products. So has insurance. Toffee is an innovative insurance delivery FinTech in India that acts as a bridge between low-income customers and traditional insurance companies, offering a simplified sign-up and easy access. The company provides simple insurance policies to protect customers against common diseases, such as dengue and malaria, or life events such as bicycle damage and theft.[23]

Latin America has experienced an 80% jump in the number of financial apps installed between the first quarter of 2020 and the first quarter of 2021. Mexico has led this growth (from a lower base), doubling in the number of installs, while the number of installs of financial apps in Brazil grew 65%. Overall, Latin America experienced 850 million financial app installs between the first quarter of 2019 and the first quarter of 2021, no doubt accelerated by COVID-19. Interestingly, for the first time in the time series, the share of digital banking apps became the largest category within financial apps in Brazil in 2021 (Figure 2).

Traditional banks in Brazil and other regions have experienced stability or even sometimes a contraction in the total number of their clients. Challenger banks, on the other hand, are experiencing outstanding growth in the number of their clients. However, average tickets for newcomers tend to be lower, especially given the limited exposure to lines such as mortgages and car loans, which tend to drive higher tickets (Table 2).

The idea of platform banking and the rise of superapps is inseparable from the ubiquitous usage of cell phones, in particular smartphones. Under platform banking, an entity allows other companies, such as FinTechs or other banks, to offer their products via its online platform. This integration provides several benefits to the platform: it becomes a central integrated point of sale for customers, who can find a one-stop shop, develop loyalty to the platform, share their

---

[22]D'Acunto *et al.* (2019). The promises and pitfalls of robo-advising. *The Review of Financial Studies*, *32*(5), 1983–2020. doi: 10.1093/rfs/hhz014.

[23]CGAP (2021). Fintech and financial inclusion. A funder's guide to greater impact. *Focus Note*, June 2021, p. 11.

Table 2: Number of Clients at Main Brazilian Financial Institutions: Digital Banks Have Experienced Exponential Growth

	Number of Clients with Outstanding Loan			Growth (2020/2019)	Clients with Outstanding Loan (%)	Avg Ticket (US$, k)	Household Loan Market Share
	2018	2019	2020				
Traditional banks							
Itaú	34,769	38,467	36,489	−5%	44%	1,860	15%
Bradesco	39,047	37,725	33,334	−12%	34%	1,558	11%
Santander Brasil	17,730	20,328	21,383	5%	42%	2,135	10%
Calixa Economica Federal	17,299	18,080	18,694	3%	13%	6,470	26%
Banco do Brasil	13,838	16,131	16,013	−1%	23%	4,952	17%
Banrisul	2,662	3,001	3,016	0%	59%	1,883	1%
Challenger banks							
Nubank	4,641	8,043	12,061	50%	NA	256	1%
Banco Pan	3,106	3,840	5,104	33%	72%	1,062	1%
Inter	436	797	1,404	76%	17%	916	0%
Digio	—	1,120	1,365	22%	93%	286	0%
C6	—	63	1,201	1806%	27%	712	0%
Agi	785	753	634	−16%	62%	709	0%
Banco Original	184	327	501	53%	14%	1,545	0%

Source: Company data and UBS research.

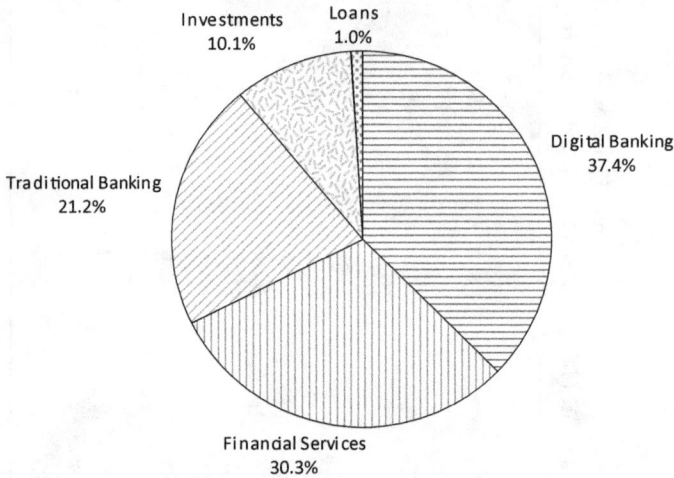

Figure 2: Downloads of Financial Apps Show the Lead of Digital Banking in Brazil

Source: Appsflyer.com.

data and preferences with the platform as well as remunerate it for providing a distribution channel. This is also a smart way for the central player to benefit from third-party innovation and offer it to its clients. Platform banking follows a collaborative logic. The financial services are not necessarily produced or originated by the legal entity with whom the customer has a relationship. For example, a platform bank could simply distribute to its customer a loan that was originated by another bank, an insurance policy underwritten by an external carrier, or a robo-advisory service offered by a FinTech. Different entities are in charge of the manufacturing and distribution of the financial service. Some financial institutions have adopted the approach of platforms, such as Nu or Inter in Latin America.

Nubank was founded in 2013 as a credit card issuer. It is the largest neobank globally outside of China, with 48 million clients as of the end of 2021 and a mission to reinvent financial services and "fight complexity and empower people in their daily lives," according to the company's founder David Vélez. Vélez emphasizes that Nubank is a "tech company that happens to be in financial services," stressing the focus on data analysis and technology. The institution is already one of the largest credit card issuers in Brazil, with a 10% market share, adding more than two million new clients per month in the third quarter of 2021 in Brazil, Mexico and Colombia. Vélez explains the decision-making process around manufacturing or distributing select services. Nubank manufactures products is they meet three conditions: the product is good for the customer, Nubank has a competitive advantage, and the service has favorable unit economics. If the product is good for the customer but the other conditions are not met, the company would look for partnerships and distribute the service. According to Vélez, Nubank has a strong comparative advantage in credit, while other products such as insurance or secured lending can benefit from partnerships.[24]

Inter is a financial platform in Brazil, with close to 15 million clients and is present in 99% of Brazilian municipalities. CEO Joao Vitor Menin explains that "the purpose of Inter as a superapp is to become a provider of financial solutions and not a mere factory of financial products." Offerings encompass an e-commerce gateway, insurance, an investment platform, mortgage lending, where the demand from clients is met by products crafted by Inter or by other financial institutions. Such a strategy requires the FinTech to offer core banking products but the focus is on client satisfaction. Inter's stated goal is to "be the best gateway to financial products for its clients." This asset-light vision allows to keep a smaller capital base and, in the view of his CEO, allows Inter to counter a potential "uberization," in other words to be displaced by cheaper and more agile financial institutions.[25] In order to avoid competition based purely on pricing, a platform will aim at adding new financial services, competing on customer experience and brand loyalty.

Intermedium was born in 1994, initially a non-bank financial institution active in mortgage and payroll-deducted lending and SME factoring. The institution received a full banking license in 2008. The bank diversified its strategy to retail after 2008. Banco Inter launched its digital account in 2014, with the slogan to offer a product that is "digital, complete and free." Launching a retail online strategy represented a "low-cost option with a large upside potential," according to Inter CEO. The bank completed its initial public offering on the

---

[24]Interview with Nubank's founder and CEO David Vélez, November 17, 2021, and SEC F-1.
[25]Interview with Inter's CEO João Vitor Menin, December 13, 2021.

São Paulo stock exchange in 2018. Banco Inter increased its product offering to include investments and insurance. The digital bank then became a superapp, with the addition of e-commerce. Permanent innovation allowed the company to evolve, offering "new layers of services to its customers," as financial services were becoming embedded or "invisible." In fact, e-commerce was a natural next step for the superapp, as e-commerce is closely linked to payments and credit, both activities already offered by Inter.

Innovation and disruption are a "natural process," according to Menin, and lead companies to adapt to a new environment or disappear, following the logic of creative destruction. While this movement is not linear, finance is experiencing a "transformational moment," and "incumbents will be the losers of this evolution," for lack of agility. Importantly, innovation does not lie essentially in technology or in the products, as all players have access to the same resources and ideas. For Menin, innovation is essentially related to internal processes, and can be encapsulated in the "culture of the company." Menin emphasizes that a successful culture gives ample autonomy to employees and fosters horizontal structures where interactions are easier.

While Brazil has been at the forefront of innovation in Latin America, other countries in the region have been home to fast growing and successful challengers. Ualá in Argentina was created in 2017 by Pierpaolo Barbieri. The neobank had issued more than three million cards at the end of 2021. While the company started as a debit card issuer and personal finance manager, the company invested decisively in its technology stack to be able to launch more products, including insurance brokerage, mutual funds, credit products, merchant acquiring, and new geographies, including Mexico and Colombia.

Neobanks and superapps are reinventing the user experience in financial services. They leverage big data and technology, the ubiquity of mobile, customer appetite for simple delivery of financial products, and disrupt the existing status quo with traditional banks. They simplify the financial life of millions of users, while including customers who were previously unbanked or underbanked.

Chapter 2

Benefits and Limits of Financial Inclusion

The Three Dimensions of Financial Inclusion

Financial inclusion is a public policy objective that fosters development through access to financial services for all. A common definition of financial inclusion includes the three dimensions of access, usage, and quality of financial services. Inclusion of individuals and small enterprises has made considerable progress in emerging markets over the past two decades, but it has also reached excesses in some cases. Regulatory changes, technological innovation, and disruptive business models have helped the expansion of financial services and the rising FinTech sector brings the promise of enhanced access and usage. Has financial inclusion reached a limit? Is access to finance robust enough to serve consumers and unlock the potential of companies? Can the revolution that is currently taking place in payments and FinTech foster more inclusion?

Financial inclusion has become a consensual policy objective. There is a large literature offering support for a link between financial inclusion and development, while excessive or inappropriate inclusion can also bring risks. Access to financial services has improved thanks to deeper branch networks and the rise of banking correspondents. Over the past two decades, technology and regulations have boosted inclusion. While access has improved, it is far from ubiquitous, and actual usage remains a challenge.

There are several definitions of financial inclusion. Some define it simply as the use of formal accounts.[1] We find that the definition of the Consultative Group to Assist the Poor (CGAP) best describes the phenomenon. CGAP defines financial inclusion as the process whereby "households and businesses have access [to] and can effectively use appropriate financial services. Such services must be provided responsibly and sustainably, in a well-regulated environment."[2] The Center for Financial Inclusion (CFI) at Accion provides a complementary dimension, explaining that financial inclusion allows everyone to have "access to a full suite of quality financial services at affordable prices, with convenience, dignity, and consumer protection, delivered by a range of providers in a stable, competitive market to financially capable clients."[3] In fact, financial inclusion is much more than banking the unbanked and the CFI defines five dimensions to advance financial inclusion: develop financial capabilities, attend customer needs, technology-enabled businesses, credit reporting, and customer protection.

The definitions illustrate that being financially included is different from — and much more complex than — being banked: having a bank account at a formal banking institution. Being banked is a state where individuals have a relationship with a formal financial institution, including banks, cooperatives or credit unions. Financial inclusion consists in having access to a wide range of financial services, not just credit, and bank branches are just one channel through which customers can take advantage of those services.

There are three critical dimensions of financial inclusion: access, usage and quality of formal financial services.[4] Understandably, access to financial services has been the first focus of policymakers,

---

[1] Allen, F. *et al.* (2012). The foundations of financial inclusion: Understanding ownership and use of formal accounts. Policy Research Working Paper; No. 6290. World Bank, Washington, DC; *Journal of Financial Intermediation*, 27, 1–30.

[2] Center for Financial Inclusion (2013). Seizing the moment, on the road to financial inclusion 2020. Available at https://www.centerforfinancialinclusion.org/seizing-the-moment-on-the-road-to-financial-inclusion. Last accessed October 6, 2021.

[3] Kelly, S. and Rhyne, E. (2015). By the numbers: Benchmarking progress toward financial inclusion. Center for Financial Inclusion, ACCION.

[4] Roa, M. J. (2015). *Financial inclusion in Latin America and the Caribbean: Access, usage and quality.* Research Paper, p. 19.

especially for underserved rural and poor segments of the population. Regulations around banking correspondents, simplified financial services, mandatory free basic financial offering, investments into branch opening and mobile banking have helped increase meaningfully the convenience for citizens to be banked.

Usage, or outreach, is the willingness of people to take advantage of accessible financial services, and "those who have access, but choose not to use services pose less of a problem for policymakers."[5] While this sounds rather obvious, research shows that among survey participants without an account in the 2014 Findex survey, only 4% said they do not need one.[6]

Finally, there is the quality dimension. Users need to develop a list of financial capabilities to be able to fully take advantage of services that are offered to them. The financial capability of the customer has become an increasingly central aspect of the reflection on financial inclusion. Authors define financial capabilities for customers who "have knowledge, skills, and behaviors that enable them to make sound financial decisions."[7] Importantly and rather surprisingly, research suggests that financial education does not necessarily precede an uptake of financial services and that experience, word-of-mouth and trial and error, rather than formal training, is at the core of improvements in financial capability. For example, some studies in Indian microinsurance show that customers understand fairly well insurance products, and that lack of understanding is not the driver of the low uptake in the product.

Data on the penetration of financial services, such as bank accounts, credit, insurance or payments, all point to a meaningful improvement over the past 20 years globally. Electronic payments can be an entry door for inclusion and access to a wide range of financial services, including — but not limited to — credit. Electronic payments include credit, debit, prepaid cards, and other electronic means such as online and mobile payments. Measures that promote

---

[5]See footnote 1.

[6]Demirgüç-Kunt, A., Klapper, L. F., Singer, D. and van Oudheusden, P. (2015). The Global Findex Database 2014: Measuring financial inclusion around the world. *World Bank Policy Research Working Paper No. 7255*, Available at SSRN: https://ssrn.com/abstract=2594973.

[7]See footnote 3.

electronic payments include simplified accounts, mobile banking, and the formalization of the economy with mandatory salary payments or government subsidies on accounts. The rise in electronic payments goes hand in hand with higher financial inclusion and brings various development-related benefits to a country, while cash usage is generally associated with informality. There is a close connection between electronic payments, financial inclusion, and access to credit. In fact, the payment sector has seen the emergence of disruptive business models that flourish at the intersection of banking, retail and social media.

A key element to explain the growth of financial services has come from the distribution outside of the traditional brick-and-mortar bank branches. Different types of providers have emerged, including cooperatives, community-based development institutions, insurance and credit-card companies, telecommunications and wire services, post offices, and other businesses that provide point-of-sale (POS) access. Those businesses that are not regulated as banks are often referred to as Non-Bank Financial Institutions (NBFIs) or the shadow banking sector. Technology, with the advent of the Internet and mobile solutions, has played a critical role in the recent growth of those channels.

With the expansion of branches and other points of sale, outreach has benefited millions of customers and companies. Financial inclusion considers all economic agents, either individuals or corporates, with special attention for the more vulnerable and excluded segments, such as the poorer segments of the population in emerging markets. The reverse concept of financial exclusion is a growing concern, especially in developed economies such as the US.[8] Data show that roughly 20% of the US adult population is underbanked, defined as having a bank account but using financial services from another alternative non-FDIC insured financial provider.[9]

Within corporates, the research on financial inclusion focuses especially on small- and medium-sized enterprises (SMEs). The literature on asymmetries of information shows that SMEs are at a

---

[8]Burhouse, S. and Osaki, Y. (2014). FDIC National survey of unbanked and underbanked households. Federal Deposit Insurance Corporation.

[9]World Bank Group (2013). *Global Financial Development Report 2014: Financial Inclusion* (Vol. 2). World Bank Publications.

disadvantage when it comes to accessing financial services.[10] Akerlof, in an influential paper, noted that information asymmetry can be detrimental to the market as a whole.[11] Paraphrasing Stiglitz, the credit market is imperfect in a sense that there may not be a price that clears the supply and demand for credit, if banks simply refuse to lend for lack of information. Research even suggests that credit market conditions amplify and propagate the effects of real monetary shocks under a phenomenon described as the financial accelerator. Borrowers who face relatively high agency costs in credit markets will bear the brunt of economic downturns.[12] Agency costs stem from the situation where a principal (the lender) cannot costlessly acquire information on the agent (the borrower). SMEs have a particularly difficult time accessing sources of funding, either via bank credit or the capital markets. "Bank characteristics can have a large impact on the provision of credit," strengthening the hypothesis of a bank lending channel.[13] Credit is different from other goods, due to the central role of information, and sunk costs from information gathering act as barriers to entry for borrowers.[14] The existence of asymmetries of information means that some customers are "informationally captured," stressing the importance of credit registries or credit bureaus, and differentiating between negative information, used for enforcement, and positive information, used

[10]Stiglitz, J. E. and Weiss, A. (1981). Credit rationing in markets with imperfect information. *The American Economic Review, 71*(3), 393–410; Stiglitz, J. E. and Weiss, A. (1992). Asymmetric information in credit markets and its implications for macro-economics. *Oxford Economic Papers, 44*(4), 694–724.

[11]Akerlof, G. A. (1970). The market for "Lemons": Quality uncertainty and the market mechanism. *The Quarterly Journal of Economics, 84*(3), 488–500.

[12]Bernanke, B. S. *et al.* (1991). The credit crunch. *Brookings Papers on Economic Activity, 1991*(2), 205–247; Bernanke, B. *et al.* (1994). *The financial accelerator and the flight to quality*, Working Paper 4789, National Bureau of Economic Research. doi: 10.3386/w4789; Bernanke, B. S. and Gertler, M. (1995). *Inside the black box: The credit channel of monetary policy Transmission*, Working Paper 5146, National Bureau of Economic Research. doi: 10.3386/w5146.

[13]Gambacorta, L. and Marques-Ibanez, D. (2011). The bank lending channel: Lessons from the crisis. *Economic Policy, 26*(66), 135–182.

[14]Greenwald, B. and Stiglitz, J. E. (2003). *Towards a New Paradigm in Monetary Economics*. Cambridge: Cambridge University Press.

for credit scoring.[15] Meanwhile, SMEs are the larger providers of employment in most economies and therefore play a key role in development. At the intersection of individuals and SMEs, the segment of micro-entrepreneurs has received a high level of attention.

However, the most recent research brings a more complex analysis on relationship lending and goes against a common paradigm. In fact, the specialization of banks in the SME segment may not lead to superior efficiency.[16] The focus on one segment of the market does not necessarily lead to superior bank performance. In fact, research shows that sectorial specialization increases volatility and systemic risk exposures, while not leading to higher returns. Banks that are specialized in niche segments such as SMEs are not at an advantage compared to banks with more traditional intermediation models. Data on US banks from the Survey of Small Bank Finance confirm the view that specialized banks may not be at an advantage compared to more universal players, suggesting that large banks are perhaps using new lending technologies, such as scoring, the use of collateral in order to offset the potentially less detailed personal knowledge they have of borrowers.[17]

Despite the considerable progress, around 1.7 billion people still do not have access to formal financial services, or 31% of adults globally.[18] In the lower-income segments, more than 50% of adults in the poorest households are unbanked. What is the main reason for financial exclusion?

There are three main reasons for being unbanked: the costs associated with bank accounts, distances traveled to reach a bank or financial agent, and the various requirements involved in opening a financial account. Those three reasons alone explain 73% of the cases of unbanked people. Moreover, one-fourth of people with an account either have a dormant or low-use account.

---

[15]Pinheiro, A. C. and Moura, A. R. (2001). *Segmentation and the Use of Information in Brazilian Credit Markets.* Rio de Janeiro: Banco Nacional de Desenvolvimento Econômico e Social.

[16]Beck, T. and De Jonghe, O. (2013). Lending concentration, bank performance and systemic risk: Exploring cross-country variation.

[17]Berger, A. N. *et al.* (2014). Do small businesses still prefer community banks? *Journal of Banking & Finance, 44*, 264–278.

[18]Demirgüç-Kunt, A. *et al.* (2018). The Global Findex Database 2017: Measuring financial inclusion and the FinTech revolution. World Bank, April.

Account ownership naturally translates into usage of financial services: 34% of firms in developing economies have a bank loan, versus 51% in developed markets.[19] For firms, especially small and medium-sized enterprises, improving access to credit is likely to have significant growth effects, as "200 million enterprises in developing economies are still constrained in terms of financing, even though small and medium enterprises generate the greatest number of new jobs, employ the largest number of people in aggregate." Retailers can play a central role "not only in increasing consumer acceptance of payments, but [they] can also contribute to improved supply chain efficiency by paying their suppliers electronically and, ultimately, can encourage financial inclusion."[20]

Data availability is critical to understand the progress of inclusion. The Global Financial Inclusion database was created by the World Bank and provides in-depth data showing how people save, borrow, make payments and manage risk. The Findex database was launched with the first survey in 2011, followed by surveys in 2014 and 2017. The 2017 edition shows that 69% of adults worldwide have an account. Between 2011 and 2017, one billion adults became account holders.[21] The 2014 survey showed that in developing countries, "1.3 billion adults with an account pay utilities bills in cash and more than half a billion pay school fees in cash." When people participate in the financial system, they are better able to start and expand businesses, invest in education, manage risk and absorb financial shocks.[22]

Being financially excluded is linked to income level: the richest 20% of adults in developing countries are more than twice as likely to have a formal account as the poorest 20%. Yet, while the poor do not have the same access to financial products as wealthier individuals, their need for financial services may be even greater.

---

[19] World Bank Group (2013). *Global Financial Development Report 2014: Financial Inclusion* (Vol. 2). World Bank Publications.

[20] World Bank Group (2016). *Innovation in Electronic Payment Adoption: The Case of Small Retailers*. World Bank Publications.

[21] Demirgüç-Kunt, A. *et al.* (2018). The Global Findex Database 2017: Measuring financial inclusion and the FinTech revolution. World Bank, April.

[22] Bacchetta, P. and Gerlach, S. (1997). Consumption and credit constraints: International evidence. *Journal of Monetary Economics*, 40, 207–238. doi: 10. 1016/S0304-3932(97)00042-1.

Research shows that access to savings products — and, in particular, to "commitment" savings, in which individuals restrict their right to withdraw funds until they have reached a self-specified goal — can have important benefits beyond simply increasing one's amount of savings: it can also help empower women, increase productive investment and consumption, raise productivity and incomes, and increase expenditures on preventive health.[23]

The three main barriers to savings have included branch location with the need to deposit small funds frequently close to home or work, cost with a reluctance to open a formal savings account that bears costs, and liquidity with the ability to withdraw part of the savings at any time. Studies suggest that overcoming those three barriers has more weight than behavioral incentives, such as when savings are earmarked for a specific finality like education expenses or when goals are defined.[24]

Financial inclusion is much broader and ambitious than just providing formal bank accounts. Greater financial inclusion, especially "among those most likely to be excluded: poor, rural, female or young individuals," is associated with lower account costs, greater proximity to financial intermediaries, stronger legal rights, and more politically stable environments.[25]

Benefits and Limits of Financial Inclusion

The case for inclusion is both ethical and economic

The ethical current suggests that inclusive societies can be seen as fair and allow people to fulfill their potential.[26] John Rawls builds his theory of justice in contrast to the utilitarian view. Rawls defines

---

[23]Better Than Cash Alliance (2015). An inclusive approach to digital payments ecosystems: Accelerating the transition from cash requires an ecosystem approach. Working Paper.

[24]Beck, T. (2015). Microfinance: A critical literature survey. IEG working paper, 2015/No.4. Washington, DC: Independent Evaluation Group, World Bank Group, p. 14.

[25]Allen, F. *et al.* (2012). The foundations of financial inclusion: Understanding ownership and use of formal accounts.

[26]Rawls, J. (1971). *A Theory of Justice*. Harvard: Cambridge Press; Rawls, J. (1988). La théorie de la justice comme équité: une théorie politique et non pas

a hypothetical initial state, where the wealth of the economy has not been shared, and all participants in a society agree on the essential basic treatment that should be offered to each of them. This "veil of ignorance" allows to define the basic level of inclusion and comfort that an individual would accept in a given society. There is a pragmatic basis for the theory, which does not have to rely on a religious or philosophical prerequisite. Rawls underlines that his theory of justice is political in essence, and not metaphysical. His theory can be defined as an implementation of the game theory to a view of justice and is based on a principle of fairness. The basic principles of justice "are the principles that rational and free persons concerned to further their own interests would accept in an initial position of equality as defining the fundamentals of the terms of their association." Authors have also linked the emergence of a middle class, linked to inclusion, to benefits in terms of institutions and adoption of democracy through a contribution to "economic growth, as well as social and political stability."[27]

The economic arguments can be divided into three broad groups, depending on the mechanism by which financial inclusion leads to a positive outcome for society.

The first and most studied set of arguments links financial inclusion with higher economic growth. Levine, in a seminal paper, analyzed the channel between the financial sector and economic growth, contrary to the previous literature that focused more on the relationship between money and growth. According to him, the financial system is a "real" sector, and does not respond passively to economic growth. The author suggests a "positive, first-order relationship between financial development and economic growth."[28] The argument is particularly present in the literature produced by

---

métaphysique. In *Individu et justice sociale*. Le Seuil (programme ReLIRE), pp. 277–318.

[27]Pressman, S. (2007). The decline of the middle class: An international perspective. *Journal of Economic Issues*, *41*(1), 181–200; Chun, N. *et al.* (2016). The role of middle class in democratic diffusion. *International Review of Economics & Finance*, *42*, 536–548.

[28]Levine, R. (1997). Financial development and economic growth: Views and agenda. *Journal of Economic Literature*, *35*(2), 688–726.

the World Bank.[29] The current consensus is that financial inclusion has a positive impact on a host of well-being and economic development metrics, such as income generation or protection from hardship. Authors suggest that "under normal circumstances, the degree of financial intermediation is not only positively correlated with growth and employment, but it is generally believed to causally impact growth," due to lower transaction costs and better distribution of capital and risk across the economy.[30] Emerging evidence indicates that access to financial services through formal accounts can enable individuals and firms to smooth consumption, manage risk, and invest in education, health and enterprises. Authors investigated the effect of access to finance on job growth in 50,000 firms across 70 developing countries and found that "increased access to finance results in higher employment growth, especially among micro, small, and medium enterprises."[31] A growing number of randomized evaluations supports the consensus that financial services have a positive impact on a variety of microeconomic indicators related with development, including self-employment business activities, household consumption, and well-being.[32] The impact varies across individual financial product categories. Randomized controlled trials to date have largely been conducted at individual product levels, whereas some observers would argue that research ought to measure whether access to a broad range of services improves the household ability to make appropriate choices. Controlling for other relevant variables, almost 30% of the variation across countries in rates of

---

[29]Beck, T. and Demirgüç-Kunt, A. (2008). Access to finance: An unfinished agenda. *The World Bank Economic Review, 22*(3), 383–396; Cull, R. *et al.* (2012). Financial inclusion and stability: What does research show? CGAP Brief. Washington, DC: World Bank; Demirgüç-Kunt, A. and Singer, D. (2017). Financial inclusion and inclusive growth: A review of recent empirical evidence.

[30]CGAP (2014). Financial Inclusion and Development: Recent Impact Evidence, No. 92, April 2014, p. 6.

[31]Ayyagari, M. *et al.* (2016). Access to finance and job growth: Firm-level evidence across developing countries. Policy Research Working Paper; No. 7604. World Bank, Washington, DC.

[32]CGAP (2015); Bauchet, J. *et al.* (2011). Latest findings from randomized evaluations of microfinance; Angelucci, M. *et al.* (2013). Win some lose some? Evidence from a randomized microcredit program placement experiment by Compartamos Banco (No. w19119). National Bureau of Economic Research.

poverty reduction can be attributed to cross-country variation in financial development.[33]

The second argument links financial inclusion with a reduction in inequalities. Indeed, higher financial inclusion impacts disproportionately more the poorer segments of the population and therefore can contribute to reducing inequality. While a reduction in poverty rates is good *per se*, a reduction in inequality has also been demonstrated to have positive effects on society. The reflection on inequalities has experienced a renewed focus with historic analyses on the distribution of income and wealth, finding strong evidence for a rise in inequalities in the past three decades.[34] Data support that "the rise in income inequality in high-income countries as well as in large emerging economies, combined with the reduction of average income inequalities between countries, transformed the geography of global inequality over the past few decades." In other words, there are now "global poor in rich countries".

Equal societies reach higher growth rates and achieve higher income levels and more stable growth.[35] Easterly finds that a "higher share of income for the middle class and lower ethnic divisions are associated with higher income and higher growth." He also finds evidence that the middle-class consensus leads to "more education, better health, better infrastructure, better economic policies, less political instability, less civil war and ethnic minorities at risk, more social "modernization" and more democracy." Data also show that "countries with higher inequality at a given point in time tend to have lower intergenerational mobility rates."[36]

Chancel notes that the richest 1% of Western Europeans and North Americans captured around 17–20% of national income a century ago. This value decreased to 8% in the 1970–1980s before returning to 10–20% in the late 2010s. Between 1980 and 2017, the

---

[33]Beck, T. *et al.* (2007). Finance, inequality and the poor. *Journal of Economic Growth*, *12*(1), 27–49.

[34]Piketty, T. (2013). *Le capital au XXIe siècle*. Le Seuil.

[35]Easterly, W. (2001). The middle class consensus and economic development. *Journal of Economic Growth*, *6*, 317. doi: 10.1023/A:1012786330095.

[36]Chancel, L. (2021). Ten facts about inequality in advanced economies [Chapter 1], in Rodrik, D. and Blanchard, O. (Eds.), *Combating Inequality: Rethinking Government's Role*. Cambridge, MA: MIT Press, pp. 171–176.

income share of the poorest 50% of Europeans rose by 40%, while
the income of the bottom 50% of Americans grew just by 3% over
the same period. In the United States, the wealth share of the top
1% has risen from 25% in the late 1970s to around 40% today, a
rise almost entirely driven by the top 0.1%. The share of wealth of
the top 1% of Europeans increased from 15% to 20–25% over the
same time period (late 1970s to today). Researchers such as Piketty
or Chancel have brought a unique contribution to the field by gathering longer time series and allowing for cross-country comparisons,
showing that "capital is back". This trend is not driven by the Global
Financial Crisis, nor it is an inevitable consequence of global trade
or technology, as evidenced by the diverging trends between the US
and Western Europe.

The third argument links higher financial inclusion with a better efficiency of policymaking and stability. With higher access to
financial services, levels of formality increase in the economy and
more people fall within the reach of government policies. Authors
highlight a relationship between financial inclusion and sought-after
policy outcomes, such as women empowerment, health, education,
gender equality, and peace.[37] Broad access to bank deposits can have
a positive effect on financial stability. By moving away from cash payments to digital to distribute government wages and cash transfers
such as pensions, "governments can cut costs and reduce leakage".[38]
Importantly, wider inclusion and lower levels of informality also make
monetary policy more effective, as reference rates defined by monetary authorities impact more economic agents.

It is therefore not a surprise that financial inclusion has become
in the past three decades a growing focus of public policy. At the G20
Summit in Seoul in 2010, financial inclusion was recognized as one of
the main pillars of the global development agenda. The Maya Declaration was signed in 2011 in Riviera Maya, Mexico. The document
has become an important international framework for including the

---

[37]Han, R. and Melecky, M. (2013). Financial inclusion for financial stability:
Access to bank deposits and the growth of deposits in the global financial crisis;
Klapper, L. *et al.* (2016). Achieving the sustainable development goals.
[38]Klapper, L. and Singer, D. (2014). The opportunities of digitizing payments.

unbanked in order to "unlock their full economic and social potential while contributing to reduced income disparities, inclusive development and overall national financial stability."[39]

However, financial inclusion has not always met its claimed objectives.

Evidence has shown mixed conclusions on the relationship between financial inclusion and poverty reduction. For example, data on Mexican microcredit did not show a statistically relevant correlation between access to credit and higher revenues or financial resilience of borrowers.[40] Moreover, the risks of excessive or inadequate financial inclusion have led policymakers to focus not just on access and usage, but also on the quality of financial services and capabilities of users. Capabilities put the emphasis on the abilities of consumers to select, identify and use services that are tailored to their needs. In some cases, consumer lenders bear responsibility in situations of over-indebtedness.[41] Some authors add that the "emerging field of behavioral economics has identified biases that can lead borrowers to take on more debt than is good for them." In extreme cases, high growth in microcredit has led to multiple lending, defined as borrowers taking credit from multiple sources at once, excessive leverage for households, leading to massive consumer defaults, and tragic incidents in some instances, as in the case of India in 2010. Morocco, Bosnia and Pakistan have also experienced episodes of massive consumer delinquencies in microcredit, and authors have recommended that microfinance institutions improved their marketing and underwriting, designing "products that better match client needs and cognitive abilities," improving credit reporting, and developing "early

---

[39]Alliance for Financial Inclusion (2014). The 2014 Maya declaration progress report: Measurable goals with optimal impact.

[40]Angelucci, M. *et al.* (2013). *Win some lose some? Evidence from a randomized microcredit program placement experiment by Compartamos Banco* (No. w19119). National Bureau of Economic Research.

[41]Rhyne, E. (2001). Mainstreaming microfinance: How lending to the poor began, grew, and came of age in Bolivia (No. 332.1 R4). Bloomfield, CT: Kumarian Press. On the Bolivian microfinance crisis and de Mariz, F. *et al.* (2011). Discovering limits. Global microfinance valuation survey 2011. Available at SSRN: https://ssrn.com/abstract=2654041 for India.

warning systems."[42] Countercyclical policies can also bear risks when using credit to support consumption.[43]

Financial inclusion increases economic growth up to a point, and access to credit without proper supervision can have a negative impact on financial stability. In contrast to credit, other types of access to financial services do not seem to impact financial stability adversely. Credit has a bell-shaped impact on growth, while other financial services such as savings or payments have a linear relationship. As we now know, "not all financial products are equally effective in reaching development goals, such as reductions in poverty and inequality."[44]

Inclusion Through Which Products

At the global level, a higher GDP per capita is associated with higher usage of electronic payments and higher levels of banking penetration. Penetration of financial services varies widely between countries. More than 80% of Brazilian adults have some kind of active relationship with a financial institution, according to data from the Central Bank as of September 2020. This is much higher than the banking rate in the rest of Latin America. Moreover, 70% of Latin American adults have a smartphone, compared to 66% for the world average.

Data from the Findex database from 2017 show the disparity between countries, even within developing economies. While account ownership is close to 100% in OECD countries, the percentage goes down to less than 40% in Nigeria or Mexico. Similarly, the reliance on mobile banking services is widespread in richer economies, with more than 90% of adults receiving or making a digital payment in the past year. This compares with less than 20% in countries like India or Mexico (Figure 1).

---

[42]CGAP (2011). Too much microcredit? A survey of the evidence on over-indebtedness. No. 19, September 2011.
[43]Bonomo, M. *et al.* (2015). Macroeconomic and financial consequences of the post-crisis government-driven credit expansion in Brazil.
[44]Demirgüç-Kung, A. and Singer, D. (2017). Financial inclusion and inclusive growth: A review of recent empirical evidence.

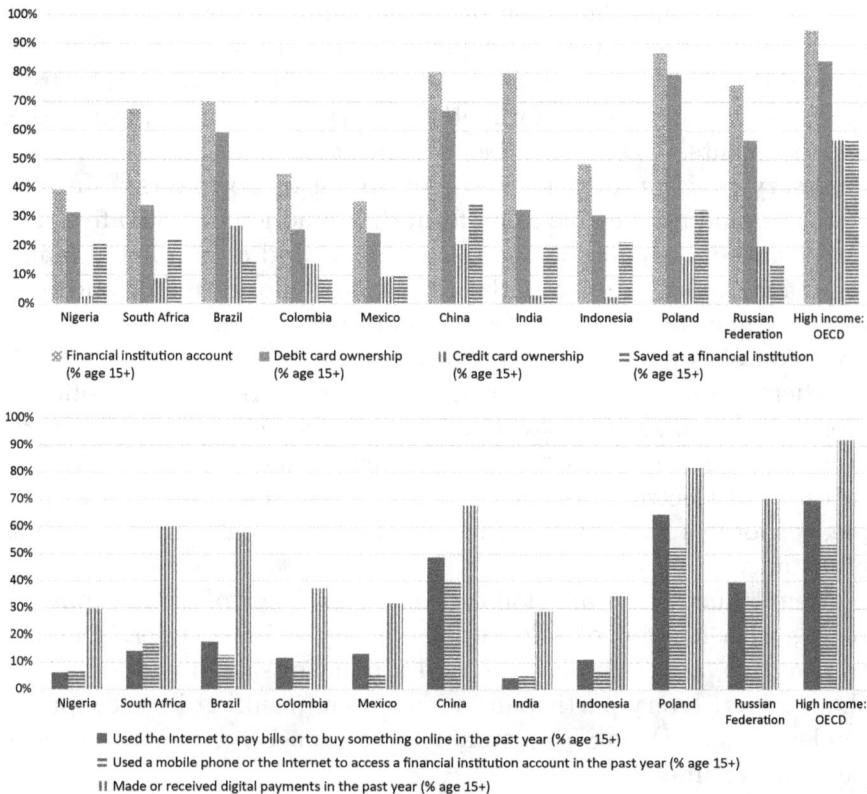

Figure 1: Metrics of Adoption of Financial Products (2017)

Source: Findex database. Demirgüç-Kunt *et al.* (2018). The Global Findex Database 2017: Measuring financial inclusion and the FinTech revolution. World Bank, April.

There are many faces to financial inclusion. The theme encompasses cases such as microcredit concession by non-bank financial institutions and public banks, transfers and payment capabilities offered via mobile connectivity, government transfers via electronic payments and banking correspondents, or life microinsurance policies. Other examples include wealth management products in money market funds with no minimum investment balance, or supply chain finance that uses receivables as a collateral for credit.

The traditional definition of financial intermediation focuses on its credit function. Klein developed a theory of the banking firm and showed that banks are not simply allocators of capital and differ from funds in that they can perform other functions such as deposit-taking and payments.[45] Diamond had the intuition that banks perform a necessary function of delegated monitoring of borrowers.[46] In fact, lenders would not be able to perform that function or would free ride. Other authors expand on the role of banks and argue that it makes sense for banks to offer both credit and deposits under one roof, as those may be the "manifestations of one primitive function: the provision of liquidity," with potential synergies between functions.[47]

Microfinance is evolving and becoming more complex, offering more products, such as savings, insurance, such as life, agricultural crops, and property and casualty, and electronic payments. This last category of electronic payments includes transfers from and to people, corporates and governments, and international transfers such as remittances.

Remittances typically follow a complex layer of market participants, with a point of sale in the country of the sender, a money transmitter, a money business, and a point of sale in the country of the receiver. Every participant adds its fee, resulting in a fee for the sender of as much as 8% on transactions from US dollars to Mexican pesos for example.

Microfinance providers are also incorporating the benefits of technology, even though they maintain their significant branch networks to attend customers. Research suggests that "much of the value created with digital implementations is associated with the credit process," in the form of efficiency gains for the agents through automated underwriting and approval process and leveraging existing data from returning customers. The mobile app of Bancamía in Colombia digitized the workflow of commercial officers and "increased their

---

[45]Klein, M. A. (1971). A theory of the banking firm. *Journal of Money, Credit and Banking*, *3*(2), 205–218.

[46]Diamond, D. W. (1984). Financial intermediation and delegated monitoring. *The Review of Economic Studies*, *51*(3), 393–414.

[47]Kashyap, A. K. *et al.* (2002). Banks as liquidity providers: An explanation for the coexistence of lending and deposit-taking. *The Journal of Finance*, *57*(1), 33–73.

productivity by 27% and decreased loan processing time by over 50% within one year."[48]

Savings are an essential financial service for poorer households, since building assets over time allow to face emergencies or large expenses, such as marriage, sickness or death in the family. Women play a critical role within households "as money managers, juggling day to day needs while making sure that school fees are paid and health emergencies are covered."[49] Not only do women have less access to financial services, but research shows that women's decision-making on spending and investment brings better development outcomes than men's as they tend to focus on the household, dedicating spending for education and health. Repayment rates are usually higher for women than for men.

In poorer communities, savings mechanisms are often informal and unreliable. Poorer segments tend to save at home, by buying excess inventory for their businesses, or livestock. They also rely on neighborhood savings clubs. The small amounts are often seen as the main barrier for consumers to bring their savings to a bank branch, especially as the time spent to deposit the cash is a real disincentive. Cash-in and cash-out capabilities offered by financial institutions or cooperatives are essential for consumers to be willing to save with official mechanisms; in other words, it must be easy, cost-efficient and convenient to make deposits or withdraw cash.[50]

Households in emerging markets often resort to savings mechanisms outside of the banking sector. The most widespread mechanisms include savings clubs and RoSCAs. But not all of those are informal, as in the case of "consorcios," a form of RoSCA popular in Brazil, which are regulated by the Central Bank. "RoSCA" stands for Rotating Savings and Credit Association, which are common across emerging markets, including Africa or South Asia. Members save a defined amount every period and the total amount saved in each

---

[48]Flaming, M. and Jeník, I. (2021). Digitization in microfinance: Case studies of pathways to success. Working Paper. Washington, D.C.: CGAP.

[49]Women's World Banking (2014). Savings: A gateway to financial inclusion. Available at http://www.womensworldbanking.org/wp-content/uploads/2014/0 1/Womens-World-Banking-Savings-Gateway-Financial-Inclusion-new.pdf. Last accessed October 6, 2021, p. 3.

[50]Mas, I. (2009). The economics of branchless banking. *Innovations*, *4*(2), 57–75.

period is given to one of the members. This continues until every-one receives the "prize," at which point the RoSCA comes naturally to an end. One of the key features of the RoSCA is that it com-bines the accumulation of small amounts with the extension of a large lump sum, "blurring the distinction between saving and bor-rowing."[51] RoSCA and consorcios group like-minded savers under the same mechanism, with every participant turning into a borrower when receiving the prize. A variation on the theme allows members to bid to receive the lump sum, essentially accelerating the date of the "prize," known as ASCA (Accumulating Savings and Credit Associ-ation): this is an auction RoSCA.

Both RoSCA and ASCA differ from the concept of a savings club also known as self-help groups (SHGs) — also very common in emerg-ing markets — where all members of the group save a small sum at frequent dates and retrieve the large lump sum at the end of the period, and where peer pressure plays a key role in ensuring that participants do save.

Mycon is a Brazilian fully digital originator of consorcios and defends that the product fulfills a social mission in so far as they allow customers to have access to durable goods when a credit would have been too expensive or simply not approved by any bank. Consorcio is a way to socialize the acquisition of a large ticket asset, such as a car or a house. Consorcios are a popular retail product in Brazil, with annual growth above 10% over the past decade, despite macro-economic volatility (Figure 2). The product has anticyclical charac-teristics for banks, as it performs well when credit concession becomes more stringent.

Experiments with mobile banking in Africa show the potential that new technology offers for savings and transfers. Services such as M-Pesa have allowed to increase meaningfully financial inclusion in Kenya, where a fifth of the country's GDP is estimated to flow through this service and close to two-thirds of the adult popula-tion uses mobile payments. The use of M-Pesa is negatively related with the use of informal saving mechanisms, positively associated with the probability of being banked, and its widespread use has

---

[51]Collins, D. *et al.* (2009). *Portfolios of the Poor: How the World's Poor Live on $2 a Day.* Princeton University Press, p. 123.

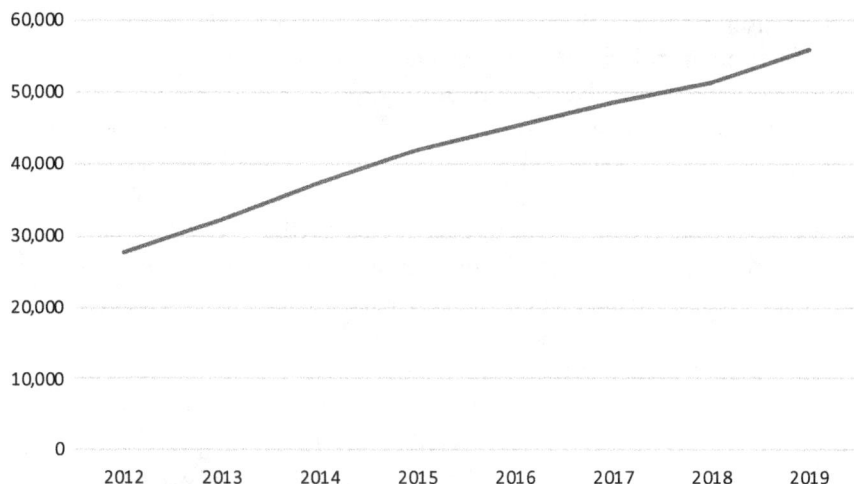

Figure 2: Growth of Consórcio in Brazil (R$, bn)
Source: Central Bank of Brazil.

created competitive pressure on traditional providers such as Western Union to reduce their prices.[52] The introduction of M-Pesa has led to a reduction in transaction costs for transfers in Kenya and has been associated with a better ability by users to absorb negative income shocks, especially among lower-income households.[53] Research suggests that recipients benefit from both a higher quantity of remittances received in the case of negative income shocks and a higher variety of remittance senders, showcasing the positive impact of M-Pesa. Electronic payments reduce transaction costs, widen the network of assistance in the case of shocks, and can possibly lead to better development outcomes because of changes in intrahousehold decision-making induced by mobile delivery of grants.[54] With

---

[52]Mbiti, I. and Weil, D. (2011). Mobile banking: The impact of M-Pesa in Kenya. NBER Working Papers 17129, National Bureau of Economic Research, Inc.

[53]Jack, W. and Suri, T. (2014). Risk sharing and transactions costs: Evidence from Kenya's mobile money revolution. *The American Economic Review*, *104*(1), 183–223 (41 pages).

[54]Aker, J. *et al.* (2013). How do electronic transfers compare? Evidence from a mobile money cash transfer experiment in Niger. Tufts University Working Paper. Find that randomly switching to mobile delivery of cash grants in Niger leads to a change in consumption patterns, toward a more diversified diet, possibly

"33 million people using the mobile wallet and 96% of households outside the capital Nairobi having at least one M-Pesa account," the innovation impacted Kenya's economy.[55]

In southern Mozambique, "vulnerable households experiencing emergency shocks received 210% greater value of remittances and maintained 39% higher consumption in regions with mobile money access than those in regions without."[56] Studies identified the mechanisms through which digital services improve welfare, i.e. faster and cheaper transfers received in response to household shocks, coming from a diverse network. Several studies show the unmistakenly positive impact of digital financial services on users.

The example of M-Pesa shows how a society leapfrogged the regular brick-and-mortar banking infrastructure to build a digital banking platform, initially focused on payments and then expanding into credit with M-Shwari. In Guatamala, Banco de los Traballadores launched "Yolo," a simplified digital banking offering, which attracted 250,000 users within 60 days of its launch, with online services, prepaid cards and access to a network of ATMs.

Insurance is another important channel for financial inclusion and can offer a financial mechanism to protect consumers against unforeseen hardship. Banco Compartamos in Mexico is one of the largest micro insurers globally and includes life microinsurance coverage in every credit operation. In the case of a borrower's death, the credit is forgiven and her family receives a cash amount of 15,000 pesos, meant to cover burial expenses. In fact, on top of the emotional challenge brought by death, the departure of a household member, in particular a breadwinner, can be a financially insurmountable event for families. Research has shown the financial distress brought to families by death in South Africa, as social convention requires expensive

---

because of changes in intrahousehold decision-making induced by mobile delivery of grants.

[55]Monteiro, F. and Carrick, A.M. (2019). Digital Transformation in Latin America: Leapfrogging and Social Impact, Case Study, INSEAD.

[56]World Bank Group (2021). Why with such robust evidence isn't digital finance more ubiquitous across poor countries? World Bank Blogs. Available at https://blogs.worldbank.org/allaboutfinance/why-such-robust-evidence-isnt-digital-finance-more-ubiquitous-across-poor-countries. Last accessed October 6, 2021.

burial ceremonies, in a context of rising death rates under AIDS. InsurTech companies, such as Vitality in South Africa, are leveraging technology to change the distribution of policies, pricing of risk, and after-sale service.

Microinsurance constitutes somewhat of a puzzle to researchers, as the need for the product, its benefits and the large size of the potential market make it look like the next big opportunity in microfinance. For example, research in rural Kenya on index-based drought insurance shows that "insured households are on average 36 percentage points less likely to anticipate drawing down assets, and 25% points less likely to anticipate reducing meals upon receipt of a payout".[57] However, the existing coverage has met with limited enthusiasm and low take-up. Research suggests that this is not because users do not understand the benefits, as was sometimes stated by the proponents of an academic vision of financial education. That said, it appears that households — especially poor households — may find it difficult to pay today for something they hope they will not have to use in the future. Findings by field experiments have several implications for the design of insurance products. First, trust and word-of-mouth are essential drivers of product adoption, and products that are designed to pay fairly often can engender trust in users. Having a well-known underwriter also helps client trust and adoption. Second, payouts conditions need to be simple, clear and payments needs to be fast, as users value rapid liquidity in the event of a disaster.

Financial inclusion has graduated from its seminal focus on microcredit to incorporate other products such as remittances, savings and insurance.

---

[57] Janzen, S. and Carter, M. (2013). After the drought: The impact of microinsurance on consumption smoothing and asset protection. NBER. Working Paper 19702.

Chapter 3

Microcredit 15 Years After
the Nobel Prize

Lessons Learned and Latest Trends in Microcredit

When Grameen Bank and Muhammad Yunus won the Nobel Peace
Price in 2006 for outstanding achievements with microcredit, the
world came to know the concept of small loans and the potential
they could have to lift millions out of poverty. Those loans were
meant for consumption or for microentrepreneurs to launch or grow
their businesses. In his acceptance speech at the Nobel Committee
in Oslo on December 10, 2006, Yunus emphasized that poverty was
a threat to peace and a denial of all human rights. By 2006, the
bank he had created had given "loans to nearly 7 million poor people, 97% of whom women, in 73,000 villages in Bangladesh," with
the goal to "make a break in the historical continuation of poverty"
and "put poverty in the museums".[1] The bank focused on housing,
student and micro-enterprise loans, savings, pension funds and insurance products. Cumulated loans had reached $6 billion by then, with
a repayment rate of 99%. As Banerjee and Duflo put it, "from its
modest beginnings with the Bangladesh Rehabilitation Assistance
Committee (universally known as BRAC) and the Grameen Bank

---

[1]Yunus, M. (2006). Nobel lecture. Available at https://www.nobelprize.org/
prizes/peace/2006/yunus/26090-muhammad-yunus-nobel-lecture-2006-2/. Last
accessed November 16, 2021.

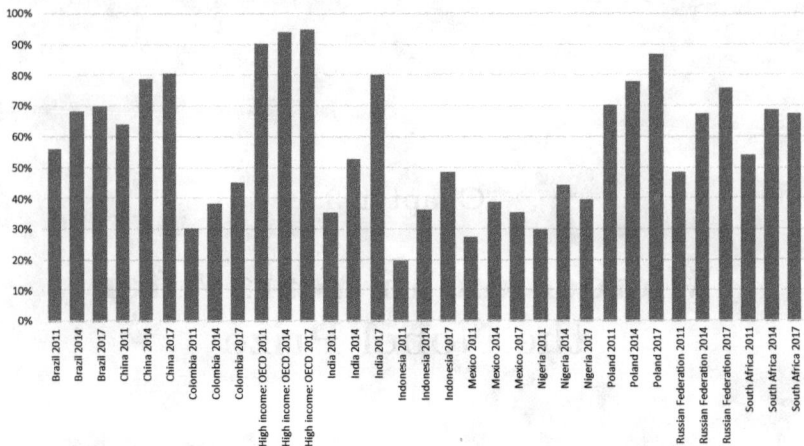

Figure 1:   Growth in Financial Access Metrics (Financial Institution Account,
% Age 15+)

Source: Findex database, Demirgüç-Kunt *et al.* (2018). The Global Findex
Database 2017: Measuring financial inclusion and the FinTech revolution. World
Bank, April.

in the mid-1970s in Bangladesh, microcredit is now a global phenomenon," having reached between 150 and 200 million borrowers,
mainly women, and available to many more."[2] The percentage of
citizens, aged 15 and more, who have an account at a formal financial institution has grown steadily over time and across geographies
(Figure 1).

Microfinance can be defined as "attempts to provide financial services to households and micro-enterprises that are excluded from
traditional commercial banking services, [...] typically low-income,
self-employed or informally employed individuals, with no formalized
ownership titles on their assets and with limited formal identification
papers."[3] Microcredit focuses on lending, while microfinance has a
broader goal of providing different financial services to customers.
Microcredit was viewed as an alternative to shark loans in communities, with a potential to alleviate poverty, especially for women. Its
focus is the low end of the market, or the so-called bottom of the

---

[2]Banerjee, A. V. and Duflo, E. (2011). *Poor Economics*. New York: Perseus Books.
Chapter 7 on microcredit.
[3]Beck, T. (2015). Microfinance: A critical literature survey. IEG Working Paper,
2015/No.4. Washington, DC: Independent Evaluation Group, World Bank Group.

pyramid. High costs, both operating expenses and losses from non-repayment of loans, create a high barrier for the supply of micro-finance services. On the demand side, financial literacy is often a barrier for users. Microfinance is based on the idea that the financial sector could play a key role in poverty alleviation and income generation, by promoting wider access and a more efficient capital allocation. As Amartya Sen explains, poverty is not just a lack of money, it's not having the capability to realize one's full potential.[4]

The Grameen Bank was founded in 1983 by Muhammad Yunus, who began the project in the town of Jobra, using his own money to deliver small loans in the amount of $27 at low-interest rates to the rural poor. Other microfinance organizations were started a few years before, including BRAC, founded in Bangladesh in 1972 and ASA in 1978. In Indonesia, microcredit began in 1984 with the formation of Unit Desa at Bank Rakyat Indonesia, offering microloans at market rates. In Latin America, PRODEM was established in Bolivia in 1986; a bank that would transform into for-profit BancoSol. Other organizations included NGOs, such as Women's World Banking (WWB), present in 31 countries today across continents. Pro Mujer was founded in 1990 and is present across Latin America. Both WWB and Pro Mujer target women in priority. More actors work with the concept of a double bottom line, targeting financial and social objectives, and even sometimes a triple bottom line, including environmental considerations.

Microcredit *per se* was not totally new in the 1970s. Earlier attempts to provide loans to a broad base of customers with a social objective included examples such as credit unions and cooperatives. Raiffeisen founded the first cooperative lending bank for farmers in rural Germany in 1864, and gave its name to several systems of cooperatives, including Rabobank in the Netherlands. The combined ideas that small borrowers could be good credit, that they could represent a huge untapped business opportunity and that credit could have a tremendous positive impact on the lives of millions of individuals and families bore a revolutionary promise.

Microcredit covers a variety of business models and realities. Some institutions focus on microentrepreneurs while others disburse microloans for consumption also. Rates vary widely, from low levels,

---

[4]Sen, A. (1999). *Development as Freedom*. New York: Knopf.

often supported by donors and a philosophy to reinvest profits into the institution. On the other side of the spectrum, some institutions charge interest rates similar to market practices, spurring vehement controversy in the sector such as the debate that opposed Compartamos at the time of its successful IPO in 2007 and Yunus and his philosophy of social businesses.

Compartamos is the largest microfinance institution in Latin America, headquartered in Mexico, with operations also in Peru. The company was founded in 1990, initially as a not-for-profit institution focused on offering financial services to women, especially in the southern and poorer states of Mexico. The status of the entity evolved to a for-profit non-banking financial institution. In 2006, Compartamos became a fully regulated bank and the company went public on the Mexican stock exchange in 2007. Compartamos currently offers working capital loans, insurance, savings, payment channels and financial education to more than three million clients, "with the objective of improving the life quality and development opportunities of people, generating shared value," according to the company. The group reported total loans of approximately 1.9 billion dollars as of the third quarter of 2021. Patricio Diez de Bonilla, CEO of Banco Compartamos, recognizes the continuous challenge to serve the bottom of the pyramid with adequate financial products in Latin America. He notes that FinTechs can help solve some painpoints, but FinTechs will need to follow strict regulations, while a physical presence continues to favor existing players in an economy that is still cash-based. The "jury is still out" to determine the role of FinTechs in a fast evolving financial sector. He notes that COVID-19 accelerated digitization of some processes, such as credit committees or "virtual visits" which, in many cases, worked just as well as in-site visits, increasing the productivity of employees. Diez de Bonilla highlights that "the engagement from customers was impressive". On the flip side, the pandemic increased the cash usage in day-to-day transactions, as uncertainty led households to stack more cash for precautionary purposes.[5]

---

[5] Interview with Patricio Diez de Bonilla, CEO of Banco Compartamos, November 23, 2021.

The exclusion from formal sources of financial services does not mean that lower-income citizens do not use any financial services at all. Quite the contrary. Financial diaries of the poor show that the financial situation of poor households varies widely from one month to the next and that they use a complex array of informal financial providers, such as money lenders, deposit collectors, stores providing credit, pawnshops, and friends and family.[6] Managing their finances is a "fundamental and well-understood part of everyday life" for the poor.[7]

In their research on the portfolios of the poor, Collins, Murdoch, Rutherford and Ruthven analyzed the financial activity of more than 250 poor households in Bangladesh, India and South Africa. In the colorful description of personal journeys, their influential book emphasized that although poor, households are financially active, using several financial tools with microfinance institutions, moneylenders and often with informal counterparts such as family members, neighbors, or employers. One of the key insights of their analysis is that it is not just the low value of cash flows that is a challenge for poor households, but also their uncertain timing or unpredictability. With their careful analysis of cash flows, the authors note that poor households require financial services that offer flexibility (in repayment for example), stressing that "if you are poor, managing money well is absolutely central to your life — perhaps more so than for any other groups."[8]

Empirical studies show that social classes are often transitory states, with a meaningful income variability from one month to the next.[9] In particular, the literature has focused on the intra-generational social ascension of people who are not yet firmly established in the middle class and are at risk of falling back below poverty levels. This class is sometimes described as the "strugglers"

---

[6]Collins, D. *et al.* (2009). *Portfolios of the Poor: How the World's Poor Live on $2 a Day.* Princeton University Press, p. 26.

[7]CGAP. (2014). Financial inclusion and development: Recent impact evidence, No. 92, April 2014, p. 2.

[8]Collins, D. *et al.* (2009). *Portfolios of the Poor: How the World's Poor Live on $2 a Day.* Princeton University Press, p. 4.

[9]Plano CDE (2012). Gestão financeira entre as classes de baixa renda no Brasil: Abrangente, diversificada, engajada. Bankable Frontier Associates.

or the new vulnerable class, by opposition to the new middle class in countries such as China, India, or Brazil. Research identifies a "group of people in Latin America that are not poor but not middle class either — namely "strugglers" in households with daily income per capita between $4 and $10, at constant 2005 PPP. Strugglers will "account for about a third of the region's population over the next decades" and run the risk of falling back into poverty and being marginalized. Importantly, the "cash transfers they receive are largely offset by indirect taxes" and "the benefit of schooling and other in-kind transfers they receive is questionable after adjusting for quality."[10]

For poor households, the diaries helped uncover several lessons, including the idea that price is just one of the factors considered by customers and rarely the "overriding determinant of financial choices," as poor households consider "convenience, flexibility and reliability."[11] For very small sums and short durations, price is "more sensibly understood as a fee than as annualized interest."[12] Poor households face a daily challenge to match uncertain cash inflows with regular expenses, such as food, but also larger lump sums in the event of sickness, marriage or death, among other events of life. While microfinance institutions may have focused too much on wealth accumulation, with the offering of loans to microentrepreneurs, diaries show how much cash flows (rather than balance sheets) matter for poor households. The rising offering of formal services for the poor provides more reliability, offers consumer protection and allows users to build a credit history.

Models have included group lending, which met with success as a way to reach scale faster, in a context where the small size of microloans is one of the more relevant barriers for lenders, as operating costs make the business model unsustainable. Group loans also have the advantage to offer a group guarantee, where members of the group support each other in the case of default of a member. In fact,

---

[10]Birdsall, N. *et al.* (2014). The strugglers: The new poor in Latin America? *World Development*, *60*, 132–146.

[11]Collins, D. *et al.* (2009). *Portfolios of the Poor: How the World's Poor Live on $2 a Day*. Princeton University Press, p. 153.

[12]Collins, D. *et al.* (2009). *Portfolios of the Poor: How the World's Poor Live on $2 a Day*. Princeton University Press, p. 22.

borrowers often do not have a real guarantee to offer for the loan. The group also plays a key role to monitor the activity of fellow group members and exert peer pressure for repayment, lowering the cost of monitoring for the financial institution. Studies show that individuals with stronger social connections to their fellow group members due to geographic or cultural proximity have higher repayment and higher savings rates.[13]

Microcredit presents some key differences versus traditional credit operations, which explains in part why traditional banks have either avoided this segment or been rarely successful at offering microloans in a sustainable and profitable way. Microcredit by definition considers average loans that are meaningfully smaller than personal or corporate loans disbursed by traditional banks, varying from a few hundreds to thousands of dollars. The average loan of Banco Compartamos in Mexico reached $600 in the second quarter of 2021 (12.7 thousand Mexican pesos), serving 3.5 million customers. There are several operating characteristics that differentiate microfinance from traditional banks, which translate into four essential gaps. We capture those four gaps via metrics of net interest margins, asset quality, efficiency and leverage.

Starting with asset quality, the probability of borrowers to default on their loans is higher in microfinance than for traditional commercial banks, but manageable. Considering a sample of 45 microfinance institutions with data provided by MIX, authors find that the non-performing loan ratio — a common measure of asset quality that divides problematic loans by total loans — reached 3.7% in 2007, compared with 2% for traditional emerging market banks. While the ratio is higher, microfinance institutions adopt strategies to control asset quality, such as joint liability and peer monitoring in the case of group lending, as well as dynamic incentives, such as the promise of a future and larger loan. This supports the idea that microloans and poorer households are not necessarily bad credit.

On the flip side, there have been examples of countries with rapid deterioration of microfinance asset quality. Research shows non-performing loan ratios in 2009 reaching 7% in Bosnia-Herzegovina,

---

[13]Karlan (2007). Social connections and group banking. *The Economic Journal,* *117*(517), F52–F84. Using data for microborrowers in Peru.

10% in Morocco, 12% in Nicaragua and 13% in Pakistan. The case of India has been well documented. Following a rapid expansion of the microcredit industry, the State of Andhra Pradesh saw a major crisis in 2010, exacerbated by improper regulation, government intervention, and a lack of transparent and centralized credit reporting. The crisis of 2010 in Andhra Pradesh was a repeat of previous crises, and not dissimilar to situations observed in other countries, with tragic instances of farmer suicides used as an argument by politicians to attack MFIs, which in turn led repayments to stop once the government stepped in.[14] Episodes of multiple lending with inappropriate supervision have demonstrated the limits of financial intermediation.

While microcredit can experience volatile asset quality, especially in the case of excess lending or natural disasters, evidence suggests that the loan portfolio can also show resilience, as shown in a study of the impact of COVID-19 published by CGAP and Symbiotics in April 2021 analyzing more than 300 microfinance institutions up to December 2020. Microfinance institutions recovered in the second half of 2020, particularly in Africa, but the recovery remained fragile, with questions about how restructured portfolios will impact MFIs' longer-term solvency. Country-specific issues at the macro level and the slow rollout of vaccines in some countries added to fragility.[15]

Deborah Drake, from the Center for Financial Inclusion at Accion, notes that "one of the highest priorities microfinance providers have faced in the midst of the COVID-19 crisis has been access to funding," while "debt investors, particularly microfinance investment vehicles (MIVs), responded quickly and effectively to provide breathing room to microfinance providers through a coordinated effort." Moreover, she highlights the important role of DFIs during COVID-19, but also the evolving mandates of DFIs, which have had to incorporate new considerations into their scope, including climate,

---

[14]Banerjee, A. V. and Duflo, E. (2011). *Poor Economics*. New York: Perseus Books, p. 177; CGAP (2010). Growth and vulnerabilities in microfinance. No. 61 February 2010; de Mariz, F. *et al.* (2011). Discovering limits. Global microfinance valuation survey 2011. Available at SSRN: https://ssrn.com/abstract=2654041.
[15]CGAP (2021). Analyzing the 300 MFIs in symbiotics portfolio and how they fared during COVID. COVID-19 Briefing, July 2021. Available at https://www. cgap.org/sites/default/files/datasets/2021_07_COVID_MFI_Symbiotics.pdf. Last accessed October 6, 2021.

alongside financial inclusion. The uncertainty brought by COVID-19 as well as moratoria and regulatory relief measures made it more difficult for investors to assess the financial strength of MFIs. She notes that Tier II and III microfinance providers were more affected by the crisis and may face potential solvency risks, which could lead to asset sales, while mergers are less likely to occur due to uncertainties about asset quality, the difficulty of aligning the interests of all stakeholders, a lower appetite for brick-and-mortar and labor considerations. Having digital channels was a gamechanger for microfinance providers during COVID-19. Offering credit in a digital form is complemented by other services, including payments, savings, while insurance remains difficult to scale. Partnerships with FinTechs can offer interesting opportunities, as FinTechs can enable outreach, provided there is a sense of purpose.[16]

In the case of Banco Compartamos, COVID-19 had a strong but short duration impact on the bank, due to the nature of loans, which have a short maturity and fully amortize, and the swift actions taken by the bank. On March 17, 2020, Gentera — the parent company of Banco Compartamos — transitioned all 22,500 employees to remote working. The company defined three priorities: care for employees, care for customers, care for the company. The first pillar included no reduction to the workforce nor to benefits. Patricio Diez de Bonilla, CEO of Banco Compartamos, explains that COVID-19 represented a huge challenge and moment of uncertainty, it was also a key opportunity for the company to "live by its values" and care for its people. Loan officers were required to make sure there was a communication channel with every customer, mostly via WhatsApp.[17]

---

[16]Interview with Deborah Drake, November 2, 2021. Deborah Drake is VP, Investor Engagement and Research at the Center for Financial Inclusion (CFI) at Accion. Accion is a global nonprofit committed to creating a financially inclusive world, with a pioneering legacy in microfinance and FinTech impact investing. She also directs the Financial Inclusion Equity Council (FIEC). See also Drake, D. (2021). COVID-19 and microfinance: What's next for equity investors? CGAP Blog Series. Available at https://www.cgap.org/blog/covid-19-and-microfinance-whats-next-equity-investors. Last accessed 21 October 2021.

[17]Interview with Patricio Diez de Bonilla, CEO of Banco Compartamos, November 23, 2021.

The second pillar involved a suspension of principal and interest repayments offered to all customers for 10 weeks, with no penalty and no additional fee. Loan repayment schedule would be reevaluated after 10 weeks. About two-thirds of customers used this benefit, while one-third continued to pay their installments as initially planned. The company maintained insurance coverage. All the implied costs were incurred by the company.

The third pillar consisted in protecting the company and included the drawdown of preexisting funding facilities and the maintenance of a high position of liquid assets. For Compartamos — as for all MFIs — liquidity was a top-of-mind concern. While Compartamos had a good access to lines of funding, smaller microfinance institutions suffered from the contraction in preexisting lines, be it from development banks or from commercial banks and capital markets. Uncertainties around asset quality trends, especially as portfolios were being restructured, complicated further the flow of liquidity.

Following a first phase focused on people, which corresponded to the second quarter of 2020, the bank targeted the restructuring of its client base and loan book. In the third quarter of 2020, about 85% of the loan book was restructured. Loans that could not be restructured led to additional levels of provisions, as the bank decided to "take the hit fast and rebound". This led the bank to recognize the first quarterly loss in its history in the third quarter of 2020.

The fourth quarter is traditionally a critical quarter for microfinance customers, with several holidays and Black Friday, which required financing solutions for borrowers. After caring for people and restructuring the loan book, the bank therefore focused on reactivating its client base. This would allow the bank to "start 2021 with a clean sheet".

Overall, Diez de Bonilla noted that as of the end of 2021, the microfinance sector had not experienced a full recovery yet and borrowers had adjusted down their demand for loans. At the end of 2021, the non-performing loans for Compartamos were back to 3.0% — a very strong level — compared with 6.9% in the third quarter of 2020,[18] with outstanding customer satisfaction with a net promoter

---

[18]Non-performing loans defined as loans with a late repayment over 90 days.

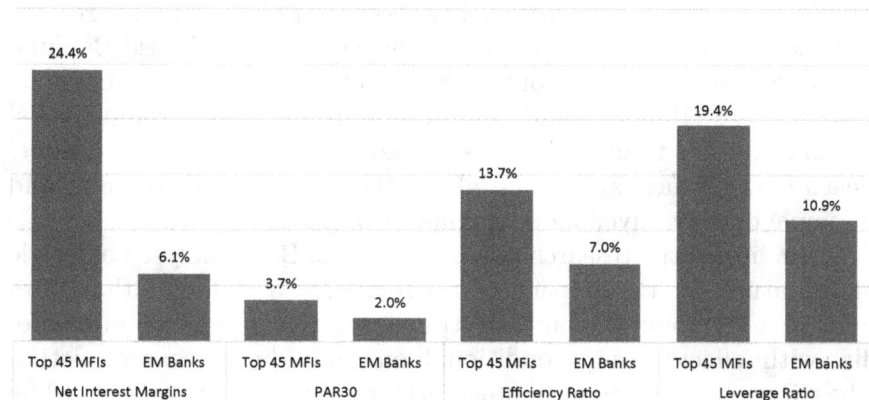

Figure 2:   Key Ratios Comparing Microfinance and Banks
Source: CGAP (2009). Net interest margins defined as net interest income divided by average interest earning assets. PAR30 stands for the portfolio at risk with a late payment over 30 days and is a measure of asset quality. Efficiency ratio is defined as operating expenses divided by gross loans. The leverage ratio is defined as equity to assets. Raw data from MIX, as of 2007.

score of 92, and Compartamos earned once again the number one spot in the "Great Places to Work" both in Mexico and in Peru.

Interest rates tend to be meaningfully higher for microloans, with an average net interest margin (difference between rates charged to borrowers and the cost of funding) of 24.4% for the same sample of 45 largest MFIs, compared with just 6.1% for traditional emerging market banks (Figure 2).

Moreover, the efficiency ratio — a ratio of administrative and personnel expenses divided by total loans — is meaningfully higher for microlenders than for traditional banks. Top MFIs reported an efficiency ratio of 13.7%, versus 7% for banks. In fact, higher interest rates do not mostly remunerate a higher potential risk, as most believe, but the higher cost of operations.

Microlenders also tend to have a more limited access to market funding, in the form of interbank liquidity or bonds, and therefore operate with a higher base of capital, which makes the operation less profitable for shareholders. Top MFIs reported a leverage ratio (ratio of equity to total assets) of 19.4%, compared with 10.9% for traditional emerging market banks.

While microfinance growth has been impressive, many remain excluded from traditional financial services. Women's World Banking estimates that 1 billion women remain outside the formal financial system today. Banerjee and Duflo therefore ask if "microfinance [is] less of a miracle than we have been told".[19] 15 years after the Nobel Peace Prize, what can be said about the growth of microcredit and its impact on the livelihood of millions of people?

In an influential research paper from 2015, Beck analyzed a decade of literature on the impact of microfinance and found that data pointed to "moderate but not transformative effects of microcredit, with effects being conditional on individuals' characteristics. The effects of microsavings interventions seem more promising, while microinsurance interventions suffer mostly from limited take-up. The biggest impact seems to come from expanding payment services."[20]

In the world of social sciences and development, the gold standard to analyze additionality — the impact an intervention had on a sample population above what would have happened otherwise — is the randomized controlled trial (RCT). Borrowed from exact sciences such as medicine, RCT captures and quantifies how much a population benefited from interventions such as a public policy, a vaccination program or a microcredit initiative. RCTs are a powerful tool, which "give researchers, working with a local partner, a chance to implement large-scale experiments designed to test their theories." In a RCT, "individuals or communities are randomly assigned to different treatments," and "since the individuals assigned to different treatments are exactly comparable because they were chosen at random, any difference between them is the effect of the treatment."[21]

One of the first studies by Pitt and Khandker of Grameen Bank and two other MFIs in Bangladesh in 1998 showed a small but significant and positive effect of the use of credit on household expenditures, household assets, labor supply, and the likelihood that children attend schools. This study is subsequently criticized for

---

[19]Banerjee, A. V. and Duflo, E. (2011). *Poor Economics*. New York: Perseus Books, p. 159.
[20]Beck, T. (2015). Microfinance: A critical literature survey. IEG Working Paper, 2015/No.4. Washington, DC: Independent Evaluation Group, World Bank Group.
[21]Banerjee, A. V. and Duflo, E. (2011). *Poor Economics*. New York: Perseus Books, p. 14.

issues related to the identification strategy of credit recipients. An influential research paper from Angelucci, Karlan, and Zinman published in 2015 used a randomized program placement by Compartamos and found modest effects on socioeconomic outcome variables after two to three years, including no statistically significant effect on household income, while there is positive and significant modest increase in female intrahousehold decision-making power.[22]

Many studies using the innovative technique of the RCT have been published over the past 15 years, bringing hard evidence to confirm or criticize economic hypotheses. Studies aggregating the conclusions from dozens of other analyses on the impact of microcredit — also called meta-studies — have also been published. Research by the Abdul Latif Jameel Poverty Action Lab (J-PAL) suggests a mixed impact from microcredit on revenue generation and other economic outcome variables for borrowers.[23] Beck explains that "the initial expectations on microcredit being able to pull millions out of poverty by giving them access to credit have not been fulfilled,"[24] while Banerjee, Karlan, and Zinman stated that there is "a consistent pattern of modestly positive, but not transformative, effects." Beck recommends "to move up the firm ladder toward small enterprises, which might have more potential to be transformative and create jobs."[25]

Although there is no firm evidence that direct access to credit always improves recipients' welfare, there is some tentative evidence that financial deepening can reduce income inequality and

---

[22]Angelucci, M. *et al.* (2013). Win some lose some? Evidence from a randomized microcredit program placement experiment by Compartamos Banco (No. w19119). National Bureau of Economic Research; Banerjee, A. V. *et al.* (2010). *The Miracle of Microfinance? Evidence from a Randomized Evaluation.* Cambridge, Mass.: Abdul Latif Jameel Poverty Action Lab and Massachusetts Institute of Technology, June.

[23]J-PAL (2015). Abdul Latif Jameel Poverty Action Lab, "Where credit is due". *Policy Bulletin*, February.

[24]Beck, T. (2015). Microfinance: A critical literature survey. IEG Working Paper, 2015/No.4. Washington, DC: Independent Evaluation Group, World Bank Group, p. 24.

[25]*Ibid.*, p. 36; Banerjee, A. *et al.* (2015). Six randomized evaluations of microcredit: Introduction and further steps. *American Economic Journal: Applied Economics*, 7(1), 1–21.

poverty alleviation indirectly. Building a cross-country dataset with 45 developed and developing countries, researchers have found that "enterprise credit is positively associated with economic growth whereas household credit is not; and enterprise credit is significantly associated with faster reductions in income inequality whereas household credit is not." In other words, the negative relationship between financial depth and changes in income inequality goes through enterprise and not household credit. This suggests that a key mechanism to spur growth and reduce income inequality comes from financial deepening and its indirect effect on employment growth.[26] This also questions if the most powerful tool related to growth is a "democratization of credit" or rather a more effective credit allocation, implying that microcredit is not necessarily the most important policy area to reap the benefits of financial deepening for poverty alleviation.

The microcredit sector has evolved and two trends have become clear over the past decade, including a broader product offering beyond credit alone, and digitization. International expansion of microfinance operations, in turn, seemed plausible 15 years ago, but has experienced limited success, due to varying regulatory and cultural contexts.

The broader offering now goes beyond credit, and includes payments, transfers, and insurance. Financial deepening has been enabled by the growing sophistication of essential intermediaries known as financial market infrastructure, such as credit bureaus and registries. Credit bureaus, such as Experian, are looking into non-traditional datasets to predict credit behavior, bringing the promise to include more users into the credit market. They facilitate the good functioning of the financial system and have gained renewed importance in the era of data.

Overall, there is a wide consensus that microfinance contribution is "beyond dispute,"[27] even though some may argue that microcredit overemphasized the focus on micro-enterprises or was slow to

---

[26]Beck, T. *et al.* (2012). Who gets the credit? And does it matter? Household vs firm lending across countries. *B.E. Journal of Macroeconomics: Contributions*, 12, May 2012.

[27]Collins, D. *et al.* (2009). *Portfolios of the Poor: How the World's Poor Live on $2 a Day*. Princeton University Press, p. 26.

embrace other services such as savings or insurance. Tellingly, Banerjee and Duflo conclude that "microcredit has earned its rightful place as *one* of the key instruments in the fight against poverty."[28]

Financial Services Engaging in the Transition to ESG

Similar to the mantra in the field of education that school enrollment is not the same as learning, access to finance is a necessary but insufficient condition for inclusion, which brings the necessity of impact measurement. How does the financial sector measure its own impact? This evolution is inserted into the broader trend of growth in sustainable finance. What is the connection between the ubiquitous concern with environment, social and governance (ESG) and the financial sector? What are the metrics that financial institutions should report on when it comes to inclusion?

For a long time, the positive impact of microfinance was mostly defined as access to finance for a population that had been historically excluded from those services. Beyond reporting a number of branches, bank accounts and app downloads, researchers have also analyzed the impact of microfinance on other measures of welfare, such as income generation, a higher level of education for the household's children or a stronger role and improved self-confidence for mothers within the household. In the previously quoted study on microcredit in Mexico, authors incorporated 35 outcomes, including school attendance, female decision power or subjective well-being. Financial institutions have become more cognizant of social demands beyond simple access.

The rise of sustainable finance is not restricted to public banks and development finance institutions. In fact, Sustainable Development Goal (SDG) #17 emphasizes the importance of partnerships if we are to reach the established goals before 2030. SDG #17 is a call to "strengthen the means of implementation and revitalize the global partnership for sustainable development." The financial sector, which is by essence an activity of intermediation, plays a key role to achieve those goals. Banks — and Central Banks — play a role to

---

[28]Banerjee, A. V. and Duflo, E. (2011). *Poor Economics*. New York: Perseus Books, p. 171.

finance those goals, including climate action.[29] Banks have taken on a more active role in ESG-aligned issuance of financial instruments. Over the past two decades, the banking sector has actively participated in the definition of best practices in lending and investing.

One example relates to the financing of large projects. The Equator Principles were defined in June 2003, based on existing environmental and social policy frameworks defined in the IFC Performance Standards, and propose a series of guidelines for project finance, impacting the financing of large projects such as dams, roads or drilling projects. Currently, 118 financial institutions in 37 countries have officially adopted the Equator Principles, covering the majority of international project finance debt within developed and emerging markets. The Equator Principles are a risk management framework, adopted by financial institutions, for determining, assessing and managing environmental and social risk in projects, and primarily intended to provide a minimum standard for due diligence and monitoring to support responsible risk decision-making. The principles apply globally, to all industry sectors and to five financial products: project finance advisory services, project finance, project-related corporate lending and bridge loans, and project-related refinance and acquisition finance.

In their lending activities, financial institutions are increasingly relying on independent sectorial certifications, such as the Forest Stewardship Council (FSC) for forestry companies or Roundtable for Sustainable Palm Oil (RSPO) for palm oil producers. Those independent certifications are typically maintained by not-for-profit entities and ensure that corporates follow best standards, in particular related to labor standards, protection of biodiversity, absence of deforestation and controlled use of chemicals.

More than 230 banks have also signed the Principles for Responsible Banking (PRB) launched in 2019 and more than 1800 signatories follow the Principles for Responsible Investing launched in 2006 (PRI), which incorporate ESG considerations into their activities and

---

[29]Lagarde (2021). Speech by Christine Lagarde, President of the ECB, at the International Climate Change Conference in Venice, Climate Change and Central Banks: Analysing, Advising and Acting. Available at https://www.ecb.europa.eu/press/key/date/2021/html/ecb.sp210711~ffe35034d0.en.html. Last accessed October 6, 2021.

align with the Paris Agreement and SDGs. PRI apply to asset management, while PRB cover a broader spectrum of banking activities. The first step of PRB is to require signatories to undertake a thorough impact analysis, determining where the bank has more impact on people and planet. Banks subsequently define targets. Finally, they are required to publicly report on their progress.

In April 2021, a group of 43 banks founded the Net-Zero Banking Alliance, representing over US\$29 trillion in assets from 24 countries. Banks reaffirmed their commitment to aligning their lending and investment portfolios with net-zero emissions by 2050.

On top of those wide-ranging commitments, financial institutions have developed and structured a growing field of sustainable finance. The growth in "green, social, sustainable, and sustainability-linked bonds" reached 212% in 2021 versus 2020 in annualized terms, with a particular emphasis on green bonds and the noticeable innovation of sustainability-linked bonds (Figure 3).[30]

The financial sector has therefore been active in integrating considerations of sustainability. The ubiquitous letters ESG have conquered the financial sector in at least three ways. First, banks and financial institutions are rethinking how they operate, incorporating metrics on a broad range of topics including CO_2 emissions and workforce diversity. Second, banks are reviewing their lending portfolios, incorporating the ESG dimension into their risk and resilience analyses. Third, financial intermediaries are analyzing their portfolios of securities and investments. Banks have developed a series of impact metrics covering a broad range of topics related to sustainability.

FinTech institutions also routinely incorporate metrics related to financial inclusion, such as the number of customers who are using a financial product for the first time, and client net promoter score (NPS) in their reports as a proxy for impact. Brazilian FinTech

---

[30]There is a large literature on green finance and the initiatives of the Network of Central Banks and Supervisors for Greening the Financial System (NGFS) and it is the exclusive topic of several books. For a recent overview of the sustainable bond market, see Deschryver, P. and de Mariz, F. (2020). What future for the green bond market? How can policymakers, companies, and investors unlock the potential of the green bond market? *Journal of Risk and Financial Management*, *13*, 61. Doi: 10.3390/jrfm13030061. Available at SSRN: https://ssrn.com/abstract=3565933.

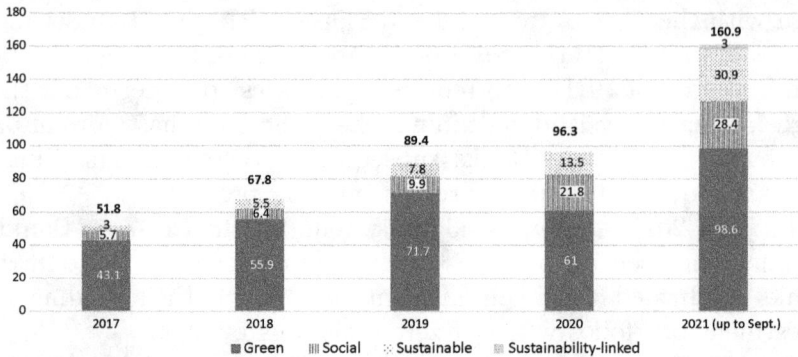

Figure 3: Issuance by Financial Institutions of Sustainable Bonds (US$, bn)
Source: Bloomberg, data up to September 2021.

PagSeguro underlined in its initial public offering filing that according to a survey conducted by them in June 2017, "75% of merchants who own [the] entry-level mPOS device did not accept card payments prior to signing up with PagSeguro."

Similarly, in the public filings for its initial public offering in 2021, Nubank considers first-time access as an important metric, but goes well beyond in terms of scope and wealth of considered metrics.

Nu defines its impact in two main categories, considering its employees and direct operations, and considering the impact it has on the lives of its clients. For its direct operations, Nubank discloses metrics including diversity and company ownership among others, with 61% of employees in leadership positions being from underrepresented groups, and 76% of Nu employees owning a stake in the company.

In terms of impact on the lives of its clients, Nubank considers access or outreach as a first key metric, with 48 million users of its service, complemented by active usage and first-time access. As of September 30, 2021, "5.1 million people had selected [Nu] as their first bank account or credit card." Nubank reports that it has "become the *primary* banking relationship[31] for over 50% of [its]

---

[31]Primary relationship is defined as active customers who had at least 50% of their post-tax monthly income move in or out of their NuAccount in any given month.

active customers who had been with [Nubank] for more than 12 months as of September 30, 2021." The business reaches 100% of municipalities in Brazil.[32]

Adding to access, the company also aims to define and report metrics that illustrate the true impact of its services, ultimately leading to "more money in people's pockets to be invested in their families, education and healthcare," improving the "quality of life for millions of people, lower-income inequality and adding several points of additional GDP growth over time." Nubank defends the approach of "profits with a purpose," creating value for all stakeholders and calculated that they had "saved their customers over US$5 billion of banking fees" and "113 million hours of waiting time inside bank branches or on hold with call centers." Internal survey data suggest that "67% of customers say they have gained more financial independence due to the use of [Nubank's] financial services and 80% reported they could overcome unforeseen financial issues as a result of the access to [Nubank's] credit products." Overall, usage and client satisfaction are encapsulated in the net promoter score, which reached 90 in Brazil and 94 in Mexico, far exceeding incumbent banks' scores. On the financial side, the company reported metrics that are essentially customer-centric, as opposed to product-centric, such as lifetime value of client and customer acquisition cost, and estimates a ratio of LTV/CAC "greater than 30x," or a monthly average revenue per active customer (ARPAC).

Moreover, Nu sees its role as an enabler for other FinTechs in the Brazilian and Latin American market, shedding light on the formidable potential of digitization and smart innovation in Latin America, and attracting first-time investors into the region.

For Menin, CEO of Inter, values are essential to justify the "social license of the company" and support its very existence in society. He notes that impact metrics still lack clarity and standardization. However, the codification of impact metrics, once it happens, will represent a "disruption of business models," as did accounting standards in the past.[33]

We provide the case study of Latin American bank Itaú in Table 1, with a selection of detailed self-reported metrics defined and tracked

---

[32]Interview with Nubank's founder and CEO David Vélez, November 17, 2021, and SEC F-1.

[33]Interview with João Vitor Menin, CEO of Inter, December 13, 2021.

Table 1: Case Study of Metrics Included in a Sustainability Report (Banco Itaú)

Category of Commitment	Materiality and Positive Impact Commitments	Example of Selected Targets and Metrics
Reporting	Transparency of reporting and communications	– 2020, we implemented 79% of the projects in response to TCFD recommendations. – 4.5 is the overall satisfaction score on surveys conducted in 2020. The satisfaction survey, using a scale from 0 to 5, has five evaluation criteria: IR team service, financial statements and notes, conference calls, questions & answers of investors, and ESG content.
Positive impact through our business	Responsible investment	– ESG integration distributing impact investment products to reach 3% of out total assets under management (WMS) by 2022.
	Financing in positive impact sectors	– Allocating R$100 billion, through products and services, to positive impact sectors by 2025, including R$15 billion to renewable energy generation and services by 2025.
	Inclusion and entrepreneurship	– Impacting 70,000 entrepreneurs with management, training and online or in-person networking solutions by 2020. – increasing the volume of credit for women-led small and medium-sized business, reaching R$11 billion in total credit by 2024 (21% of the total portfolio).
	Financial citizenship	– Providing differential offers for delinquent clients or those heavily in debt, using a preventive approach to avoid nondelinquent clients falling into debt. – Encouraging the use of the financial management tool Minhas Finanças (My Finances).
Conduct and way of acting	Ethics in relations and business	– Training 90% of employees in topics impacting our integrity and Ethics Program every two years, including ethics, anti corruption, AML.

Responsible management	– Reduction of electric energy consumption by 15% in 2013–2021.
	– By 2021, purchase 96% of electrical energy for administrative buildings from renewable sources.
	– Reduced absolute Scope 1 emissions by 21% in 2018–2020. 100% of emissions of Scope 1 are offset by the purchase of carbon credits.
	– Reduced water consumption by by 62% in 2013–2020.
	– Reduced waste generation 31% in 2017–2020.
	– Reduced the absolute number of kilometers traveled by 38.5% in 2018–2020.
	– Encourage our supply chain to adopt positive environmental and social impact commitments and practices. For five years, we have been part of the CDP Supply Chain Program, an initiative aimed at discussing climate change with the suppliers of our supply chain. Last year, 93% of invited suppliers participated in the program.
Inclusive management	– High scores on employee satisfaction and engagement surveys e-NPS of 84.2 (employee satisfaction).
	– Increasing the number of women in leadership positions. 57.5% of employees are women; 51.4% of women in management positions; 14.0% women in executive positions. 89.7% of post-maternity retention (12 months).
	– Percentage of black employees 23.4% in 2020; development program for 150 interns black people.
	– Volunteering 200 actions, totaling more 10,000 donated hours.
Private social investment Amazon	
Development of the country	– Launched in June 2020, supporting environmental preservation and the development of a bio-economy; investing in sustainable infrastructure; and helping ensure the population's basic rights.

Source: Itaú, ESG Report 2020.

in its sustainability report. Itaú approaches its impact through four large categories of reporting, business, conduct and philanthropy. Those broad categories are then broken down into 10 themes corresponding to the map of materiality of the bank, which in turn are approached via dozens of indicators and targets, of which we list only a few in the table above.

Deborah Drake from the Center for Financial Inclusion at Accion flags the importance of providing gender-segregated data, as digital tools are not equally used by men and women. Providing data on access, even first-time access, is necessary but not sufficient, and should be complemented by metrics related to customer satisfaction, such as grievance, actual usage or drop-outs. In fact, donors and investors are increasingly asking for metrics not only about access but also impact on the end client.[34]

Some of the tools that support this engagement of banks into the ESG topic include a standardization of metrics and more transparency in reporting, being supported by global initiatives such as the Global Reporting Initiative (GRI). Behind the push for better disclosure is the idea that environmental and social considerations should be routinely incorporated into business decisions. GRI advocates in favor of a principle of double materiality, with companies reporting on metrics that are relevant from both the financial and impact perspectives.

The Task Force on Climate-related Financial Disclosures (TCFD) acknowledges that there is a threat of climate change as well as the "warming of the planet caused by greenhouse gas emissions poses serious risks to the global economy and will have an impact across many economic sectors."[35] In December 2015, nearly 200 governments agreed to strengthen the global response to the threat of climate change by "holding the increase in the global average temperature to well below 2°C above pre-industrial levels and to pursue efforts to limit the temperature increase to 1.5°C above pre-industrial

---

[34]Interview with Deborah Drake, November 2, 2021.
[35]TCFD (2017). Recommendations of the task force on climate-related financial disclosures, June 2017.

levels," referred to as the Paris Agreement.[36] The expected transition to a lower-carbon economy is estimated to require around $1 trillion of investments a year for the foreseeable future, generating new investment opportunities. In 2015, the G20 (Group of 20 Finance Ministers) and Central Bank Governors requested that the Financial Stability Board (FSB) "convene public- and private-sector participants to review how the financial sector can take account of climate-related issues."[37]

The Financial Stability Board of the Bank for International Settlements created TCFD in December 2015 to improve and increase reporting of climate-related financial information, in order to provide better information to investors and economic agents around risk management and strategic planning. Financial institutions, including credit institutions, investment firms, insurance carriers need to be better equipped to understand where climate-related risk lies in their books. In December 2016, TCFD released the first draft of its recommendations for climate-related disclosure. The task force consists of 32 members from across the G20, representing both institutions and users of financial disclosure, and is chaired by Michael R. Bloomberg. By February 2020, TCFD had gathered more than 1,000 supporters, emphasizing a market shift toward recognizing the importance of disclosure.

TCFD defines categories for climate-related risks and opportunities, as shown in Figure 4. Risks entail transition risks and physical impact of climate change. Transition risks include the impact of policy changes, judicial actions against a company, the inability to adopt an upcoming technology, market risk and reputation risk. Physical risks can impact the premises of a company or its staff. Climate-related opportunities include energy efficiency programs and savings, waste reduction, the development of new products and services under the mechanism of creative destruction or building resilience along the

---

[36] United Nations Framework Convention on Climate Change (2015). The Paris agreement, December 2015.
[37] G20 (2015). Communiqué from the G20 finance ministers and central bank governors meeting in Washington, D.C., April 16–17, 2015.

Figure 4: TCFD: Climate Related Risks and Opportunities: How to Report Them?

Source: Adapted from TCFD.

company's supply chain. Overall, TCFD emphasizes the impact of climate changes on four categories of financial data, namely companies' revenues, expenses, assets and liabilities, and capital and financing.

The Task Force developed voluntary, consistent climate-related financial disclosures that are useful to investors, lenders, and insurance underwriters in understanding material risks. Recommendations target the governance created by a company, potential impact of climate change on its strategy, risk management and definition of metrics related to assessing climate-related aspects. TCFD will be completed in the future by metrics focused on biodiversity, developed by the task force for nature-related financial disclosure (TNFD). TCFD also highlights the role of regulators across jurisdictions to mandate new types of disclosures, as detailed in Table 2.

Asset managers and allocators play a key role in the debate around the selection of metrics and reporting. Christina Leijonhufvud, CEO of BlueMark, highlights that both standards and verification are essential for impact, as "robust impact management systems and practices are critical to scaling the impact investing industry." BlueMark developed a benchmark for impact management, closely aligned with the Impact Management Principles, launched by the IFC in 2019. She adds that limited partners, asset

Table 2: Select Disclosure Frameworks: Governments

Region: Framework	Target Reporter	Target Audience	Mandatory or Voluntary	Materiality Standard	Types of Climate-Related Information	Disclosure Location	External Assurance Required
Australia: National Greenhouse and Energy Reporting Act (2007)	Financial and non-financial firms that meet meet emissions of energy of production of consumption thresholds	General public	Mandatory if thresholds are met	Based on emissions above a certain threshold	GHG emissions, energy consumption and energy production	Report to government	Regulator may, by written notice to corporation, require an audit of its disclosures
European Union: EU Directive 2014/95 regarding disclosure of non-financial diversity information (2014)	Financial and non-financial firms that meet size criteria (i.e. have more than 500 employees)	Investors, consumers and other stakeholders	Mandatory; applicable for the financial year starting on Jan. 1, 2017, or during the 2017 calendar year	None specified	Land use, water use, GHG emissions, use of materials, and energy use	Corporate financial report or separate report (published with financial report or on website six months after the balance sheet date and referenced in financial report)	Member States must require that statutory auditor checks whether the non-financial statement has been provided. Member States may require independent assurance for information in non-financial statement

(Continued)

Table 2: (*Continued*)

Region: Framework	Target Reporter	Target Audience	Mandatory or Voluntary	Materiality Standard	Types of Climate-Related Information	Disclosure Location	External Assurance Required
France: Article 173, Energy Transition Law (2015)	Listed financial and non-financial firms, Additional requirements for institutional investors	Investors, general public	Mandatory	None specified	Risks related to climate change, consequences of climate change on the company's activities and use of goods and services it produces. Institutional investors: GHG emissions and contribution to goal of limiting global warming	Annual report and website	Mandatory review on the consistency of the disclosure by an independent third party, such as a statutory auditor
India: National Voluntary Guidelines on Social, Environmental, and Economic Responsibilities of Business (2011)	Financial and non-financial firms	Investors, general public	Voluntary	None specified	Significant risks, goals and targets for improving performance, materials, energy consumption, water, discharge of effluents, GHG emissions, and biodiversity	Not specified; companies may furnish a report or letter from owner/chief executive officer	Guidelines include third-party assurance as a "leadership indicator" of company's progress in implementing the principles

| United Kingdom: Companies Act 2006 (Strategic Report and Director's Report) Regulations 2013 | Financial and non-financial firms that are "quoted companies," as defined by the Companies Act 2006 | Investors, shareholders ("members of the company") | Mandatory | Information is material if its amission or misrepresentation could influence the economic decisions shareholders take on the basis of the annual report as a whole (section 5 of the UK FRC June 2014 Guidance on the Strategic Report) | The main trends and factors likely to affect the future development, performance, and position of the company's business, environmental matters (including the impact of the company's business on the environment), and GHG emissions | Strategic Report and Director's Report | Not required, but statutory auditor must state in report on the company's annual accounts whether in the auditor's opinion the information given in the Strategic Report and the Director's report for the financial year for which the accounts are prepared is consistent with those accounts |

(Continued)

Table 2: (*Continued*)

Region: Framework	Target Reporter	Target Audience	Mandatory or Voluntary	Materiality Standard	Types of Climate-Related Information	Disclosure Location	External Assurance Required
United States: NAICS, 2010 Insurer Climate Risk Disclosure Survey	Insurers meeting certain premium thresholds - $100 mn in 2015	Regulators	Mandatory	None specified	General disclosures about climate change-related risk management and investment management	Survey sent to state regulators	Not specified
United States: SEC Guidance Regarding Disclosure Related to Climate Change	Financial and non-financial firms subject to SEC reporting requirements	Investors	Mandatory	US securities law definition	Climate-related material risks and factors that can affect or have affected the company's financial condition, such as regulations, treaties and agreements, business trends, and physical impacts	Annual and other reports required to be filed with SEC	Depends on assurance requirements for information disclosed

Source: Adapted from TCFD (2017).

owners and asset allocators are leading the demand for verification. She explains that "the challenges we collectively face can't be solved with a "business as usual" approach to financial and investment decisions." For asset managers, understanding the context of the invested company as well as defining and tracking the proper metrics are key.

Leijonhufvud flags the importance to harmonize frameworks and standards in impact metrics, combining the efforts of organizations such as SASB, WEF, SDGs or IFRS. Transforming impact into monetary metrics will be challenging and could even be undesirable as asset owners pursue impact not just for financial motivation. Going forward, as impact investing matures, there will be "increased accountability" as actors in the impact field will be more careful and specific about their claims, with a clearer labelling. She defends the view that ESG will look increasingly not just at optimizing risk and return but more and more incorporate a focus on outcomes and true impact.[38]

Financial institutions have gradually developed a host of metrics to follow and disclose their impact. Those metrics have focused on financial inclusion, such as providing numbers around first-time access and customer satisfaction. Banks have used a wide range of metrics to capture the entirety of their activities, including their own operations, their loan book and their investment portfolios. Several initiatives have been developed to streamline and standardize how those metrics are monitored and reported.

The Role of Development Finance Institutions

Development Finance Institutions (DFIs), together with public development banks (PDBs), have played a key role in the growth of sustainable finance, including microfinance, and have set early on a focus on fostering financial inclusion. How do they interact with more traditional pockets of capital and what impact do they pursue?

---

[38]Presentation by Christina Leijonhufvud, CEO of BlueMark and co-founder of Tideline, at Columbia University, November 4, 2021. BlueMark is a leading provider of impact verification. See also BlueMark (2021). Making the mark 2021. Available at https://bluemarktideline.com/making-the-mark-2021/.

DFIs and PDBs meet five criteria. First, they have a separate legal personality, which sets them apart from government credit programs and aid agencies. Second, they deploy financial instruments that suggest a "reflow relationship," such as loans, equity, guarantee, or insurance, and they monitor their customers, different from most grant-making aid agencies. Third, their funding sources include the ability to finance themselves, with a complete balance sheet, which is different from select agencies that rely exclusively on budget transfers. Fourth, they follow a public policy mandate, different from commercial banks. Finally, they have government sponsorship.[39]

Development-focused institutions play a role in countercyclical policies. There are more than 450 PDBs and DFIs worldwide from about 150 countries with total assets of nearly $12 trillion, and accounting for about 10% of the world's investment, or $2.3 trillion in 2018 (Table 3).[40] China alone represents 35% of that total, roughly four trillion dollars, with China Development Bank being the largest PDB globally with $2.355 trillion in assets in 2018. Europe (27 countries) represents roughly the same amount at close to $4 trillion, including in particular the European Investment Bank (EIB) and European Bank for Reconstruction and Development (EBRD). The majority of DFIs and MDBs are much smaller. At the low end, the development agency of the State of Roraima in Brazil has a balance sheet of $2 million. Some have a long and well-established history like the Caisse des Dépôts et Consignations established in France in 1816, or the Banco de la Provincia de Buenos Aires, established in Argentina in 1822. Those institutions vary by ownership, with multinational, national or sub-national control. Multinationals are the most renowned and include the IBRD, IDA, IFC, MIGA, and the New Development Bank (or "BRICS" Bank).

Ninety percent of institutions apply one or several of the following four mandates. SME financing is the core mandate for 35% of those institutions, behind a general mandate of development (36%), but ahead of export financing (10%) and agriculture financing (9%).

---

[39]Xu, J. *et al.* (2020). Identifying and classifying public development banks and development finance institutions. AFD Editions, Research Papers, No 192, November 2020.
[40]*Ibid.*, p. 4.

Table 3:   Landscape of Development Banks

Continent	Number of PDBs and DFIs	%	Total Assets (US$, mn)	%	Number of Countries	Average Number of PDBs and DFIs per Country
Africa	95	21	131,357	1	54	1.8
America	100	22	1,378,639	12	35	2.9
Asia Pacific	146	32	5,611,406	48	64	2.3
Europe	102	23	3,494,058	30	50	2
Global	9	2	958,879	8	NA	NA
Total	**452**	**100%**	**11,574,340**	**100%**	**203**	**2.2**

Source: Xu *et al.* (2020).

Grant-making and not-for-profit played a key role in the initial growth of microcredit, with key players such as Accion, Pro Mujer, WWB. Development Finance Institutions providing a large support to the sector.

Public finance has generally shifted its focus from building institutions to a market development approach. Initial capacity building and funding to institutions gave rise to some criticism, as DFIs may have been crowding out private players from the sector and focused their efforts only on the most credit-worthy microfinance institutions.[41] DFI funding is meant to remedy a market failure and enable business models that may not naturally find funding until they become financially sustainable. The strategy of institution-building led to successful cases, such as Compartamos, initially set up as a not-for-profit in 1994 in Mexico, which received funding from USAID and Accion. DFIs were essential for the early growth and financial sustainability of the company. Its growth, transformation into a for-profit organization and subsequent IPO in 2007 have vastly amplified its ability to tap private markets for funds.

In the case of ACLEDA, a promising Cambodian microfinance institution, three DFIs (FMO, KfW, and IFC) engaged and funded

---

[41]Microrate (2011). Role reversal revisited. Available at http://www.microra te.com/media/downloads/2012/10/MicroRate-Role-Reversal-Revisited.pdf. Last accessed October 6, 2021.

the institution in the mid-1990s, which subsequently played a key role in advocating for "policy and regulatory changes that ultimately created a robust microfinance industry" in Cambodia.[42] The National Bank of Cambodia eventually created a new legal structure, Microfinance Deposit Taking Institution, for regulated MFIs. ACLEDA was born as NGO and then transformed into a specialized bank and then a commercial bank. The MFI engaged actively with policymakers and created educational programs known as ACLEDA Institute of Banking. Over time, private investors entered the capital table of Acleda, allowing the DFIs to exit and redeploy their funds in other ventures. Acleda reported $4.5 billion in total loans with 319 offices in Cambodia, Lao and Myanmar at the end of 2020.

DFIs have played a key role to foster inclusion. Critics flag that, despite decades of assistance, financial systems are still imperfect and that DFIs cherry-pick the best recipients. DFIs may also be investing in projects that have an uncertain impact. Data from the MIX suggest that most funding for inclusive finance goes to sub-Saharan Africa, but within the region, funding is directed to the countries with the highest levels of financial inclusion such as Kenya and Tanzania, as opposed to countries like Ethiopia where inclusion is meaningfully lower.[43] A critical view on DFIs' funding allocation would benefit from more impact studies.

DFIs have reviewed their role in supporting well-functioning financial markets and target an ever bigger impact. DFIs are increasingly looking at a systemic approach to foster enabling factors for inclusion, also known as horizontal policies in a sense that they benefit all players. The desired impact of DFI funds includes additionality (to existing sources of capital) and catalysis (to attract or crowd in other investors). Enabling investments include activities such as capital markets, credit information systems, payment infrastructure, on top of technical assistance.

Other enabling solutions include mechanisms that facilitate onboarding, Know Your Customer (KYC), or registration of assets,

---

[42]CGAP (2017). Development finance institutions and financial inclusion: From institution-building to market development. *Focus Note No. 105*, March 2017, p. 2.
[43]MIX (2020). Fintech, digital finance and funding: How the development sector is channeling money to digital financial services. *MIX*, July 2020, p. 6.

among other examples. Mobile technology is a powerful tool to include millions of new users and provide adequate financial services. In the case of India, the Aadhaar biometric identification system provides the foundation for an integrated set of APIs and is the basis for customer identification, enabling authentication for account openings and financial transactions.[44]

Hector Gomez Ang, Regional Director for South Asia at IFC, highlights that IFC has developed a detailed framework to characterize its added value, including rigorous *ex ante* and *ex post* assessments and targets. In fact, DFIs aim to crowd in sources of private financing. Gomez Ang explains that for every dollar invested, IFC mobilized an additional dollar from the private sector, reinforcing the role of IFC as an enabler. For example, IFC and German insurance company Allianz announced an agreement in November 2021, during the COP26 in Glasgow, to create a "new global platform for climate smart-investment that will provide up to $3 billion to private enterprises in developing economies." The agreement will direct financial flows to emerging markets for climate-smart solutions consistent with the goals of the Paris Agreement.

During COVID-19, DFIs stepped in to support countries and invested companies. Gomez Ang highlights that COVID-19 represented an "additional layer of challenge on top of other challenges for those countries," which "impacts clients, operations and has distributional impacts." DFIs developed specific responses to help clients with their COVID-related challenges, acknowledging that "COVID-related" represented different realities for different clients. While supporting existing clients was a focus, there was limited appetite to expand to new counterparts. As COVID-19 strained the fiscal situation of governments, there is room for the private sector to be more involved.

The pandemic also "accelerated digitization by about a decade across sectors," including healthcare, agribusiness, education and financial services. IFC is prioritizing select segments, including cleaner energy and the climate agenda, gender equality and finance to

---

[44]CGAP (2021). Fintech and financial inclusion. A funder's guide to greater impact. *Focus Note*, June 2021, p. 4.

women-led businesses, transportation, cities with digital infrastructure, waste management, and municipal services, and a digital push, which includes telecom infrastructure. In South Asia, and India in particular, IFC has an ambitious agenda related to financial inclusion, housing finance, SME finance and clean energy. IFC is also increasingly looking at early-stage investments and opening up to innovation, with specialized teams dedicated to digital businesses.

FinTechs, with their potential to disrupt and bring new services to previously underserved customers, are also becoming a focus of attention for DFIs. While FinTechs present an opportunity for inclusion, it is a sector that is already attracting a lot of interest from traditional investors, and may require less investments from DFIs than other sectors. Gomez Ang believes that traditional financial players and challengers will converge, and that convergence will be "towards the more digital part of the spectrum."

Looking ahead, "DFIs will need to do more," with a rising focus on impact investing, and collaboration between DFIs and with other players, such as private foundations, as "complex problems call for effective partnerships."[45]

The challenge remains for DFIs to invest in relevant recipients that deserve to be scaled up, while at the same time picking investees that would not receive funding from regular private investors. Nick O'Donohoe, CEO of CDC Group Plc, explains that "since 2012, [CDC has] put more focus on working in the places where it is most challenging to invest, and the use of catalytic capital has been driving how [CDC] approach[es] these markets to find opportunities for investment." For example, CDC invested in Gridworks, a development and investment platform, to address the under-investment in electricity transmission, distribution, and off-grid infrastructure in Africa, potentially providing "power to half a million people in three cities in the Democratic Republic of Congo via solar-hybrid off-grid utilities." Catalytic capital allows to look at early-stage markets and businesses, where technology can help achieve transformational impact. CDC strives to remain "focused on the most challenging issues, [reach] countries where it is complex to invest, and [help]

---

[45]Interview with Hector Gomez Ang, IFC's Regional Director for South Asia, November 25, 2021.

to build long-term sustainable markets." DFIs often have similar processes to banks and need to maintain strong credit ratings. He adds that "blended finance solutions are useful for taking a flexible approach to risk, but they are complex, difficult to structure, standardize and scale." No doubt the funding gap will require collaboration between DFIs and private sector investors.[46]

---

[46]O'Donohoe, N. (2021). Driving development with flexible capital. Available at https://www.cdcgroup.com/en/news-insight/insight/articles/driving-develop ment-with-flexible-capital/. Last accessed October 20, 2021.

Chapter 4

Electronic Payments as Entry Point for Inclusion

The Preference for Electronic Payments

Cash light economies present several benefits. They favor a reduction in informality, an increase in fiscal revenues, increased access to a wide range of financial services, an increase in domestic savings, a more effective monetary policy, and a reduction in the cost of transactions.

Several countries have launched public policies directed at increasing the use of electronic payments, and therefore reducing the reliance on cash. The existing literature classifies payments in nine categories according to the sender and the recipient. These different types involve people, businesses and government (Table 1).

There is still a large opportunity from G2P and B2P to shift to electronic payments.[1] The World Bank calls for leveraging on "government payment programs to promote financial inclusion," as "the large volume of payments issued by governments, as well as the nature of some specific programs like social spending programs, represent an opportunity to promote or facilitate financial inclusion on a large scale."[2] Several governments have taken the opportunity of

---

[1] World Bank Group (2015). Innovative digital payment mechanisms supporting financial inclusion: Stocktaking report. Payment System Development Group.

[2] World Bank (2012). General guidelines for the development of government payment systems, financial infrastructure series. World Bank Publications.

Table 1:   Types of Payments

Payer\Payee	People	Business	Government
People	P2P	P2B	P2G
Business	B2P	B2B	B2G
Government	G2P	G2B	G2G

Source: Author.

redistribution programs to include a payment component into existing public policies. Other examples of successful initiatives include a policy implemented by several States in Brazil, which offers customers a tax deduction when they require a fiscal receipt from their merchant, essentially reducing informality and removing one of the key benefits of cash payments.

In Brazil, the Bolsa Familia is a case study in G2P transfers, as 99% of the recipients receive digital payments into a card or bank account.[3] In Brazil, among the 15% of adults receiving any type of government transfers — Bolsa Familia or others, 88% receive them into an account. The Bolsa Familia program is the largest conditional redistribution program in the developing world and attended 14.3 million families in 2020 throughout the country. The program seeks to reduce poverty and conditions transfers on school attendance, vaccines and pre-natal visits by the beneficiaries. There are over 32,000 points where benefits can be withdrawn, and 65% of benefits are received at lottery points managed by public bank Caixa Economica Federal. G2P payments reduce the administrative cost of the program for the government, reduce fraud and offer an entry point into the financial system for recipients. According to the World Bank, "moving to electronic payment and consolidating four programs into one reduced administrative cost from 14.7% to 2.6% of the value of the grants disbursed."

However, research shows that Bolsa Familia has not been a successful entry point for financial services.[4] The Bolsa Familia program delivers financial assistance to nearly a third of the total population

---

[3]World Bank (2015). Payments aspects of financial inclusion, committee on payments and market infrastructures. World Bank Publications.
[4]World Bank (2015). Innovative digital payment mechanisms supporting financial inclusion: Stocktaking report. Payment System Development Group.

via digital transfers, representing a public policy success. However, the poorer the household, the more likely they are to withdraw their full transfer at once, as opposed to using their bank account for cash management. Among Brazilian adults receiving government transfers, 88% withdraw all the money right away.

Likewise, while other international experiences have been successful for G2P disbursements, they have not always led to a true financial inclusion of beneficiaries. In Colombia, the Daviplata program launched by privately-owned bank Davivienda initially experienced a slow uptake. Daviplata is responsible for the electronic transfer and disbursement of payments by the Colombian central government to public servants, military and retirees. Research has shown that a large part of the transfers is then withdrawn in full by recipients, thereby limiting the benefits of constituting savings and inclusion at large.

By contrast, another Colombian payment experiment has shown clear success. The Colombian banking sector and ACH Colombia — a private clearing house — have developed over the past decade an online payment instrument, which is embedded in government and business websites and allows "businesses and consumers to authorize electronic payments directly from their bank accounts to government agencies and to other businesses."[5] From 2008 to 2013, the number of "payments made this way had increased by more than tenfold to almost a million a month." The online tool is known as Secure Online Payments (Pagos Seguros en Línea, PSE), and is a private sector innovation that was supported by the Colombian government.

In Mexico, switching from cash payments to electronic payments delivered via a bank account for the Oportunidades program has had several consequences. Following the change, "participation in informal savings arrangements was reduced, the frequency of remittance reception increased and, when hit by idiosyncratic shocks, beneficiaries of bank accounts were more likely to use savings rather than contracting loans or reducing consumption to cope with the events."[6]

---

[5]Marulanda, C. P. and Meltzer (2016). Digital Colombia: Maximizing the global internet and data for sustainable and inclusive growth. Brookings Global Working Paper Series.

[6]Masino, S. and Niño-Zarazúa, M. (2014). Social service delivery and access to financial innovation. UNU-WIDER Working Paper 2014/034.

Authors assess the success of the G2P program in Mexico with its two simultaneous dimensions: a move toward electronic payments and toward centralized payments. In 2012, "97% of pension payments were made by electronic transfers."[7] The unification and digitalization of payments to government employees, retirees and social transfers were a wide success. By digitizing and centralizing its payments, the Mexican government has "saved US$1.27 billion per year," equivalent to "3.3% of all its total expenditure on wages, pensions and social transfers." Savings came in the form of "float revenues, with no more anticipation in payment, lower transaction fees, and less leakage and operational errors."

Payments made by the government (G2P, G2B) have largely benefited from a move to electronic channels as they slash the costs associated with the disbursement of benefits and wages, as in the case of Brazil, Colombia and Mexico. However, while electronic payments bring efficiency to the system, data on effective inclusion are mixed. Data from the World Bank Findex show that the poorer the household, the more likely they are to withdraw all at once. Moreover, only 41% of Findex respondents reported receiving their wage payments into an account.

For other types of payments, especially P2P and P2B, new business models are emerging and reaching scale. They are gaining share from incumbent companies, providing better products to customers, and offer a new challenge for regulators. Countries such as Kenya, China and Brazil provide world-class benchmarks for innovation in payments and FinTech, offering lessons for developing and developed markets alike. Many innovative models are also growing in developed markets, where inclusion has become a policy objective in the aftermath of the 2008 financial crisis.

From the FinTech perspective, payments present the triple advantage of having high operating margins for newcomers, requiring less capital investment from FinTech companies (than credit, for example) and gathering valuable data on customers. Not surprisingly, payments have been the first product to be offered by new FinTech players, as this is a logical entry product for customers. In fact, before

---

[7]Babatz, G. (2013). Sustained effort, saving billions: Lessons from the Mexican government's shift to electronic payments. *Better Than Cash Alliance Case Study.* http://betterthancash.org.

resorting to credit, customers need to have a transaction account and they need to evidence their ability to save over time. Most businesses have developed product innovation with simpler and more afford-able point-of-sale equipment, combined with the ubiquitous rise of e-wallets. In the most relevant development in recent years, several countries have started to implement peer-to-peer payments, includ-ing 3P systems in China,[8] while consortia are developing transfer systems based on blockchain,[9] questioning the existing models in place.

That said, emerging economies are still largely cash-based and informal, which suggests a need for adequate inclusion and regula-tion. In some cases, data suggest individuals' preference to hold cash, denoting a distrust for the banking system. Another explanation for the preference for cash usage, especially during times of economic downturn, has to do with consumer behavior. Brazilian consumers often express that they have a better control of their personal finances when using cash, as they can see and control the physical cash in their wallets. In other cases, products for the lower-income segments of the population are simply not available or too complex and costly.

What drives the adoption of electronic payments? Would a change in regulation, wider access, or change of customer preference impact adoption the most?

There is a vast literature on the availability, adoption and use of payment means and the usage of electronic payments in devel-oped countries. There are different currents explaining the drivers of payments. The first stream of research underlines the relative costs of cash and card usage.[10] Another camp takes the role of con-sumer preferences into account. Finally, some researchers say that the

---

[8]A four-party (4P) payment scheme includes a cardholder, an issuing institution (typically the bank that issued the plastic card), a merchant and the acquiring institution (typically the company that provides a POS equipment). In a three-party scheme (3P), the same institution provides acquiring and issuing services.

[9]Kenya-based startup BitPesa, for example, uses distributed ledger settlement, allowing customers to send and receive low-cost, near-instant payments without a bank account or even an enrolled wallet.

[10]Schuh, S. D. and Stavins, J. (2011). How consumers pay: adoption and use of payments. Use data from a US survey on consumer payment behavior and find that the cost associated with a payment mode is found to significantly affect payment use.

choice of a means of payments (either cash or electronic) is driven by transaction characteristics. Variables used in the literature include consumer characteristics, such as consumer preferences and socio-demographics, point-of-sale characteristics, such as type of merchant, size of transaction, card acceptance and, in the case of international comparisons, some country characteristics, such as macroeconomic variables, regulations, or innovation.

An early influential paper analyzed the determinants of the choice of payment instruments after comparing datasets from 13 industrialized countries between 1987 and 1993.[11] Using payment aggregated data, the authors built a statistical model with seven independent variables to determine the evolution of five types of payment modes. Their analysis suggested that the movement toward electronic payments was "uniform and unmistakable" across countries and led to a meaningful reduction in social cost, as the "cost of electronic payments is one-third to half the cost of other payment means." Several types of variables were studied: price and income, GDP, equipment, cash holding per person, payment availability (point of sale: POS), Automated Teller Machine (ATM) and, finally, institutional variables (crime, concentration of the five largest banks). The econometric results show in particular a positive effect of the presence of POS and ATM on the use of payment cards.

More recent research focuses not just on existing infrastructure (presence of POS and ATM), but also on customer and transaction characteristics. Cohen and Rysman using a panel of US consumers, find a negative relation between age and card use. On the other hand, they find a positive relationship between income and cards and checks use, while the relation with cash is negative.[12] Bounie and Francois use a unique dataset of 11,945 payments made from March to May 2005 in France and estimate the "determinants of the probability of a transaction being paid by cash, check or bank card at the point of sale." The authors find that transaction size

---

[11]Humphrey, D. B. *et al.* (1996). Cash, paper, and electronic payments: a cross-country analysis. *Journal of Money, Credit and Banking, 28*(4), 914–939.

[12]Cohen, M. A. and Rysman, M. (2013). Payment choice with consumer panel data. Federal Reserve Bank of Boston, 2013 Series, No. 13–6, Research Department Working Papers.

is a determinant, as well as the type of good and spending place. Transaction characteristics take center stage in their analysis.[13]

In countries like Germany, cash remains prevalent, despite the wide acceptance of electronic means, pointing to consumer preference. Researchers use a dataset that combines transaction information with survey data on payment behavior of German consumers. They note that "cash still accounts for an astounding 82% of the volume and for 58% of the value of all direct payment transactions", based on Bundesbank data, and find that "the possession of a credit card, notably in addition to a debit card, does not significantly affect the use of cash in Germany, indicating that credit cards and debit cards are close substitutes."[14] In Canada, research studies analyzed the reasons for the high cash adoption, using data from the 2009 Methods of Payment Survey, a household survey specifically designed to study payment instrument choice by Canadian households. In the survey, about "6,800 participants completed a questionnaire with detailed information regarding their personal finances, as well as their use and perceptions of different payment methods." Additionally, "3,500 participants completed a 3-day diary recording information on each transaction, including the value and the payment instrument chosen." Even though debit and credit cards account for close to 80% of all transactions in terms of total value, "cash is still the predominant payment method in terms of volume, accounting for 54% of all transactions."[15] The authors find that cash is used mostly because it is widely accepted by merchants, it is easy to use and has a low marginal cost. Those studies support the stated advantages of cash, including anonymity, convenience, universal acceptance and instantaneous settlement.[16]

---

[13]Bounie, D. and Francois, A. (2006). Cash, check or bank card? The effects of transaction characteristics on the use of payment instruments.

[14]Von Kalckreuth, U. *et al.* (2009). Choosing and using payment instruments: Evidence from German microdata.

[15]Arango, C. *et al.* (2012). Why is cash (still) so entrenched? Insights from the Bank of Canada's 2009 methods-of-Payment survey (No. 2012-2). Bank of Canada Discussion Paper.

[16]Mas, I. (2016). Strains of digital money. *Capco Journal of Financial Transformation*, No. 44, November 2016. Available at SSRN: https://ssrn.com/abstract= 1728125 or http://dx.doi.org/10.2139/ssrn.1728125.

In the US, O'Brien used a dataset from the Federal Reserve's Diary of Consumer Payment Choice, which includes all the "recorded financial transactions of approximately 2,500 individuals who participated in the diary during their variously assigned three consecutive-day periods within the month of October 2012" and found that transaction size is a key determinant and "cash continues to play a large role as a payment instrument especially in lower value transactions for all demographic groups."[17]

Research on payments in developing countries is more limited, due to smaller data samples and currency volatility.[18] Using the dataset from the Survey of Uruguayan Household Finances, authors find that "households are intensive in their use of cash while the use of credit and debit cards is low and stable," with transaction characteristics being the most relevant driver of payment choice. Consumer socio-demographics, such as age and education, play a smaller role, as well as supply-side factors, such as card acceptance at stores. The authors note that "about 30% of transactions in Uruguay are made using either credit cards, debit cards, bank transfers or direct debit, the figure is 51% in Turkey and 73% in Chile, countries with a similar level of income per capita." In Africa, authors use the World Bank's Global Findex database on 37 African countries and find that "being a man, richer, more educated and older favor financial inclusion with a higher influence of education and income." Importantly, they also

---

[17]O'Brien, S. (2015). Consumer preferences and the use of cash. San Francisco Federal Reserve.

[18]Examples include for Nigeria (Bayero, M. A. (2015). Effects of Cashless Economy Policy on financial inclusion in Nigeria: An exploratory study. *Procedia-Social and Behavioral Sciences*, *172*, 49–56), Uruguay (Lluberas, R. and Saldain, J. (2015). Paper of plastic? Payment instrument choice in Uruguay. *Revista de Economía*, *22*(1), 35), Chile (Adam, C. (2000). La Demanda por Dinero por Motivo de Transacción en Chile. *Economía Chilena*, 3(3), 33–56), Kenya (Odedra, A. J. *et al.* (2016). Determinants of payment methods on financial performance: A survey of small and medium enterprises in Kitale town. *International Journal of Scientific and Research Publications*, 6(9)), Thailand (Hataiseree, R. and Banchuen, W. (2010). The effects of e-payment instruments on cash usage: Thailand's recent evidence and policy implications), Hungary (Bodi-Schubert, A. (2010). Factors behind high cash usage in Hungary. *MNB Bulletin (discontinued)*, *5*(1), 20–28) and a regional study for Africa (Zins, A. and Weill, L. (2016). The determinants of financial inclusion in Africa. *Review of Development Finance*, *6*(1), 46–57).

show that "mobile banking is driven by the same determinants as traditional banking," suggesting that mobile banking is not a more inclusive channel. They observe that "the determinants of informal finance differ from those of formal finance."[19]

A recent current of research focuses on consumer surveys and diaries and individual transaction data, already mentioned in some studies above. Despite the growing literature on the demand for payment instruments, data on individual consumer payment behavior are difficult and costly to obtain. Consumer surveys gather information on consumer habits, preferences and socio-demographics characteristics via a questionnaire. These surveys have gained in frequency and details since the first ones commissioned in the US in a systematic manner in the 1990s. Consumer diaries are more recent and consist in asking the consumer to record all the transactions done during a period of time, typically a few days, as well as asking those same consumers some questions about their characteristics and preferences. Such diaries are particularly helpful to analyze actual transactions, as opposed to recorded or self-reported information from surveys. Diaries are also more complete as they aim at capturing all payment modes, including cash.

The Quality Dimension of Payments

Understanding the quality dimension of payments is essential, as "access refers to supply, whereas use is the intersection of the supply and demand schedules."[20] Quality of a financial service is the catalyst that converts the existing access to actual usage. There are various aspects of quality, including availability, convenience, affordable cost, speed of settlement, design, privacy, security, consumer protection or reliability. How can quality payment systems drive higher adoption? What are the characteristics of good quality payment systems? What best practices can be shared when establishing new payment systems and regulations?

---

[19]Zins, A. and Weill, L. (2016). The determinants of financial inclusion in Africa. *Review of Development Finance*, 6(1), 46–57.

[20]Claessens, S. (2006). Access to financial services: A review of the issues and public policy objectives. *The World Bank Research Observer*, 21(2), 207–240.

The high inflation experienced in Brazil in the 1980s and 1990s and banking consolidation have led Brazilian banks to invest heavily in technology, especially in fast and secure payment systems. Moreover, a high level of frauds pushed issuers and acquirers to invest in technology. The deep and innovative reform of the Brazilian Payment System (SPB) in April 2002 was an important regulatory development in this process. The focus of policymakers and companies was to incentivize the penetration of card products, by affiliating more merchants. During the following decade, Brazilian regulators focused more and more on the contestability of the market, acknowledging the high prices paid by merchants and customers. In Brazil, studies suggest that a lower cost of financial services leads to higher levels of formalization and higher levels of credit.[21] In fact, the Brazilian card market is marked by a higher level of pricing and higher profitability than other payment markets globally.

The Central Bank of Brazil dedicates a section of its annual Report on Financial Inclusion to payments. Transfers represent the most used electronic payment mode and include products known as available electronic transfers (Transferências Eletrônicas Disponíveis: TEDs), credit documents (Documento de Crédito: DOC) and invoices (Boletos). The last category of invoices is the largest one: there are close to 10 million "boletos" liquidated every day in Brazil. Cards, be it credit or debit, be it present or not-present, are progressively replacing cash and checks. Presential payments mean that the customer or cardholder is physically present at the merchant location to make his payment. The Central Bank notes a large increase in card not-present payment models, such as payments through call centers or online payments. Internet transactions represented 39.2% of total transactions in 2010, while mobile transactions represented an additional 10%. In the case of not-present payments, an active credit card is still required, but not the use of a point-of-sale terminal. Until 2013, credit cards were used more frequently than debit cards. The curve then inverted with debit cards being the most used electronic payment mode, in terms of the number of active plastic cards and in terms of the number of transactions. The Central Bank explains that the rise in debit card usage suggests the substitution

---

[21]D'Erasmo, P. (2013). Access to credit and the size of the formal sector in Brazil.

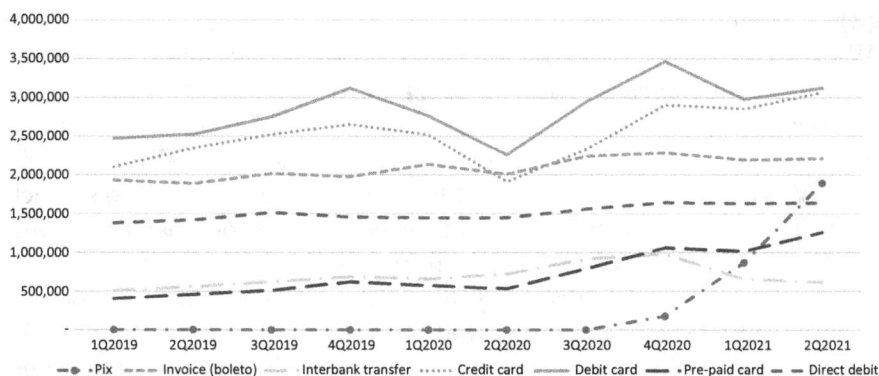

Figure 1: Number of Payment Transactions with Non-Cash Instruments (Thousands of Transactions)

Source: Central Bank of Brazil.

of cash and check payments by debit, which is viewed as more cost effective and secure.[22]

Innovation has played a key role in the evolution of payment means. Digital banking experienced exponential growth in the recent past. According to the Brazilian Card Association ABECS, contactless payments grew by almost six times between 2019 and 2020, reaching R$41.0 billion in 2020. The number of banking accounts with mobile access also expanded considerably, reaching 94 million accounts in 2019, up from 33 million in 2015. The Central Bank of Brazil expects to launch new functionalities of its peer-to-peer payment system Pix by 2024, including cash withdrawal, salary accounts, contactless and international payments. As of March 2021, Pix had reached 206 million registered keys, processing almost 400 million transactions in the month, totaling R$278 billion in volume, almost 10x higher than the month of its launch in November 2020 when the figure was just R$29 billion (Figure 1).

Assessing the quality dimension of payments can mostly be approached via surveys. The Bank for International Settlements defines four elements of infrastructures that effectively support financial inclusion: (1) interoperability and coverage, (2) accessibility,

---

[22]Banco Central do Brasil (2015). Relatório de inclusão financeira.

(3) efficiency and standardization, and (4) safety and reliability.[23] We illustrate how those four elements apply to high quality payment systems with the case study of Brazilian payments.

Technology companies have invested in new forms to capture or acquire transactions, that is to say, connect electronically a buyer's and a seller's bank accounts. This requires acquiring tools, such as a point-of-sale terminal accepting card swipe or near-field communication. Other participants in the ecosystem include processing companies and antifraud systems. Policymakers have supported interoperability as a basis for well-functioning payment systems. In Brazil, a joint effort of the Central Bank, the Ministry of Finance and the Ministry of Justice mandated in 2009 that the largest payment networks be open. Any acquiring system could capture a transaction stemming from a plastic card from any issuer and card network. Previously, payment systems were vertically integrated and worked in silos, preventing the entry of new acquirers and resulting in higher costs for users.[24]

Means of payment imply various types of costs, implicit and explicit for both parties in a transaction. Electronic payments imply an explicit cost for merchants in the form of a merchant discount rate paid by the merchant to the companies participating in the card ecosystem, such as the card acquirer, processor, brand and issuer. Moreover, merchants pay for the rental or acquisition of POS equipment. In Brazil, the merchant discount rate reached 2.1% of the transacted volumes for credit transaction and 1.1% for debit transactions at the end of 2020. While rates have come down since the opening of the market, they still compare unfavorably with developed countries. Other costs include frauds, which can be paid for by merchants or banks, depending on the rules of the payment ecosystem. Printing, embossing and shipping plastic cards also represent a cost for the issuing bank (Figure 2).

For a cardholder, the cost associated with a card consists in card fees paid to the card issuer. Card fees depend on the card network,

---

[23]World Bank Group (2015b). Payments aspects of financial inclusion, committee on payments and market infrastructures. World Bank Publications.

[24]Santos, E. L. D. and Cavalcanti, L. F. (2020). *Payments 4.0. as forças que estão transformando o Mercado brasileiro*. São Paulo: Linotipo Digital. For a detailed account on the Brazilian card market.

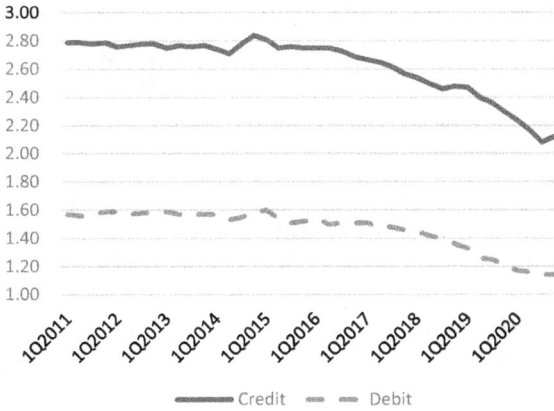

Figure 2: Cost for the Merchant (Gross Merchant Discount Rate, %)
Source: Central Bank of Brazil.

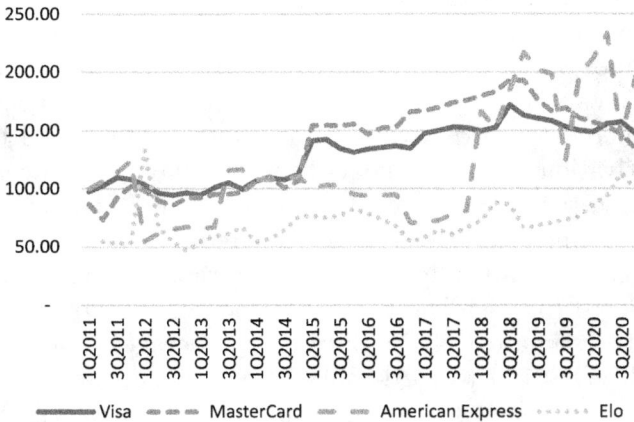

Figure 3: Cost for the Cardholder (Annual Card Fees in R$)
Source: Central Bank of Brazil.

the type of plastic card and the benefits it provides. Contrary to the merchant discount rate, card fees paid by the cardholder are fixed in nature and do not depend on transacted volumes. Card fees in Brazil typically ranged between $20 and $40 per annum at the end of 2020 (Figure 3).

On the flip side, merchants and customers tend to underestimate the explicit and implicit costs of cash and checks. These costs include cash management, safety and fraud. Different studies suggest that banning cash would lift GDP by 0.7% to 1%, due to lower cost of cash management.[25] In the case of checks, frauds related to unfunded checks represented 6% of total cleared checks by volume, according to the Central Bank of Brazil, a percentage that has been remarkably high and stable over time (Figure 4). Checks present the disadvantage of complicating cash management for whoever writes the check, as there is no defined date for those to be cashed in.

Cash payments are common in the informal economy — not just for tax evasion purposes — and sometimes explain the discounts or rebates offered to customers when they pay in cash. In Brazil, Regulation MP764/2016 authorized merchants to charge different prices depending on the means of payment, thereby giving an incentive for higher cash usage. This law is contrarian to the trend observed in most countries, where authorities have incentivized the use of electronic payments against cash. The main justifications for the regulations were to put pressure on card companies to lower their prices, as well as avoid cross-subsidies. In fact, a single price policy leads cash payers — most often from lower-income segments — to subsidize card payers — most often from higher-income segments, who capture the rewards offered by card payments. The regulator decided to favor a social motivation, against a goal of tax and payment efficiency.

Studies in the US confirm the hypothesis of cross-subsidies. Data highlight the inefficiencies brought by credit card usage, as reward programs generate an "implicit monetary transfer to credit card users from non-card (or cash) users," when there is a unique price for all users. Data estimate that in the US, on average, "each cash-using household pays $149 to card-using households and each card-using household receives $1,133 from cash users every year." Moreover, "because credit card spending and rewards are positively correlated with household income, the payment instrument transfer also induces a regressive transfer from low-income to high-income households."[26]

---

[25]Banco Central do Brasil (2007). *Custo e Eficiencia na Utilizacao de Instrumentos de Pagamento de Varejo*. Reforma do sistema de pagamentos de varejo; Garcia-Swartz, D. D. *et al.* (2006). The move toward a cashless society: A closer look at payment instrument economics. *Review of Network Economics* 5(2): 175–198.

[26]Schuh, S. D. *et al.* (2010). Who gains and who loses from credit card payments? Theory and calibrations.

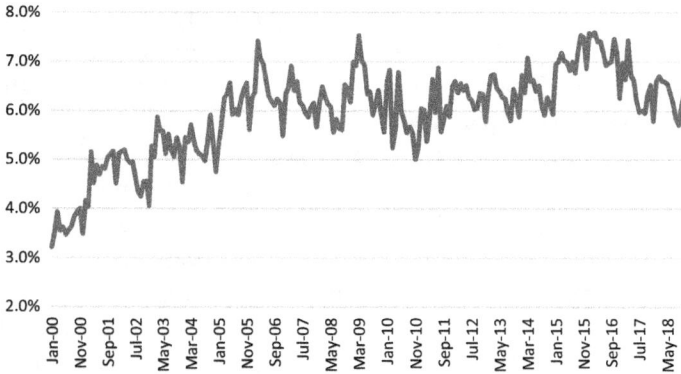

Figure 4: Unfunded Checks in Brazil (% of Unfunded Checks/Total Checks)
Source: Central Bank of Brazil.

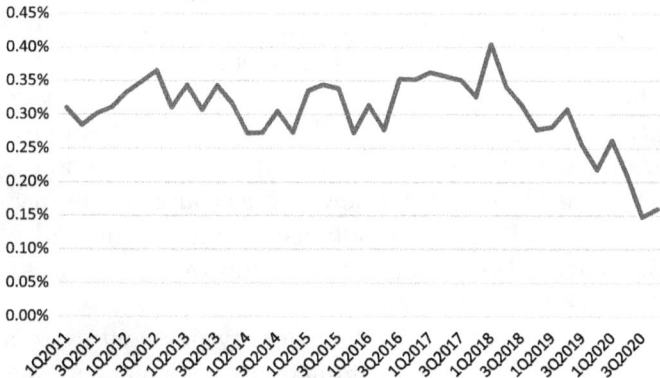

Figure 5: Spending by Card Issuers in Loyalty Programs (% of Total Card Volume)
Source: Central Bank of Brazil.

From the point of view of the cardholder, direct and explicit benefits of card usage include the rewards and loyalty points accumulated in the case of payment by credit cards (Figure 5). Rewards have experienced a decrease in Brazil in the recent past in percentage terms. In percentage terms, rewards paid by issuing banks to credit cardholders represent approximately 15 basis points of transacted credit volumes.

Another important advantage of electronic payments for a customer is the possibility to build her credit score, which often proves essential for the subsequent approval of credit application. Credit scoring is not only built on negative information on credit repayment, but also on positive information, such as timely payments of bills, or patterns of payments and savings.

From the point of view of merchants, the use of electronic payments allows to gather information and intelligence on customer trends and preferences. Big data enables the design of customized discounts in order to increase traffic at the point of sale. Moreover, electronic payments enable retailers to develop "a comprehensive solution for managing their business, such as better inventory and sales management." Small merchants are "more likely to adopt electronic payments if they are combined with other services and business intelligence": the value proposal needs to be strong, with big data allowing for business intelligence or facilitating their access to credit.[27] Offering intelligence and services on top of payment solutions is a global trend in the acquiring and processing industry, it can facilitate cash and inventory management for example.

Cross-border payments have experienced rapid growth and led to innovation in digital payments. Ebanx is a leader in cross-border payments in Latin America and defends that innovation is just an enabler, and it is fostered by a new mindset and regulatory changes. For FinTechs, the challenge is not just about pricing and winning a race to the bottom, but about offering innovative services and payment experience to the end customer.

Speed is another key element for quality payment systems. While cash presents the advantage of immediate settlement at the point of sale, it needs to be withdrawn from ATMs by the payer in a transaction, while the merchant needs to bring it to a bank to earn interest and be safe. The lifecycle of cash and banknotes represents an implicit cost for economic agents.

There is conflicting evidence from surveys about which payment modes users find easier. Ease of use includes elements such as the wide acceptance of electronic payments, the ease to swipe and process a payment, or the convenience of carrying around cards or cash. Card acceptance at the point of sale has become widespread

---

[27]Demirgüç-Kunt, A. and Singer, D. (2017). Financial inclusion and inclusive growth: A review of recent empirical evidence.

in Brazil, providing ample access to this means of payment. Acceptance also includes a technology component, as downtime prevents electronic transactions to be processed, especially in rural areas, with poor network connectivity. Downtime has often more to do with telecommunication infrastructure than with payment networks. Some research stresses that users find cash payment easier, as it is universally accepted and does not require reliance on infrastructure. Other research stresses that users value the convenience of carrying a plastic card in their wallet and not needing to withdraw physical cash. Users also sometimes express their preference for plastic cards over QR codes, as cards provide a convenient experience. Technology can make electronic payments more convenient, for example via near-field communication or biometry, boosting the dimension of ease of use. Electronic payments and card payments stored in online wallets are particularly useful for recurring payments, for services such as Uber or Spotify, and for e-commerce.

Due to slow legacy payment systems, most countries, including many developing countries, settle financial transaction in one or more days. In Brazil, debit card transactions settle on the following day (T+1), while credit card transactions settle one month later (T+28, on average), implying a large cost in terms of working capital for merchants. In fact, merchants accumulate receivables in the case of credit card transactions, which they often anticipate in order to receive cash immediately, thereby generating another high-margin source of revenues for card companies and banks, known as anticipation of receivables.

Electronic payments can provide superior safety to users. Card payments offer the ability to track transaction information, confirm, revoke, cancel transactions in case of errors or frauds. They enable reports on transactions and maintain audit trails, providing full transparency, being a tool to fight criminal activities. In the list of benefits of card usage, customers spontaneously quote the safety concerns related to carrying cash. This is particularly true in Latin America where the risk of crime and theft is elevated. Cash does not provide audit trails, preventing to revert a transaction. Defining audit trails allows to comply with tax rules, in particular. Audit trails are essential to grow businesses out of informality and fight criminal activities.

For merchants, the use of cards brings security, as card-present payments are covered by the issuing bank in the case of defaults. In other words, if the payer is not able to settle a card payment, the merchant has the certainty to receive her funds from the issuing bank. Contrary to card-present payments, in the case of online purchases or card-not present payments, the merchant incurs the cost of defaulting payers.

On the flip side, the use of cash maintains due anonymity and protects users' personal information, including payment details and preference for consumption. In emerging markets, concerns around privacy are rarely mentioned in the preference for cash and seem to be more of a concern in developed countries, such as Scandinavia. The concern for privacy stems from the legitimate desire of users to not contribute their personal data and preferences to merchants and service providers without their consent. In fact, data on payments can be used by companies to map preferences and design products and special offers.

Overall, means of payment bear implicit and explicit costs for parties involved in a transaction, including merchant discount rates, card fees, cost of cash management and safekeeping, costs related to thefts and frauds. The preference for electronic payments over cash is complex and takes into account benefits, such as rewards, building a credit history and customer preference. There is a complex tension between the legitimate concern for privacy and the need to offer safe payment modes and avoid informality, tax evasion and criminal activities.

Variety of Payment Methods

The reference Findex research at the World Bank defines three main measures of financial inclusion.[28] *Formal account* refers to the fact that the individual has an account either at a financial institution or through a mobile money provider. *Formal saving* refers to the fact that the individual saved, using an account at a financial institution

---

[28]World Bank Group (2013). *Global Financial Development Report 2014: Financial Inclusion* (Vol. 2). World Bank Publications.

in the past 12 months. *Formal credit* refers to the fact that the individual borrowed from a financial institution in the past 12 months. A formal account is the basis for payments, which are a powerful vector of financial inclusion, as discussed earlier. Globally, 1.7 billion adults do not have access to a transaction account, even though 1.1 billion of them have a mobile phone, turning phones into a portable bank branch.[29]

Electronic payments include money transfers and online transfers, card-based instruments, such as debit, credit or prepaid cards, and e-money. Electronic payments, also referred to as digital payments, are often opposed to cash usage and payments by checks. Electronic payments can be completed in the real world at brick-and-mortar stores with plastic cards, or online via mobile phones or the Internet in card-not-present transactions, as in the case of e-commerce transactions or online transfers and online payments of bills, such as *boletos* in Brazil. The payment market is a classic example of a two-sided market, which implies that "to succeed, platforms in industries such as software, portals and media, payment systems and the Internet, must get both sides of the market on board."[30]

Payments are essential in any economic transaction involving the exchange of services and goods but also in the case of government transfers or remittances, increasing the efficiency of economic transactions. The World Bank explains that "not all financial products are equally effective in reaching development goals, such as reductions in poverty and inequality," and "current evidence suggests that the biggest impacts come from savings accounts — provided that they are inexpensive and serve a specific purpose — and digital payments."[31] This requires owning a transaction account to perform all payment needs and safely store some value. While 31% of the

---

[29]Demirgüç-Kunt, A. *et al.* (2018). The Global Findex Database 2017: Measuring financial inclusion and the FinTech revolution. World Bank, April.

[30]Rochet, J. C. and Tirole, J. (2003). Platform competition in two-sided markets. *Journal of the European Economic Association*, *1*(4), 990–1029.

[31]Demirgüç-Kunt, A. and Singer, D. (2017). Financial inclusion and inclusive growth: A review of recent empirical evidence.

adult population worldwide still does not have an account, transaction accounts are "the cornerstone for providing electronic payment services."

Analyzing payment systems is important for economic models. Costs incurred for payments, both direct and indirect, go against the efficient, rational and frictionless classical economic theory. An essential goal of electronic payments is to reduce the friction, with better convenience and cost for users. Studying payment systems is of particular interest when considering new institutional economics, which focus "explicitly on transaction costs, taxes, computational limitations, and other frictions." Meanwhile, the paradigm of behavioral economics "introduces non-rational and systematically uninformed behavior by agents."[32] Some evidence is provided by a report analyzing 12 European countries, which estimated a reduction in operating costs of € 32 billion, or 0,38% of GDP, between 1987 and 1999, driven by the 36% increase in electronic payments.[33]

Electronic payments represent a very large market. The World Bank estimates that the "global market opportunity for expanding the adoption of electronic payments by merchants is large, estimated at $19 trillion of payments made and accepted in cash and checks by micro, small and medium retailers (MSMRs) in 2015."[34] The authors calculate that in 2015, "MSMRs made and accepted around $34 trillion in supplier payments, wages and salaries, and customer payments." This total amount of $34 trillion is split between $15 trillion that were made electronically and the remaining $19 trillion in cash and checks. There are two legs to digitalize at the level of merchants: funds they receive as payments and funds they transfer to employees or suppliers. Grocery retailers have a higher usage of cash and checks. Latin America represented $3.5trillion, of which just 46% was already electronic, a figure that increased during the Great

---

[32]Merton, R. C. and Bodie, Z. (1995). A conceptual framework for analyzing the financial system. *The global financial system: A functional perspective*, 3–31.

[33]Humphrey, D. B. *et al.* (1996). Cash, paper, and electronic payments: A cross-country analysis. *Journal of Money, Credit and Banking*, *28*(4), 914–939.

[34]World Bank (2016). *Innovation in Electronic Payment Adoption: The Case of Small Retailers*. World Bank Publications.

Lockdown. This compared with an average of 71% for high-income OECD countries. In particular, B2B transactions represent a large opportunity, especially for cross-border payments, and new models are emerging for online payments.

The payment industry generates vast amounts of plastic. The number of issued cards continues to increase, while the number of active cards grows at a slower pace. In Brazil, the percentage of activation started to decrease after 2010 and reached 48% for credit cards and 37% for debit cards in 2020, implying that more than half of all plastic cards are unused. Credit or debit cards are considered active when there has been at least a transaction in the 12 months preceding the reporting date. Those datapoints suggest a potential large cost saving for issuing banks to switch to digital payment means, such as virtual cards or QR codes, as well as a reduction in produced plastic.

Issuers, card networks, acquirers and processors have invested massively in order to develop new payment systems that would bring more convenience, safety and transparency to users. Investments have revolved around three main elements: infrastructure (such as switching systems), ecosystem (analytics, risk, authorization of transactions), and front-end (with a wider category of point-of-sale equipment and better user experience). Payment capture has broadened from card swipe and chip-and-pin to include biometrics-based payments, near-field communication and payments without cards, such as QR codes.

In September 2020, Amazon Go piloted in Seattle a contactless identity service linking the credit cards of customers with their palm print to create a unique biometric signature. It allowed customers to pay in a store by holding their palm above a "One" palm reader, reinforcing the potential of touchless and secure means. Artificial intelligence (AI) also represents an opportunity for payment companies and merchants, providing smarter tools for fraud monitoring and enabling higher approval rates. AI can provide new revenue opportunities for retailers and advertisers, by allowing to map customer preference, providing on-demand analytics for merchants and turning pricing and promotion campaigns more effective. For example, Visa used artificial intelligence and machine learning models to "examine over 500 transaction attributes in real-time for indicators of fraud, averting \$25 billions of fraud in 2019."[35]

Cards have shown their resilience over the past decades and while the current payment ecosystem is working well, payments are experiencing four main improvements, with easier access to payment solutions for merchants, faster speed of settlement, lower cost of transactions and new ways to capture of transactions.

---

[35]McKinsey (2021). Technology-led shifts and opportunities in card-based payments. Available at https://www.mckinsey.com/industries/financial-services/our-insights/banking-matters/technology-led-shifts-and-opportunities-in-card-based-payments. Last accessed October 6, 2021.

Chapter 5

Cryptocurrencies: A Natural Evolution for Payments?

Distributed Ledger and Its Use Cases in Finance

Blockchains are distributed ledgers, operated within peer-to-peer networks to offer a decentralized way to verify or exchange ownership securely and efficiently. While most innovations bring no real changes, some have the power to disrupt businesses, as did the internet a couple of decades ago, and blockchain is certainly one of those disruptive technologies. Distributed Ledger Technology (DLT) proposes a fundamentally new architecture to record transactions. Can it foster more inclusion and development?

DLT creates a reliable and distributed record of transactions, or ledger, which replaces centralized, closed databases. In the DLT, nodes in the system collaborate to reach a consensus on the truth. Distributed ledgers overcome the shortcomings of both centralized and decentralized architectures. The downside of centralization can include slow decision-making due to bottlenecks, increased systemic risk through concentration, dominant positions, and barriers to entry and contestation. Decentralized systems present other shortcomings, such as when different nodes reach different and inconsistent outcomes. DLT combines encryption with economic incentives to create a widely accessible and error-proofed system. The incentives are used to verify and confirm data entered into the ledger under a validation performed by "miners" in the case of Bitcoin. Every transaction is assigned a unique hash or identifier once it is verified. All those validated transactions are then stored and maintained by miners on the open network and all changes are broadcast to all other participants in the system. In the case of Bitcoin, blocks of around 500 valid transactions are added to the chain, hence the name of the technology.

A key innovation of DLT is that it eliminates the need for a central authority to perform tasks such as certifying identities and ownerships, i.e. provenance, and authorizing transactions. DLT distributes trust, it can be open, with anonymous participants accessing the ledger with encryption keys.

In other cases, the ledger can be permissioned, and only predefined authenticated users can participate. Permissioned models, sometimes referred to as closed or consortium ledgers, have a strong potential in the financial space. Users must receive permission from an administrator to be part of the consortium and operate a node. Permissioned systems follow a gated approach, with known validators, which is more appropriate to legally registered assets. It is unlikely that open ledgers, such as the one used by Bitcoin, will be widely adopted by large financial institutions or States, but permissioned ledgers defined by a consortium of institutions could meaningfully improve processes and efficiency in select products and business segments. In a permission-based system, the administrator can allow nodes to perform a lighter validation than in a fully open system, as there would be some level of trust between participants, with commensurate reduction in resource usage and potentially higher performance. Providing incentives to innovators within a consortium will be key in order to avoid free riding. Pricing could evolve so that clients pay for actual value-added services and not for simple ancillary services, such as record-keeping, which could be performed on the DLT. This would imply smarter pricing systems and would incentivize companies to embrace innovation in value-added services to differentiate themselves from their competitors.

The most relevant application of DLT so far has had to do with virtual currencies. Several regulators have called for comments and published views on virtual currencies and DLT.[1] Bitcoin is the most

---

[1]IMF (2016). Staff discussion, virtual currencies and beyond: Initial considerations, January 2016.

famous application of the DLT. It is a virtual currency developed to "allow online payments to be sent from one party to another without going through a financial institution."[2] In Nakamoto's view, the ledger's architecture and its validation logic are meant to avoid the issue of double spending. Shortly after the pseudonymous white paper was published in October 2008, the software was released in January 2009 and the first bitcoin was minted.[3] Strictly speaking, the blockchain is a type of distributed ledger, which records transactions made with the virtual currency bitcoin. In the case of virtual currencies, the ledger keeps all past transactions and the balance of each participant. The ledger is decentralized and is accessible by any participant. DLT is the technological basis for the more than 6,000 virtual currencies (VC) currently traded, for a market cap exceeding 2 trillion dollars, of which bitcoin has more than 40% of the market.[4] Research notes that "the database has never been hacked and currently settles roughly the same value of transactions each year as PayPal, all without a single employee or central organizing figure."[5] The bitcoin software guarantees that there will never be more than 21 million bitcoins.

The virtual currency is mostly a speculative asset today, while it is marginally a tool for exchanging goods and services, and does not perform the other classical functions of currencies, being a store of value and a unit of measurement. While the virtual currency market is attracting a lot of interest, it is far from reaching wide acceptance, with just over 100,000 merchants accepting payments by bitcoins globally.[6] By comparison, brand network Visa claims more

---

[2]Nakamoto, S. (2008). "Bitcoin: A Peer-to-Peer Electronic Cash System," white paper, Bitcoin.org (31 October 2008). Available at https://bitcoin.org/bitcoin.pdf.

[3]CFA (2021). Cryptoassets, the guide to bitcoin, blockchain, and cryptocurrency for investment professionals. Matt Hougan, David Lawant, CFA Institute Research Foundation.

[4]Bank for International Settlements (2015). Mark Carney: Introduction to the open forum. Available at https://www.bis.org/review/r151116c.htm. Last accessed October 6, 2021.

[5]CFA (2021). Cryptoassets, the guide to bitcoin, blockchain, and cryptocurrency for investment professionals. Matt Hougan, David Lawant, CFA Institute Research Foundation, p. 7.

[6]Data available at http://spendbitcoins.com/. Accessed on September 7, 2021.

than 2 billion Visa cards globally, while card acquirer Cielo counts 1.3 million affiliated merchants in Brazil alone. Bitcoin offers a solid proof of concept, but its architecture offers only limited applicability for financial institutions and States.

Blockchains offer a new way to transfer assets and money in the digital era. The decentralized and anonymous characteristics of DLT are particularly disruptive compared to the existing centralized issuance of fiat money performed by Central Banks. The centralization of currency issuance is a relatively recent event, dating from the 19th century for developed economies, while today, numerous companies issue what can be assimilated to currencies in the form of loyalty points or rewards.

DLT is particularly useful in businesses based on a centralized authentication and approval system, involving the ownership of some asset, with a multiplicity of participants leading to errors and reconciliation, and processes that present a delay in settlement due to technological inefficiency. DLT allows for a consensual verification of information and an open access to this information. The open access to records, in turn, reduces the risk and timing of transaction settlement.

In order to be adopted, a new technology needs to be cheaper, safer, faster, more convenient, or any combination of those. If not, market participants will not incur the switching costs. In the case of DLT disruptions, consensus among market participants points to potential use cases in securities settlement and custodian activities, trade matching and confirmation for low-volume securities or private markets, corporate actions, issuance of securities, remittances, and virtual currencies.[7] The World Federation of Exchanges also points to a potential in crowdfunding, any type of low frequency trading, trade registration, regulatory reporting, compliance functions, asset or registration facilities.

There are three interesting characteristics in the DLT. The first one is speed, as DLT allows transactions to happen fast, as ownership and payment records are open and accessible. Settlement can therefore be near-instantaneous, making it much more convenient for

---

[7]World Federation of Exchanges (2016). Financial market infrastructures and distributed ledger technology, WFE. August 2016.

economic agents than traditional settlement systems using T+1 for card payments or T+3 for transaction on stock exchanges. In the case of payments, DLT does not require transaction information to travel through a complex ecosystem of participants. The higher speed removes settlement risk, reduces collateral management, frees up capital and reduces reconciliation errors. Some regulators recognize the advantage of speed in the case of virtual currencies: the speed of VC-based financial asset transactions is higher than traditional financial asset transfers and takes place within a couple of hours at most.

Cost can be a second key differentiator of virtual currencies. The cost of transactions seems to be "currently somewhere around a couple of Euro cents."[8] Functions involving data manipulation, reconciliation, custody, record keeping could be simplified or eliminated. Costs stemming from counterparty risk in slow settlements and collateral management would also be reduced considerably. The R3 consortium is working to develop Corda, a shared ledger platform designed to record, manage and synchronize financial agreements dedicated to regulated financial institutions. David Rutter, CEO of R3, notes that "distributed and shared ledger technology can transform the way in which Financial Market Infrastructures [...] issue, record and transfer assets, enabling transactions and reference data to be visible to all relevant parties on the ledger, and "this can cut [..] costs dramatically."[9] Regulatory reporting could become easier, cheaper, and more effective as records are shared. The lower cost base would be a key incentive to financial inclusion, as it could trigger micro-payments or allow micro-issuances on capital markets. When the EBA examined cross-border payments, it estimated that DLT could lower the cost of those transfers "well below 1%, compared to the traditional 2–4% for online payment systems, and to more than 7% on average for the cross-border transfer of remittances."[10] On the flip side, virtual currencies and the activity of mining consume

---

[8]European Securities and Markets Authority (ESMA) (2015). Investment using virtual currency or distributed ledger technology. July 2015.

[9]ISF (2016). LatAm bourse becomes first exchange to join R3 blockchain consortium.

[10]European Banking Authority (EBA) (2014). Opinion on virtual currencies. July 2014.

high amounts of energy, bringing the question of their compatibility with climate targets.

Finally, DLT's characteristics can make it a safe transaction means. Transactions are irrevocable since every past transaction has been verified by nodes and cannot be modified. A hacker would need faster and higher computing power than the majority of the validators in the system. Contrary to centralized systems, getting control of one node — however relevant — would not be enough. Records are shared by nature, which removes the need for a centralized trust structure and once a consensus has been formed among the validators, it reduces the risk of information losses and makes it impossible to have two inconsistent records for the same transactions or ownership title. Moreover, the encryption technology, while not exclusive or new to the DLT, makes identities non-forgeable as long as the owner protects their private keys or authentication information. By using encryption, DLT makes it possible to protect privacy while authenticating users.

The DLT could also host smart contracts. Smart contracts have programmed logic stored on the ledger itself along with the data. Smart contracts execute instructions when some pre-defined conditions are met. The instruction, once executed, is also recorded and becomes immutable. Shares paying a dividend, derivatives exercising at maturity, transferring collateral for a margin call are common examples of the so-called smart contracts. To some extent, any work or supplier contract could be enhanced as a smart contract living on the DLT, which could reduce considerably the costs related to payroll and accounting. Ethereum is the most famous platform that runs smart contracts, which it defines as "applications that run exactly as programmed without any possibility of downtime, censorship, fraud or third-party interference."[11]

That said, actual business applications are still scarce today. Several exchanges have launched initiatives to implement DLT. In the US, the DTCC is considering changes to its CDS settlement system, while the Australian Stock Exchange (ASX) invested in 2016 in Digital Asset Holdings. The ASX initiative aims at creating a private DLT where nodes will have limited capabilities to update its clearing

---

[11]Data available at https://www.ethereum.org/. Accessed October 6, 2021.

and settlement system. Nasdaq announced in December 2015 that it had made the first ever share trade using a ledger involving the shares of a company called Chain, using the Open Assets protocol. HSBC launched in November 2019 its Digital Vault service in Asia, which digitizes the transaction records of private placement assets including equity, debt and real estate. The Digital Vault enables global custody clients to access details of their private assets directly and in real-time instead of having to request information or search records. In 2019, Deutsche Bank also announced the deployment of DLT for custody services. However, while some players have started to launch pilot projects, the larger disruption could take years to appear.

In some cases, DLT is not performant enough. Roundtrips on stock exchanges for equities trades (the time needed for a message to travel from the broker to the matching engine of the exchange and back to the broker) are close to one microsecond. The current latency of DLT, which ranges typically from a few seconds to minutes to settle a transaction, is not appropriate for low latency trading.[12] The distributed nature of DLT, with its handling of messages and transactions by multiple nodes, is inherently slower than messaging a single matching engine, although technology could evolve and improve the latency of DL-based systems. John Fildes, CEO of Chi-X Australia, explains that "Blockchain has potentially fabulous application in the settlement realm but it's a big stretch to try and use blockchain for clearing because it means you need real-time payment systems."[13]

In other cases, DLT's speed is not a desired feature. According to Bog Greifeld, Nasdaq CEO, "blockchain technology has the potential to assist in expediting trade clearing and settlement from the current equity market standards of three days to as little as ten minutes [..], settlement risk exposure can be reduced by over 99%, dramatically lowering capital costs." He adds that the "reduction in settlement period will have deep consequences for market

---

[12]Etherscan indicates the age of pending transactions on its website: https://eth erscan.io/txsPending.

[13]GBST (2016). Four scenarios for blockchain in capital markets, white paper. Available at https://www.gbst.com/wp-content/uploads/2016/05/GBST-Block chain-Whitepaper.pdf. Last accessed October 6, 2021.

participants and systemic risk."[14] However, clearing presents the key benefit of netting positions for brokers and counterparties, reducing the number of payment transactions, therefore making final netting cheaper. According to DTCC, netting of payments among market participants reduces meaningfully the value of securities and payments to be made. In other words, having an instantaneous settlement could lead to higher costs as netting does not take place. As a result, moving settlement processes to T+0 may not be desirable, as it would remove benefits from netting, require pre-funding, change the workflow for securities lending, and require material investments from participants, among other impacts.

Most regulators have demonstrated interest in DLT and some have published their views on virtual currencies and DLT. Market participants have launched collaborative efforts to test the DLT, such as R3, the Hyperledger Project or the Post-Trade Distributed Ledger.[15] However, like many other innovations, the DLT brings uncertainty together with opportunities. Despite its potential use cases, DLT presents four important barriers to overcome: interoperability, regulations, privacy and irrevocability.

DLT enthusiasts mention the lower cost as a key advantage of the technology. However, developing the DLT will imply significant upfront investments from all financial participants to train staff and interoperate the DLT with existing and legacy systems. There will most likely be a large number of ledgers that will interoperate and it is unlikely that existing systems would be entirely decommissioned. Moreover, energy consumption, disk space and computing power have been raised as potential issues in order to process and store a growing body of messages. Additionally, the function of validation bears costs, either explicit or implicit. In the case of Bitcoin, miners are remunerated with bitcoins for validating transactions and performing an essential function as compliance officers on the DLT. In permissioned

---

[14] Nasdaq (2015). Press release, Nasdaq Linq enables first-ever private securities issuance documented with blockchain technology. Available at http://ir.nasdaq.com/releasedetail.cfm?releaseid=948326. Last accessed October 6, 2021.

[15] Among other initiatives, R3 groups over 50 financial institutions (https://r3cev.com/), the Hyperledger groups close to 80 institutions (www.hyperledger.org), while the PTDL groups nearly 40 financial institutions (www.ptdlgroup.org).

ledgers, market structure companies will justify part of their fees with the function performed as miners.

Counter-intuitively, and contrary to what DLT apparently stands for, the system will need a central body to define rules of the ledger. This paradox and the need for a governance of the ledger begs questions such as the following: Who controls the ledger? Who regulates the ledger and enforces contracts? It will be important for a consortium to align incentives of members so that healthy competition fosters innovation between members and avoids free riding. Questions relating to anticompetitive practices, extra costs for participants, systemic risk, participants' responsibility and anonymity of customers will be just some of the key questions that regulators will have to address.

The DLT inherently allows participants to maintain anonymity. Thanks to encryption, the DLT can provide open access while still maintaining the privacy of participants. Who would have access to the true identity of participants? Who would be able to issue new encryption codes in the event a customer forgets her code? How will participants verify that privacy does not cover illicit activities? This is where permissioned ledgers can balance privacy concerns with regulatory requirements. In some countries, regulators require full transparency, as in the case of trade settlement in Brazil, which has to be done at the final beneficiary level.

Irrevocability is a great advantage but can also be an issue in the case of error management. What if an error gets booked into the ledger and needs to be revised? Irrevocability can be overcome by making opposite entries, just as it is done in current ledgers.

The unique combination of a distributed ledger, faster settlement, decentralized access, encryption, smart contracts, open numerous possibilities for businesses not just to become more efficient and create new revenue opportunities but also rethink and disrupt existing business models.

Cryptocurrency's Adoption as a Means of Payment

The growing debate around new types of currencies comes in the context of the rise in e-commerce and cross-border transactions magnified by COVID-19, the interest in private currencies such as Bitcoin and Libra (renamed to Diem, a project abandoned in February 2022) and the concern of Central Banks to offer a modern and credible form of their currency. Innovation in money can promote more efficiency in payments. While domestic payments offer real time, low cost and safe alternatives in many countries, cross-border payments or remittances continue to represent a hurdle for international exchanges and are a focus of attention for FinTech and researchers on financial inclusion.

Innovation in money includes cryptocurrencies, stablecoins and the Central Bank Digital Currencies (CBDC) — three concepts that are distinct but often considered together.

Cryptocurrencies are "token-based digital assets rather than currencies because it is far from clear that they fulfill the functions of money."[16] These digital assets exist outside the oversight of governments, as they rely on distributed networks of users, and stem largely from a crisis of confidence accentuated by the Global Financial Crisis. The very etymology of "crypo," meaning hidden or secret in greek, refers to the identity of the owner of the currency. It is not a surprise that cryptocurrencies tend to be favored in countries with a history of debasement and high inflation and a reliance on remittances. In other words, virtual currencies may have higher social acceptance than some currencies with limited convertibility and high inflation. As an example, the parliament of Salvador voted in favor of legal tender for Bitcoin in June 2021, giving economic agents three months to adapt and be able to accept bitcoins as a means of payment. Shops are required to accept bitcoins for payments and can exchange them against dollars through wallet Chivo. The Mexican exchange platform Bitso provides technological support for the wallet and developed an alliance with Silvergate Bank, a regulated US bank, to perform dollar transactions. The initial weeks of implementation showed a clear need to educate and train users. The appeal of those tokens is that they cannot be manipulated by a central issuer, their supply is fixed and predefined by an algorithm, and it can be used away from banks and tax authorities.

Adam Smith in the Wealth of Nations summarized the three traditional roles of money as store of value, medium of exchange and unit of account. Since it was idealized in 2008, bitcoin has not met

---

[16]Carney, M. (2021). *Value(s), Building a Better World for All.* Penguin, p. 112.

any of those three functions, and rather been used for speculation. Cryptocurrencies have experienced very high volatility, being therefore poorly suited to be a store of value (Figure 1). As means of payments or medium of exchange, their acceptance is currently very limited. Moreover, cyrptocurrencies can hardly be seen as a unit of account, in light of their volatility. The BIS emphasizes that "cryptoassets have served more as a highly speculative asset class for certain investors and those engaged in illicit activities rather than as a means to make payments."[17]

Mark Carney in his book Values reflects on the value of money and recollects the famous example mentioned by Adam Smith: in a barter economy, value reflects the relative quantities of labor required to produce two goods: "if among a nation of hunters, it usually costs twice the labour to kill a beaver which it does to kill a deer, one beaver should naturally exchange for or be worth two deer."[18] Whether is it

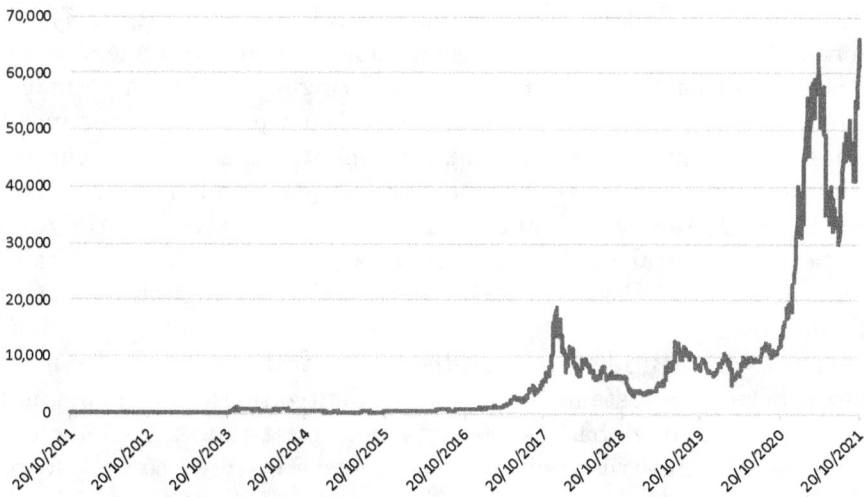

Figure 1:   Market Value of Bitcoin
Source: Bloomberg.

---

[17]Bank for International Settlements (2019). G7 working group on stablecoins. Investigating the impact of global stablecoins, p. 1.
[18]Carney, M. (2021). *Value(s), Building a Better World for All*. Penguin, p. 31.

supported by a relative comparison of labour or a theory of utility, money is used to measure value and to facilitate exchange of goods and services and graduate from a barter economy.

Stablecoins have some of the features of cryptocurrencies but they aim at a more stable price by being pegged to a currency such as dollar, gold or other types of assets. Collectively, nearly \$3 trillion in stablecoins such as Tether and USDC were transacted in the first half of 2021. Stablecoins can be used in retail transaction by any customer, or their use can be limited to a group of financial institutions or clients in the case of wholesale stablecoins. The best-known stablecoin is Libra, renamed to Diem, which is more often thought of as a payment system rather than a currency. USDC, the acronym for USD Coin, is the fastest growing stablecoin, with a one-to-one peg to the US dollar. USDC is fully backed by US dollar reserves and those reserves are audited. There is no money creation with USDC but it represents a faster and cheaper payment means than the traditional cross-border payment tracks. USDC is a digital currency representation of existing dollars, being instantaneously transferrable 24/7/365 across the globe. Visa enabled its cardholders and card issuers to use USDC in order to settle transactions, bringing stablecoin to mainstream users. Contrary to bitcoin, USDC is not just used for financial transactions but primarily for the settlement of real retail purchases. Circle — the company that manages USDC — also launched a partnership with Moneygram and Visa to offer remittances via USDC.

Several Central Banks have launched task forces to understand the benefits and risks of CBDC, a central bank digital version of the national currency, defined by some as the "most likely future of money."[19] The BIS has also created its Innovation Hub on the matter to better understand the impact of digitization in payments and highlighted that global stablecoins "may pose challenges for competition and anti-trust policies," in the case where it could lead to significant market concentration.[20] More than 80% of Central Bank respondents to a BIS survey in 2019 reported engagement in CBDC projects, with China leading the pack.

---

[19] *Ibid.*, p. 117.
[20] Bank for International Settlements (2019). G7 working group on stablecoins. Investigating the impact of global stablecoins, p. 12.

In March 2020, the Banque de France published a call for applications targeting CBDC tests "to experiment with the use of a digital euro issued for interbank settlements." The BdF explained that its aim is "to explore the potentialities offered by the technology, and to identify concrete cases integrating CBDC in innovative procedures for the clearing and settlement of tokenized financial assets." Central bank money, which is the currency issued directly by the Central Bank, is a safe settlement asset. Central bank money takes two forms: notes and coins also known as token-based money, and deposits made by commercial banks also known as account-based. In total, 95% of the money is of the second form. Banks facilitate payments by debiting the account of the payer and crediting the account of the payee, with interbank netting being done at accounts kept with the Central Bank. The call for applications of the BdF focused especially on applications for wholesale Central Bank money: "delivery versus payment of listed or unlisted securities, payment versus payment with other Central Bank Digital Currencies or other digital assets."[21] On April 19, 2021, the Bank of England and HM Treasury announced the creation of a taskforce to coordinate the exploration of a potential UK CBDC, defined as a "new form of digital money issued by the Bank of England and for use by households and businesses," existing "alongside cash and bank deposits, rather than replacing them."[22]

Within the Eurosystem, several central banks have embarked on projects to test CBDC and their potential. In June 2021, the BdF, the Swiss National Bank and the BIS Innovation Hub announced that they would conduct an experiment using wholesale CBDC for cross-border settlement, together with a private consortium. The private sector consortium was led by Accenture and included Credit Suisse, Natixis, R3, SIX Digital Exchange and UBS. The experiment

---

[21]Banque de France (2020). Call for applications — central bank digital currency experimentations, March 2020. Available at https://www.banque-france. fr/en/financial-stability/market-infrastructure-and-payment-systems/call-applic ations-central-bank-digital-currency-experimentations. Last accessed October 6, 2021.

[22]Bank of England (2021). "Bank of England Statement on Central Bank Digital Currency, 19 April 2021. Available at https://www.bankofengland.co.uk/new s/2021/april/bank-of-england-statement-on-central-bank-digital-currency. Last accessed September 6, 2021.

explored cross-border settlement with two wholesale CBDC and a digital financial instrument on a DLT platform. The test first involved "the exchange of the financial instrument against a euro wholesale CBDC through a delivery versus payment (DvP) settlement mechanism and the exchange of a euro wholesale CBDC against a Swiss franc wholesale CBDC through a payment versus payment (PvP) settlement mechanism." The transactions were settled between banks domiciled in France and in Switzerland.[23] Sweden has begun testing its CBDC, known as the e-krona.

The US is ostensibly behind other regions, with developments expected in 2022 on the back of the Project Hamilton white paper. In 2020, the Boston Federal Reserve and the Massachusetts Institute of Technology announced a joint exploration of a digital currency initiative to test CBDC. Project Hamilton is said to honor not just the founding father Alexander Hamilton, but also a female MIT scientist who played a key role in Project Apollo, Margaret Hamilton.

China is well ahead of other countries with plans to launch a digital yuan. Digital currencies are gaining traction in other emerging markets. The President of the Central Bank of Brazil Roberto Campos Neto announced in 2020 that a digital Real (BRL) was likely for 2022, coinciding with the possible launch of CBDC in China. The Brazilian CBDC are part of the initiatives to modernize the Brazilian financial system known as "Program BC#," which also includes P2P payments system Pix already launched in 2020.

Moreover, CBDC, while commonly grouped with stablecoins and cryptocurrencies, do not necessarily rely on DLT, even though most do. Bahamas launched its Sand Dollar in October 2020, being the first retail CBDC worldwide, followed by Cambodia. In March 2021, the Eastern Caribbean Central Bank launched its CBDC, available in four of the islands, namely Antigua and Barbuda, Grenada, St Kitts and Nevis and Saint Lucia. Individuals can use an app to check their account balances, make payments to merchants or person-to-person

---

[23]Banque de France (2021). Banque de France, Swiss National Bank and Bank for International Settlements Innovation Hub collaborate for experiment in cross-border wholesale CBDC. Available at https://www.banque-france.fr/en/comm unique-de-presse/banque-de-france-swiss-national-bank-and-bank-international-settlements-innovation-hub-collaborate. Last accessed October 6, 2021.

transfers. Transactions are stored on a DLT and information of identity of customers is kept separately by financial institutions. While the Eastern Caribbean example involves consumers holding accounts directly with the Central Bank, China's CBDC pilot relies on second-tier banks to maintain digital yuan accounts for end customers. Wholesale digital currencies have existed for a while, with electronic balances held by commercial banks at the Central Bank being de facto CBDC. The disruption comes from retail CBDC, with all economic agents being able to hold an account directly at the Central Bank. Those accounts could potentially bear interest, positive or negative, enhancing the effectiveness of the monetary policy.

However, three key conceptual and technical questions remain regarding CBDC. The first and obvious one is what CBDC bring to the table that digital currencies did not already offer. Central Banks have commonly stated the focus on CBDC stems from a desire to fight illegal activities and increase financial inclusion — both objectives that could be met equally well with digital currency and a reduction in cash usage. There is no doubt that private global initiatives, such as Libra, even though it was subsequently abandoned have accelerated the desire of governments to recover the lead in currencies and payment systems and displace privately created cryptocurrencies. That said, in larger economies, it is unlikely that Central Banks will offer retail CBDC.

A second question has to do with government's crowding out of private sector initiative, such as second-tier banks. Central Banks commonly publicly stress that CBDC are not meant to replace the other forms of money and in particular it is not meant to displace the role of private banks as deposit takers, but that it can provide a more efficient settlement method for payments and a direct access to the safety of Central Bank money. Is it the role of Central Banks to innovate in payments or should regulators only provide the rules of the game so that companies develop new solutions? Are Central Banks urged to launch their own currency to keep virtual currencies at bay? Would a retail CBDC displace deposits away from commercial banks over time?

A third question has to do with technological vulnerability, as Central Banks would have to increase meaningfully their efforts to serve a larger number of counterparts and respond to a higher level of cyber risk. What would be the performance of a CBDC in terms of payment transactions per second or throughput? What would be the resiliency of the system and how much time would it require to recover the system if it comes down?

Money and the value ascribed to it are ultimately a social convention, based on the solidity of institutions. The value of money is not backed anymore by a real asset, such as gold or silver. While the Bank of England currently holds 5,500 tons of gold in its vaults, the value of that gold represents less than 1% of the UK's money supply. Mark Carney therefore asks "if gold no longer backs money, what does?"[24] CBDC are only a new format for the existing currency, with the same national backing and subject to monetary policy. Private currencies beg the question of their acceptance by customers, regulatory framework, measures to prevent money laundering and terrorism financing, and may pose a risk to the effectiveness of the monetary policy.

In conclusion, cryptocurrencies bear more characteristics of speculative assets than money. Stablecoins have more to do with payment facilitators than with currencies. Finally, retail CBDC present meaningful technological risks for Central Banks and it is not clear that they can be rolled out in larger economies or that they would not compete with the activities of second-tier banks. Currencies have been at the center of innovation, and payments — in particular cross-border payments — are most likely to evolve in the short term.

---

[24]Carney, M. (2021). *Value(s), Building a Better World for All*. Penguin, p. 57.

Chapter 6

The End of Branches as We Know Them

Closing Branches

Rapid digitization can offer benefits, leading to a "less resource-intensive economy, allowing carbon emissions to be decoupled from economic growth more quickly," boosting productivity, and "democratizing access to essential services, such as health and education."[1] The Great Lockdown has accelerated trends that were visible in the financial industry, increasing the digitization of the industry and branch closures.

In general terms, commentators point to a number of changes that will impact societies and economies, defining COVID-19 as a turning point. Changes in the economy at large may include a preference for shorter and domestic supply chains, higher reliance on remote working, consumer patterns relying more on e-commerce, a different form of globalization, and more focus on sustainable practices and investment strategies, including green bonds.[2] This evolution could involve

---

[1]Lagarde, C. (2020). Keynote speech by Christine Lagarde, President of the ECB, at the European Banking Congress. Fostering sustainable growth in Europe. Available at https://www.ecb.europa.eu/press/key/date/2020/html/ecb.sp2011 20~e92d92352f.en.html. Last accessed October 6, 2021.

[2]Deschryver, P. and de Mariz, F. (2020). What future for the green bond market? How can policymakers, companies, and investors unlock the potential of the green bond market? *Journal of Risk and Financial Management*, *13*(3), 61.

large changes in retail, a return of select industries such as pharmaceuticals in developed countries, lower reliance on international air
travel, or migration to smaller cities with lower populational densities. Research also suggests a possible industry consolidation in the
hands of a small group of international companies, driven by an intensification of mergers and acquisitions, supported by the historically
low cost of financing, the search for synergies and a desire to maintain
supply chains. In the retail sector, a McKinsey survey of Brazilian
consumers showed that 40% started making online purchases during
the pandemic and plan to continue shopping online post-COVID-
19 and 35% indicated that they would visit fewer brick-and-mortar
stores in a post-COVID-19 world.[3]

In banking, the most relevant and irreversible trend that has been
visible for the past 20 years is digitization. Health and hygiene considerations are a boost to low-touch or no-touch service offerings across
industries, ranging from telemedicine and e-commerce to online education. In the financial sector, 2020 was a turning point for digital
banking and contactless payments. In the US, card-not-present transactions increased by 30% in May 2020 year over year (YoY), while
fraud attempts increased 700% YoY, suggesting a need to strengthen
risk management.[4]

There are meaningful differences in financial access among emerging economies (Table 1). While there has been a continuous increase
in loan penetration, networks of branches and ATMs have experienced diverging trends. For example, Mexico experienced an increase
in loans-to-GDP ratio from 15.9% in 2010 to 22.9% in 2020. Brazil
and India also experienced increases in the same ratio of about 10%
points over the decade. However, the usage of a physical network of
ATMs and branches has varied from one country to the other. Countries with a more abundant presence of physical channels, such as
Brazil, have experienced a contraction in the density of ATMs and

---

doi:10.3390/jrfm13030061. Available at SSRN: https://ssrn.com/abstract=35659
33.
[3]McKinsey & Company (2017). Where is technology taking the economy? Available at https://www.mckinsey.com/business-functions/mckinsey-analytics/our-i
nsights/where-is-technology-taking-the-economy. Last accessed October 6, 2021.
[4]Wyman, O. (2020). Webinar: COVID-19 and the Impact on the US Financial
System – Payments, June 3, 2020.

Table 1:   Financial Access in Brazil, India and Mexico

	2010	2011	2012	2013	2014	2015	2016	2017	2018	2019	2020
Key Indicators, Geographical Outreach, Number of ATMs per 100,000 Adults											
Brazil	118.06	116.31	115.36	118.44	117.93	114.97	112.10	107.87	106.55	102.74	96.56
India	7.24	8.82	10.95	12.82	17.73	19.64	21.17	22.00	21.65	20.95	21.50
Mexico	45.17	44.86	48.76	48.71	50.45	52.90	54.59	55.62	58.82	61.54	62.13
Key Indicators, Geographical Outreach, Number of Commercial Bank Branches per 100,000 adults											
Brazil	18.67	19.19	20.41	20.53	21.24	20.85	20.34	19.51	18.98	18.70	17.88
India	10.00	10.47	11.14	11.81	12.82	13.52	14.21	14.51	14.50	14.58	14.74
Mexico	14.09	14.41	14.89	14.83	14.73	13.92	14.02	14.03	13.86	13.73	12.79
Key Indicators, Use of Financial Services, Outstanding Loans from Commercial Banks (% of GDP)											
Brazil	31.76	33.83	36.50	38.93	40.46	41.61	39.02	36.55	35.57	35.48	42.29
India	43.82	46.65	48.30	49.19	50.39	49.95	48.87	46.33	46.42	48.63	53.71
Mexico	15.91	16.79	17.39	18.62	19.14	20.69	21.56	21.64	22.04	22.12	22.93

Source: IMF, macroeconomic and financial data.

branches. Countries that started with a lower base, such as India, continued to experience an increase in access. For example, India saw its network of commercial bank branches grow from 10 per 100,000 habitants in 2010 to 14.7 in 2020.

Innovation and technology are key enhancers of electronic payments. Card not-present channels include mobile banking, internet banking and contact centers. In 2016, in Brazil, 54.3% of all transactions were done via those remote channels. This percentage increased to 68.8% in 2020. Over the past decade, the use of mobile and internet banking has experienced an annual growth above 20% per annum. Since 2014, the mobile channel alone has experienced the fastest growth, jumping from 28.4% of transactions in 2016 to 51.1% in 2020 (Table 2). Convenience, growing trust from customers, and security protocols explain the strong growth in those channels. 80.8% of non-presential transactions corresponded to account balance inquiries (Table 3). According to the Central Bank, these channels represent a large growth opportunity.

For presential channels, ATMs represent the preferred option, representing 46.7% of presential transactions; 53.1% of transactions done via presential channels involve some kind of transfer of funds; 75.5% of cash withdrawals were made at ATMs. Naturally, cash-in and cash-out transactions, such as cash withdrawals and deposits, happen

Table 2: Number of Transactions by Type of Channel (Billions of Transactions)

	2016	2017	2018	2019	2020
Mobile banking	18.6	25.3	33.1	37.0	52.9
Internet banking	15.5	15.7	18.0	16.0	15.8
POS — Points of sale in trade	9.7	10.9	10.3	13.6	14.9
ATM	10.2	9.9	9.7	9.1	8.3
Branches	4.4	4.0	4.4	4.5	5.8
Banking correspondents	5.6	5.9	4.6	4.6	3.3
Contact centers	1.4	1.5	1.0	1.0	2.5
Total	65.4	73.2	81.1	85.8	103.5

Source: Central Bank of Brazil.

Table 3: What Channel Is Preferred for Each Transaction?

	Mobile Banking	Internet Banking	Branches	ATMs
Balance and statements	33,368	5,901	1,190	2,070
Transfer	1,997	864	47	155
Bill payment	3,257	1,428	252	547
Credit sourcing	762	147	34	44
Debt renegotiation	2,400	1,425	7,357	0
Investment sourcing	49	70	184	76
Insurance sourcing	1	0	20	0
Foreign exchange	0	0	1,882	0
Deposit	–	–	388	692
Withdrawal	–	–	188	2,123

Source: Central Bank of Brazil, Febraban survey, 2021. We indicate in grey the most used channel for each type of transaction.

via presential channels. Branches and ATMs have the same share at 42% of all deposits, with the remainder being done at banking correspondents.

The share of branches in the total number of transactions is decreasing. Digitization will lead to an acceleration in branch closures and redesign, a trend that started after the Global Financial Crisis of 2008. In Latin America, the peak in branch numbers in absolute numbers was reached in 2017 with an expected acceleration in closures, causing meaningful impact on employment or commercial real estate (Figure 1).

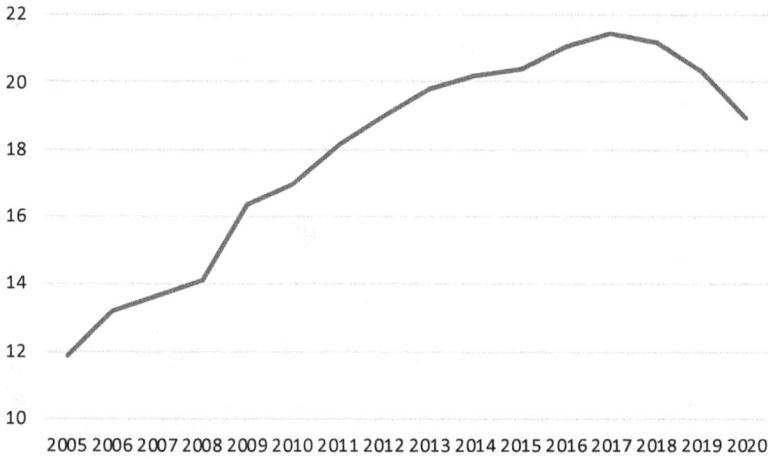

Figure 1: Branch Outreach in Brazil (Number of Branches, Thousands)
Source: Central Bank of Brazil.

The customer perception of FinTechs has also evolved as FinTechs navigate through the crisis and prove the resilience and sustainability of their business models. The 2008 crisis made apparent a trend of flight to safety, especially in deposits.[5] FinTechs' business models are based mostly on credit concession and ancillary services, such as payments, brokerage, or foreign exchange transfers. FinTechs still represent a very small percentage of deposit-taking, particularly because most of them are not formally regulated as banks, but their share of financial services is growing fast, driven by three factors: high margins in select financial products attracting new players, lower costs of technology and the ubiquity of cell phones, and a stronger support for innovation by regulators. FinTech has created high hopes.

For banks, financial innovation and digitization provide opportunities for cost savings and revenue gains, as well as transforming the customer experience. Traditional banks are innovating in order to boost efficiency gains, which are meant to offset some of the margin

---

[5]Federal Reserve Bank of Saint Louis (2010). Flight to safety and U.S. treasury securities. Available at https://www.stlouisfed.org/publications/regional-economist/july-2010/flight-to-safety-and-us-treasury-securities. Last accessed October 6, 2021.

pressures stemming from the competition. Physical branch reduction and rationalization bring meaningful cost savings for banks, while many processes are migrated to digital platforms. According to the Central Bank of Brazil, digital channels (mobile and internet) are now the main transaction channels for the largest Brazilian banks.

But it's not just branches that will be impacted. An important consequence is the impact digitization will have on back-office operations of banks. Automation of tasks will require fewer people. Studies estimate that 75–80% of transactional operations, such as general accounting operations, payments processing, and up to 40% of more strategic activities, such as financial controlling and reporting, financial planning and analysis, treasury, can be automated. Operations represent 15–20% of a bank's annual budget, and the transformation of back offices will lead to significant cost efficiencies for banks and transition and training challenges for workers.[6]

In addition to cost savings, the mobile distribution channel generates revenue opportunities. Brazilian banks originate an increasing percentage of personal loans via mobile, including payroll-deducted consumer loans. Banks have also been exploring cross-selling opportunities — for example, proposing foreign exchange or travel insurance when clients activate the international feature on their credit cards. Brazilian banks also offer loan renegotiation options on their mobile apps. Moreover, mobile banking is becoming more important for building customer relationship as a channel that can potentially engage with users 24/7, enhance the customer experience as well as customer loyalty. In Brazil, more than 100 billion financial transactions were conducted in 2020, with more than half done on mobile channels (Table 2).

Branch closure is one of the tools considered by incumbent banks to adjust to digital financial services while improving their cost base. But banks across countries start from a different base and not all experience the same trend. There is a large difference in branch presence between richer and poorer countries. While Spain counted 46 branches for 100,000 inhabitants in 2020, Brazil counted

---

[6]McKinsey & Company (2019). Banking operations for a customer-centric world.

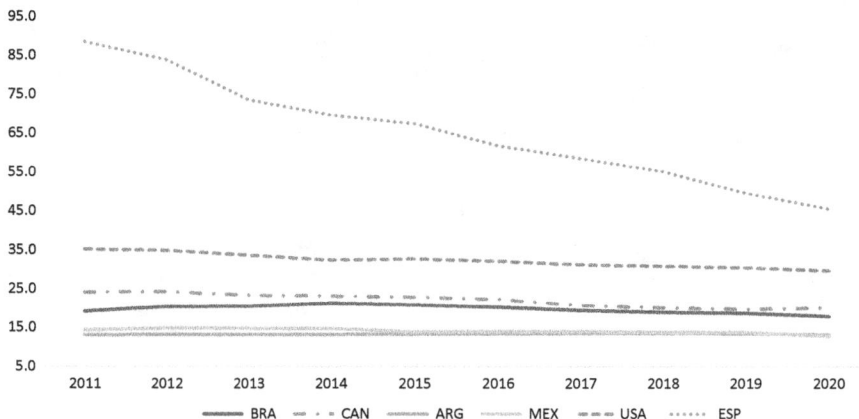

Figure 2: Comparison of Branch Outreach (Number of Branches per 100,000 Adults)

Source: World Bank.

18 branches. But even within richer countries, the US shows 30 branches per 100,000 adults, compared to 20 in Canada. This is often explained by the fact that bank branches in the US perform a wider array of services, such as providing notarizing documents.

Data on branches show a clear trend of decline in all geographies. The decline can be partly explained by a consolidation of financial institutions. In fact, the number of banks in the US or Europe experienced a meaningful contraction following the Great Financial Crisis and spurred a movement of branch rationalization (Figures 2 and 3).

Banks compete for the highest customer rankings for their apps. In lower income segments, apps are a powerful complement to nontraditional distribution channels, such as banking correspondents. While the reduction in the number and size of bank branches (and banks) is most visible in developed markets, it is a rising trend in emerging markets, where select banks have indicated the potential to close up to half of their branches within five years in the case of Brazil.

It is difficult to predict where the contribution of branches to transactions will stabilize. Technology is nowhere more disruptive than in the delivery or distribution of financial services. Naturally, there has been innovation in the design of products themselves. For example, regulators have played a key role in the development

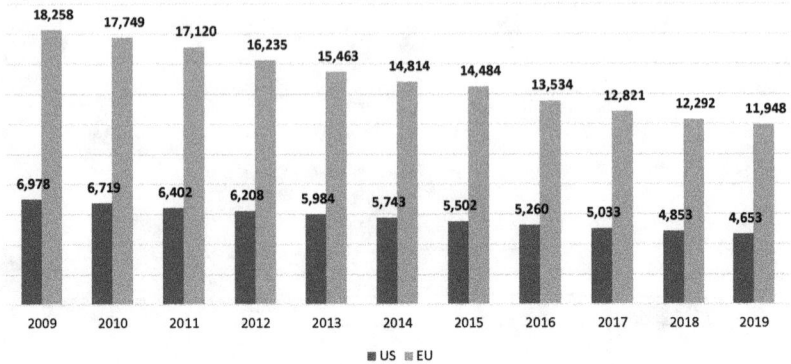

Figure 3: Consolidation in the Financial Sector
Source: World Bank.

of simplified products, such as simplified bank accounts and digital accounts, which carry no opening or maintenance fee, are easier to open and are dedicated to lower-income customers.

Since 2013, Brazilian financial institutions have been authorized to open a simplified account, called payment account, adopting 100% digital processes, following Circular 3.680/2013. This new category adds to the preexisting categories of deposits (current and savings), salary account, and simplified account. The category of payment account is meant to boost inclusion, is easier to open than other categories and incurs fees that are defined in law and standardized. The payment account can be used for withdrawals, payment by card or for transfers. Rules determining the opening, maintenance and closing of accounts were amended by the National Monetary Council in 2019 through Resolution 4.753/19 to simplify and update those processes. In particular, the new rules waive the obligation to present a physical signature card to open a bank account or the obligation for the branch officer to verify documents in paper format. With Resolution 4.753, banks can open accounts fully online. The National Monetary Council also gave more autonomy to financial institutions and determined that they were able to define the list of documents required to digitally open an account under a risk-based approach. For example, digital bank Next, owned by Bradesco, does not require proof of address as geolocalization suffices to confirm the accountholder's address. Account closure can be done digitally, even if it was initially opened at the branch, and banks have 30 days to process the closure. Similarly, in India, the government ordered the banks to offer "no frills" accounts as part of its financial inclusion policy, reducing the required paperwork and eliminating the minimum balance that was previously keeping poorer customers away.

Initiatives have been undertaken to tailor the digital financial services to low-income clients, to avoid the typical limitation of a one-size-fits-all product. For example, CGAP leveraged human-centered design to branchless banking, by learning directly from customers and promoting a fast delivery of new apps' capabilities. The frequent and careful interaction with customer groups allows for agile time-to-market of prototypes and the validation of new services. Developers can begin with inexpensive and disposable prototypes, such as sketches, and incorporate customer feedback.[7]

Digital financial services enable customers to create a financial record. The growing power and sophistication of computers have led to the rise of scoring systems based on big data. Banks have developed the understanding of their clients not just based on negative credit history, but more and more on positive data. Positive data coming from deposits, transfers, payments in general and credit repayment have allowed banks to define a more accurate portrait of their clients, thereby refining the pricing of risk at the individual level. While banks and insurance companies used to price risk in aggregate, financial institutions and FinTech now assess risk at the level of the individual. For example, some insurance companies offer auto-insurance coverage with a premium that is calculated based on the characteristics of the individual and only based on the number of kilometers actually driven.

Redesigning Branches

Is it the end for bank branches? The decline in the number of branches described previously only tells part of the story. Branches continue to play a meaningful role in the delivery of financial services.

---

[7]McKay, C. and Seltzer, Y. (2013). Designing Customer-Centric Branchless Banking Offerings. CGAP brief. World Bank, Washington, DC. Available at https://openknowledge.worldbank.org/handle/10986/18417. Last accessed October 6, 2021.

Marciano Testa, founder and CEO of Agi, one of the largest digital banks in Brazil with more than three million clients explains that branches will not disappear, they act as a gateway between the physical world and the digital world. Branches have a clear function for customers in emerging markets like Brazil, especially for previously excluded segments of customers.[8] Agi defines a "phygital" model, where the cost to serve customers declines over time, and clients typically gain the ability to fully use the digital channels of the banks after five interactions in person at the branch. Agi designs branches that are smaller than the typical bank branches, focused on interactions with an advisor and are not transaction-oriented. Caixa Economica Federal, a government-owned bank, is maintaining its network of branches unchanged (around 3,800), which it sees as a critical tool to gain business both from municipalities and from recently included customers. For example, it is an essential channel to distribute acquiring and payment services to small and medium-sized enterprises.

In the tension between the old and the new economies, many financial institutions have proposed smaller formats of brick-and-mortar presence, often supported by regulators. The Central Bank of Brazil considers six types of channels with customers: branches, service points (*posto de atendimento bancario* (PAB)), electronic service points, banking correspondents, POS and ATM. The regulator tracks and publishes the evolutions of those channels on a monthly basis. Banks require prior approval by the Central Bank to open branches. Cooperatives do not have branches, only PAB and electronic PABs.[9]

The evolution of the brick-and-mortar presence paints a more nuanced view than previously anticipated. While traditional bank branches have been declining in Brazil since 2017, thanks to digitization and partly because banks are looking for gains in efficiencies, other channels continue to strive and grow.

While banks have designed simplified, smaller and interaction-focused locations, financial institutions have also largely relied on partnerships with non-banks who can serve as distribution agents:

---

[8]Interview with Agi's CEO Marciano Testa, 28 April 2021.
[9]Data available at https://www.bcb.gov.br/fis/info/agencias.asp?frame=1.

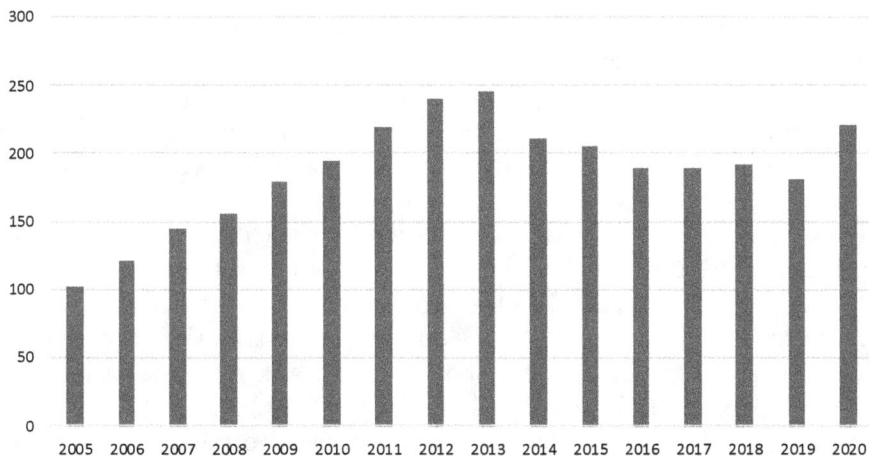

Figure 4:   Number of Banking Correspondents in Brazil (Thousands)
Source: Central Bank of Brazil.

banking correspondents. Banking correspondents retain the largest presence by far in the continental-sized country. Correspondents were implemented in the 1970s, a model that could be replicated in several other countries. Banking correspondents perform select simple financial tasks, and consist typically of smaller retailers, gas stations, or lottery stores. They complement the existing network of bank branches and fees charged on financial services complement their existing core business. The most popular types of transactions performed by correspondents consist in utilities' bills payments, transfers, top-ups of cell phones and disbursement of government benefits. According to the Central Bank data, as of 2020, Brazil had 225,000 banking correspondents, which compares with 19,000 full banking branches (Figure 4). However, banking correspondents usually do not provide more complex financial services such as credit.

Other countries have adopted and expanded the concept of banking correspondents, such as Mexico and India. In India, authors note the daunting challenge in size and scope to include the lower-income segments. The government and the Reserve Bank of India have taken "initiatives to spread banking services such as expanding the number of rural bank branches, allowing the banking correspondent model and adoption of technology."[10] Bank branches are just one channel to serve customers and are complemented by the physical presence of other players acting as banking correspondents.

Formal banks are also complemented by non-banks financial institutions (NBFI), which are financial institutions that fall under a lighter regulatory framework and typically cannot raise retail deposits. NBFI, along with other institutions such as asset managers, are sometimes described as the shadow banking system. The shadow banking system is defined as the group of agents that can offer funding to individuals and corporates outside of the traditional regulated banking sector.[11] In Mexico, the Central Bank estimates that the shadow banking represents close to 10% of the total GDP in terms of loans, while the regulated banking system represents 20% of the GDP in terms of total credit. In Brazil, the Central Bank estimates that a restricted definition of the shadow banking system represents 6.7% of total banking assets.

The redefinition of distribution channels brings large consequences to non-financial dimensions such as employment and urban planning. On the positive side, the trend also brings the promise of better customer experience and convenience. The human interaction offered at branches is being restricted to higher added-value services.

Rather than oppose in-person channels and digital means, the future will no doubt entail a distribution model that leverages digital tools, where self-service and one-on-one interactions work hand in hand.

Branchless Banking: Is It the End of Cash?

If branches are to become less important in the provision of financial services, does it mean that physical cash also known as token money

---

[10]Gwalani, H. and Parkhi, S. (2014). Financial inclusion–building a success model in the Indian context. *Procedia-Social and Behavioral Sciences*, *133*, 372–378.

[11]Fish, T., and Whymark, R. (2015). How has cash usage evolved in recent decades? What might drive demand in the future? Available at https://www.bankofengland.co.uk/quarterly-bulletin/2015/q3/how-has-cash -usage-evolved-in-recent-decades-what-might-drive-demand-in-the-future. Last accessed December 10, 2021.

is bound to lose relevance? There is a rich literature on the determinants of the demand for money and cash, mostly written by and for Central Banks, for whom understanding the issuance and monitoring of currency in circulation is essential. While money and cash are not synonymous, the demand for money provides important insights to understand the demand for cash. Why do we hold cash?

Interestingly, the Bank of England, one of the most open to financial innovation, expects cash to remain important in the future.[12] Money in circulation corresponds to coins and banknotes. In the case of England, money in circulation represents close to 4% of GDP. Coins represent 3% of total money and banknotes the remaining 97%. Money is used for hoarding and transactional purposes. Studies in the UK showed that 18% of people hoarded cash "to give comfort against potential emergencies."

In a classical paper, Baumol applied a principle of "inventory control analysis" to the theory of money.[13] He analyzes the transaction demand for cash that is dictated by rational behavior, which corresponds to holding a cash balance that can "do the job at minimum cost." The model considers the interest rate on money and the broker fee for cash withdrawal as the two drivers of the demand for cash. Inventory models, such as Baumol's, highlight the function of cash as a means of payment. Other authors have added other dimensions to cash demand, such as precautionary motivation, speculation and hoarding. In portfolio models, wealth and the relative return of other financial and real assets are also drivers of the demand for cash.[14] Many subsequent models extend the Baumol–Tobin models "where interest rates, income, and the acquisition costs of cash including "shoe leather" costs, determine the supply of money."[15]

Consumer behavior also plays a role in those drivers. Cusbert and Rohling studied the effect of the financial crisis of 2008 on the

---

[12] *Ibid.*

[13] Baumol, W. J. (1952). The transactions demand for cash: An inventory theoretic approach. *The Quarterly Journal of Economics, 66*(4) (November), 545–556.

[14] Tobin, J. (1956). The interest-elasticity of transactions demand for cash. *The Review of Economics and Statistics, 38*(3) (August), 241–247.

[15] Amromin, G. and Chakravorti, S. (2007). Debit card and cash usage: A cross-country analysis. Federal Reserve Bank of Chicago, WP 2007-04.

demand for cash in Australia.[16] The authors found that this demand "increased significantly in the last quarter of 2008 (12%), mainly due to the increase in the demand for large denomination notes." This increase was associated with precautionary motives, "originated because of the uncertainty on the financial health of banks during the crisis period."

The demand for money due to precautionary reasons according to Keynes has a different meaning and consists in the demand for money used to make unexpected expenditures. Keynes defines the precautionary cash balances as those held "to provide for contingencies requiring sudden expenditures and for unforeseen opportunities of advantageous purchases, and also to hold an asset of which the value is fixed in terms of money to meet a subsequent liability in terms of money."[17] In Keynesian economics, precautionary demand is one of the determinants of demand for money (and credit), the others being transactions demand and speculative demand. The precautionary demand for money refers to real balances held for use in a contingency. As receipts and payments cannot be perfectly foreseen, people hold precautionary balances to minimize the potential loss arising from a contingency. The precautionary demand is dependent on the size of income, the availability of credit, and the rate of interest.

Amromin and Chakravorti analyze the "change in transactional demand for cash resulting from greater usage of debit cards in 13 countries from 1988 to 2003." They note that "while check usage declined and has almost disappeared in some countries, the stock of currency in circulation has not declined as fast." The authors try to separate the use of cash as a payment mode from its use for the purpose of store of value, which are its two traditional functions, on top of being a unit of value. In fact, they note that high-denomination bank notes are usually used for store of value and explain that 60%

---

[16]Cusbert, T. and Rohling, T. (2013). Currency demand during the global financial crisis: Evidence from Australia. Reserve Bank of Australia. Available at https://www.rba.gov.au/publications/rdp/2013/pdf/rdp2013-01.pdf. Last accessed December 10, 2021.

[17]Keynes, J. M. (1936). *The General Theory of Employment, Interest, and Money*, New York: Harcourt, Brace & World, p. 196.

of the total currency in circulation in US dollars is held outside of the United States, where it has limited acceptance.[18]

The theory on the demand for cash highlights the main benefits of cash, such as convenience, universal acceptance, anonymity, or seignoriage revenues for the issuer of banknotes and coins. Another part of the literature lists the costs of cash usage from reduced fiscal revenues driven by higher informality, the cost and inconvenience of withdrawing cash from automated teller machine (ATM) and bank branches, security concerns (against thefts) and cost of printing, handling and management.[19]

There are several parallels between the demand for cash and the demand for electronic payments. However, there are some key differences. The demand for cash highlights the function of cash as a store of value, and not just of payment. Other functions of money appear, such as speculation and precaution. Cash can coexist with a host of other payment methods, such as checks, prepaid cards (in particular for food and transportation), automatic debit (for recurring bills), or invoices (*boletos* are popular in Brazil).

---

[18]Amromin, G. and Chakravorti, S. (2007). Debit card and cash usage: A cross-country analysis. Federal Reserve Bank of Chicago, WP 2007-04.

[19]Mulligan, C. B. and Sala-i-Martin, X. (2000). Extensive margins and the demand for money at low interest rates. *Journal of political Economy*, *108*(5), 961–991; Attanasio, O. P., Guiso, L. and Jappelli, T. (2002). The demand for money, financial innovation, and the welfare cost of inflation: An analysis with household data. *Journal of Political Economy*, *110*(2), 317–351; Snellman, H. (2006). *Automated Teller Machine Network Market Structure and Cash Usage*, Bank of Finland, Scientific Monographs E:38; Bounie, D. and François, A. (2008). Cash, check or bank card? The effects of transaction characteristics on the use of payment instruments, (March 2006). Telecom Paris Economics and Social Sciences Working Paper No. ESS-06-05, Available at SSRN: https://ssrn.com/abstract=891791 or http://dx.doi.org/10.2139/ssrn.89 1791, last accessed December 10, 2021; Lippi, F. and Secchi, A. (2009). Technological change and the households' demand for currency. *Journal of Monetary Economics*, *56*(2), 222–230; Briglevics, T. and Schuh, S. (2014). This is what's in your wallet... and here's how you use it (No. 14-5). Working Papers, Federal Reserve Bank of Boston.

Chapter 7

Using Data While Respecting Customers' Rights

Using Data to Reduce Asymmetries of Information

The analysis of data opens up new opportunities to better understand the risk profile of customers and also adjust a service offering to their real needs. Big data is essential to reduce asymmetries of information, but it creates new challenges in terms of customer privacy and regulation.

Credit is fraught with market failures. Stiglitz stressed the importance of asymmetries of information in the credit market, explaining that screening and monitoring clients are two essential functions of financial institutions.[1] Loans are different from other goods and markets since they are not contemporaneous: money is repaid in the future, loans are heterogeneous, they bear information problems. He developed with Weiss a theory of credit rationing.[2] According to the model, charging a higher interest rate can reduce profits for a lender, as the interest rate (price of money) does not play its normal clearing function. The authors advance two reasons for the negative correlation: an adverse selection (charging higher rates attracts the risker

---

[1]Stiglitz, J. E. (1989). Financial markets and development. *Oxford Review of Economic Policy*, *5*(4), 55–68.

[2]Stiglitz, J. E. and Weiss, A. (1992). Asymmetric information in credit markets and its implications for macro-economics. *Oxford Economic Papers*, *44*(4), 694–724.

clients) and an incentive effect (higher rates drive customers to take more risk). For Stiglitz and Weiss, credit is a real channel in a sense that monetary aggregates do not fully translate into investment, and there are two steps to influence the investment variables, from the monetary aggregate to credit, and then from credit to investment. Romer *et al.* also suggest that monetary policy impacts the total stock of deposits, but there is no clear channel between monetary policy and the stock of credit.[3]

Policymaking is therefore concerned with fostering a well-functioning credit channel. Credit bureaus and the scores they produce reduce the asymmetry of information between lenders and borrowers. Accurate and complete bureaus bear the promise of higher levels of growth via lower levels of credit rationing and lower spreads for borrowers. Asymmetries of information increase the cost of screening and monitoring and have led to the market segmentation into retail, middle market, corporate. These asymmetries mean that some borrowers are "informationally captured". This is why the establishment and strengthening of credit bureaus and credit registries have become a key focus of reform agendas in the financial sector.[4] The bureaus are often open to the largest numbers of participants, but microfinance institutions have sometimes failed to participate in those schemes mostly because of cost issues on both sides. Research demonstrates the benefits of wide-ranging bureaus. Authors show that the introduction of a credit registry for microfinance institutions in Guatemala helped reduce missed payments and delinquency by 2–3% points in one large MFI.[5]

Bureaus are adapting to a triple challenge: digitization, inflow of new information sources, and new customer-centric regulations. Bureaus verify, compile, and analyze the data to assess customers' payment ability, closing the information gap between lenders,

[3]Romer, C. D. *et al.* (1990). New evidence on the monetary transmission mechanism. *Brookings Papers on Economic Activity, 1990*(1), 149–213.

[4]Pinheiro, A. C. and Moura, A. R. (2001). *Segmentation and the Use of Information in Brazilian Credit Markets*. Rio de Janeiro: Banco Nacional de Desenvolvimento Econômico e Social.

[5]Luoto, J. *et al.* (2007). Credit information systems in less developed countries: A test with microfinance in Guatemala. *Economic Development and Cultural Change, 55*(2), 313–334.

utility providers, and users, while also empowering customers. Historically, bureaus were often developed by retail associations and then expanded to include data from utilities' providers and financial institutions. Scores represent the probability that a customer does not pay.

Scoring can be a more effective tool than the often-overrated merit of a personal relationship between a loan officer and her client. Using data for 91 large banks from 45 countries, research finds that the availability and conditions for SME lending are similar across bank types. The authors show that SME lending need not be based only on relationship lending. Consistent with these results, they "find few significant differences in the extent, type, and pricing of SME loans across bank types." Instead, they find significant differences across developed and developing countries, "driven by differences in the institutional and legal environment." They show that the small and domestic private banks are not more likely to finance SMEs because of a competitive advantage in "relationship lending," defined as a "type of financing based primarily on soft information gathered by the loan officer through continuous, personalized, direct contacts with SMEs, their owners and managers, and the local community in which they operate". In fact, large domestic banks and foreign banks have increased the use of credit scoring and collateralized lending or leasing to offer credit to SMEs, under arm-length relationships.[6]

Data also refute the common wisdom that small banks are better positioned to service small enterprises.[7] Authors formulate and test hypotheses about the role of bank type — small versus large, single-market versus multimarket, and local versus non-local banks — in banking relationships. The conventional paradigm suggests that community banks — small, single-market, local institutions — are better able to form strong relationships with informationally opaque small

---

[6]Beck, T. *et al.* (2011). Bank financing for SMEs: Evidence across countries and bank ownership types. *Journal of Financial Services Research*, *39*(1–2), 35–54.

[7]Berger, A. N. and Udell, G. F. (1994). Lines of credit and relationship lending in small firm finance; Berger, A. N. *et al.* (2005). Corporate governance and bank performance: A joint analysis of the static, selection, and dynamic effects of domestic, foreign, and state ownership. *Journal of Banking & Finance*, *29*(8), 2179–2221.

businesses, while megabanks — large, multimarket, non-local institutions — tend to serve more transparent firms. If this were correct,
banking consolidation could be an issue. Based on two types of tests,
using the 2003 Survey of Small Business Finance (SSBF), the results
are often not consistent with the conventional paradigm. Large banks
are possibly adding to the relationship the use of new lending technologies. Asymmetries of information lead some segments of the economy, such as lower-income customers of SMEs to be underbanked.

Moving from negative data to positive data has been transformational for the sector of credit bureaus in Brazil. The inclusion of
positive data into scores meaningfully enriches the traditional use
of the Credit Risk Center managed by the Central Bank of Brazil,
which has provided credit-related information since 1997. For a long
time, negative data — i.e. non-payment of loans or other debt, such
as utilities' bill — were the main basis for scores in Brazil. Positive
data allow lenders to analyze a much wider and richer set of information from clients, namely their positive behavior of payment. Quod
is the most recent credit bureau in Brazil, having been launched in
October 2018, with a view to develop scores based on positive credit
data. It is owned by the five largest banks in Brazil (Banco do Brasil,
CEF, Itaú, Bradesco, Santander). The other three bureaus are Serasa
Experian, Boa Vista Serviços, SPC Brasil. Brazilian bureaus rely on
big data analysis and artificial intelligence to transform historic payment data from close to 140 million individuals and companies into
a score that ranges from 0 to 1000.

Brazil is one of the last large economies to incorporate positive
data, with a regulation from July 2019 based on an opt-out rule.
In April 2019, Complementary Law 166/2019 was signed by the
Brazilian president enhancing the roles and responsibilities of credit
bureaus under an opt-out system. This came on the heels of years
of discussions between banks, regulators, and consumer protection
groups. Bureaus had been using positive data since 2011, though
adhesion remained low due to an opt-in system, lack of understanding
of bureaus and explicit pushback from customer protection groups.
Before the 2019 regulation, users had to voluntarily let their bank
know that they wanted their positive data to be used for scoring
purposes. Presidential Decree 9.936 was then signed in July 2019.
By November 2019, large banks and more than 100 financial institutions started contributing data from the previous 12 months. In 2021,

telecom companies joined this group, followed by cable, utilities and retailers. With this addition, credit bureaus in Brazil leapfrogged from a binary to a continuous stage.

The change in regulation (from opt-in to opt-out) had an estimated potential to include 20 million people, corresponding to individuals who did not have a traditional credit history with banks but could leverage other payment data to access credit. The regulatory change could reduce banking spreads and non-performing loans.[8] Calculations suggest that positive data could lead to an additional R$600 billion (about $115 billion) in new loan concessions, leading, in turn, to higher fiscal revenues. Credit penetration could also increase from 47% to 66% of domestic GDP.

In April 2021, less than a month after a partial lockdown in Brazil began on March 24, 91 million citizens had already experienced a late payment on a credit installment or a utility bill. This compared with 59 million in early March, and represented a jump from 39% to 58% of the adult population. Would this type of accident meaningfully impact the credit profiles of citizens following the current crisis? How should late payments resulting from the pandemic impact score? And will this change accelerate the use of positive data for credit scores in Brazil?

Smarter bureaus bear the promise of more efficient banking systems. The expectation is that complete and accurate credit scores can lead to lower banking spreads and increase financial depth. A reduction in credit rationing would translate into a higher level of credit concession for any level of overnight rate. The average corporate lending rate by regulated banks reached 15.7% in 2019. Within the large set of corporate loans, rates for the smallest category of companies (MEI) reached 58.8%. An increase in financial depth in Brazil is based on the premise that lending is mostly constrained by information. In fact, loan delinquency is the top component of banking spread, accounting for 37%, ahead of administrative expense (25%), taxes (23%) and banks' profits (15%). Several policy measures can

---

[8]BoaVista (2018). Cadastro Positivo: Entenda o que é e quais são os reais benefícios ao consumidor. Available at https://www.boavistaservicos.com.br/ blog/noticias/cadastro-positivo/cadastro-positivo-entenda-o-que-e-e-quais-sao-os-reais-beneficios-ao-consumidor/. Last accessed October 6, 2021.

reduce the impact of delinquencies, including the use of collateral as guarantees, central registries, and enhanced credit bureaus.

The second promise of positive credit bureaus has to do with competition. Better scores will be available to a wider group of financial institutions, including, in particular, FinTech companies. While dominant banks have maintained a built-in advantage in terms of information gathered on their clients, positive bureaus will create a leveled playing field for lenders. This is consistent with the worldwide trend of customer-centric regulations, where citizens can dispose freely of their data. However, Brazilian bureaus face some limitations. The new rules implemented in 2019 incorporate only 12 months of payment history, and the full benefits of positive data may take time to materialize — as long as two years, according to the Central Bank. Contributors, meanwhile, are adding their datasets gradually.

More accurate scores bear the promise of stronger financial inclusion by reducing asymmetries of information. On the flip side, scores produced by big data bear several questions around social acceptability: is it socially desirable to deny a loan to a citizen based on a score, without further explanation? Can biases be embedded into those scores? How should these scores be used in exceptional times, such as the current COVID-19 crisis?

The Legal and Ethical Limitations of Big Data

Jean Tirole, Nobel Prize winner in 2014, analyzes the questions stemming from widespread use of data and the reasons why transparency may not always be desired.[9] In favor of transparency and data disclosure, Tirole notes that people behave more pro-socially when they know they are being observed by others. He gives the examples of charitable donations, voting or blood donations. Moreover, transparency can favor allocative efficiency, and open new possibilities for inclusion, as we discussed earlier.

On the other side, Tirole makes a case against data disclosure. He defends the right to be forgotten and questions the side effects of

---

[9]Tirole (2021). Webinar organized by Fundacao Getulio Vargas with Jean Tirole, Challenges of Modern Regulation, September 14, 2021. Available at https://www.youtube.com/watch?v=Fs47pDyaByk.

social profiling based on big data and machine learning. In his view, data protection rules, such as GDPR, are well-intentioned but they do not fully solve the issue of privacy and require too much attention and expertise. Transparency can lead to excessive posturing, when individuals change their behavior from their authentic self due to social pressure, threatening individual freedom. Tirole expresses his concerns with projects such as the Chinese social score system, also called social graph, whose goal is to assign a score to citizens and companies. While some of the raw data underlying the score can be socially acceptable, such as credit history, tax compliance or traffic violations, other data points raise alarms, such as people you know or opinions. Citizens may not be given a second chance, or the right to be forgotten, as "digital record may last forever". A score may cause public stigmatization, restrict employment or access to public services. The cost of transparency may be discrimination and Tirole concludes for the strong need to "build smart regulation of privacy".

Along those lines, American psychologist and scholar Shoshanna Zuboff provides an enlightening framework to understand — and criticize — the business models of an economy based on data mining. She explains that the models of BigTech firms are based on the "extraction of behavioral surplus," in a rogue version of capitalism she defines as "surveillance capitalism".[10]

Surveillance capitalism provides "free services that billions of people cheerfully use, enabling the providers of those services to monitor the behavior of those users in astonishing detail." Human experience becomes raw material that is turned into behavioral data to feed predictive models and achieve commercial or power objectives. Zuboff explains that "although some of these data are applied to service improvement, the rest are declared as a proprietary behavioural surplus, fed into advanced manufacturing processes known as 'machine intelligence,' and fabricated into prediction products that anticipate what you will do now, soon, and later." In one of her carefully crafted formulas, she warns that "once we thought of digital services as free, but now surveillance capitalists think of us as free." The Age

---

[10]Zuboff, S. (2019). *The Age of Surveillance Capitalism: The Fight for a Human Future at the New Frontier of Power.* New York: Public Affairs.

of Surveillance Capitalism describes a new kind of commerce that depends upon surveillance at scale.

Bureaus have raised fundamental questions regarding consumer protection and data privacy. Negative data typically consist of late payments at stores and banks. But most recent trends for bureaus expand beyond credit. Alternative data sources, such as payment history, bank account records, behavioral data, and psychometric assessments, have been the most popular new avenues of research to assess creditworthiness. Consumers may worry that their data are being used in ways they do not anticipate or fully understand. They may also fear an increased risk of identity theft, especially in the case of data breaches.

In light of the real risks for privacy, regulatory oversight has been slow or incomplete. The Financial Stability Board recognized the risks to the stability of artificial intelligence and machine learning in financial services.[11] Data sharing gives rise to privacy concerns. The processing of personal data in the UK is governed by the Data Protection Act 1998 (DPA). The Information Commissioner's Code of Practice on Data Sharing highlights that the sharing of personal data can be achieved in compliance with the DPA provided that certain processes are in place to ensure it "is fair, transparent and in line with the rights and expectations of the people whose information [is being shared]."[12] Third-party access is therefore permitted by the DPA and banks do not incur potential liabilities, provided some good practices are respected. The bank must be sufficiently confident that users understand which data is being shared with a third party and give explicit and specific consent. Regulators also defend ongoing control over access to their data.

Some safeguards are in place to protect customers: the scope of data gathered is limited, and information related to health or the

---

[11]Financial Stability Board (2017). Artificial intelligence and machine learning in financial services: Market developments and financial stability implications. Annex B, November 2017.

[12]Open Data Institute and Fingleton Associates (2014). Data sharing and open data for banks, a report for HM treasury and cabinet office.

types of goods and services acquired by consumers are typically not included. In the case of Brazilian bureaus, users can choose to be removed from a given bureau at any time, and if they do, their data must be removed from all bureau databases within two business days.

On top of privacy concerns, big data and profiling also raise the question of prejudice. While data are, in theory, neutral and do not carry prejudice, data analysis can reproduce behaviors observed in human interactions. Profiling can exclude users based on their zip code, level of education or household income for example, and confirm biases of real-life interactions. Data analysis begs the question of the social acceptability of decisions that are taken by algorithms, with no space for contestation or debate. A social debate will grow around the ability of corporations and states to follow every piece of a citizen's financial life, anticipating his needs and preferences. If performed improperly, data analysis could lead to continuous exclusion of segments that are already unserved or underserved, such as microentrepreneurs, racial minorities, younger customers and women. The reliance on technology may also be a hurdle for people who do not have proper internet access, for example in rural areas, or for elderly people for whom technology may not be intuitive and suffer from a digital divide.

Another common concern with the ubiquity of data and exponential growth in data mining is the potential destruction of jobs. Is the fourth industrial revolution different from previous revolutions where creative destruction led new jobs to replace older ones? The term "technological unemployment" was coined by Keynes in a 1930 lecture, "Economic possibilities for our grandchildren," where he predicted that in the future, around 2030, the production problem would be solved and there would be enough for everyone, but machines (robots, he thought) would cause "technological unemployment." There would be plenty to go around, but the means of getting a share in it, jobs, might be scarce.[13] So far, the reality has proven him wrong, with employment still strong but in a more flexible format and with skills evolving faster than ever.

---

[13] McKinsey (2017). Where is technology taking the economy? Available at https://www.mckinsey.com/business-functions/mckinsey-analytics/our-insights/where-is-technology-taking-the-economy. Last accessed October 6, 2021.

Banks Are a Preferred Target of Cybercrime

Technology brings exciting new opportunities around data analysis, but also new types of risks for customers and financial institutions alike. As noted by the European Central Bank, "crime never sleeps, and cybercriminals are always increasing their level of sophistication and exploring new opportunities for attack."[14]

One motive of cyberattacks is financial gains. But attacks can have other motivations where hackers target infrastructures to bring down systems and destabilize a company or a State. In the case of the worldwide attack by WannaCry in May 2017, a malware spread quickly across the internet, infecting more than 250,000 computers in 150 countries in a matter of days. The malware was a type of ransomware where the software encrypts files on a computer and demands a ransom in order to receive the key to decrypt the files.

The BIS notes that the financial sector has been hit by hackers relatively more often than other sectors during the COVID-19 pandemic, being only behind the health sector. While this has not yet led to systemic disruptions, there are substantial risks from cyberattacks for financial institutions. Cyber risk is an umbrella term for failures or breach of IT systems and is a form of operational risk. Around 40% of cyber incidents are intentional and malicious, rather than accidental, in other words, they are true cyberattacks. Those include malware, which are software designed to cause damage to IT devices or steal data, cross-site scripting, phishing, or password cracking.

Attacks include account takeover, which happens when a hacker gains access to a user's account and uses the stolen credentials to complete unauthorized transactions. Another type of fraud that grew during the Lockdown by taking advantage of online retailers' refund policies occurs when a user tries to gain money back from a legitimate transaction by filing a chargeback and alleging that the merchandise was not received. Vulnerability increased as more people worked from home during the Lockdown. Moreover, there are risks related

---

[14]European Central Bank (2017). Cybercrime: From fiction to reality. In Focus, Issue no 2, June 2017, p. 2.

to clouds, and 86% of financial institutions admitted the initial mass move to remote working made their organizations less secure.[15]

Cyberattacks are different in nature from other types of operational risk. A distinguishing characteristic of sophisticated cyberattacks is the persistent nature of a campaign conducted by a motivated attacker. The presence of an active, motivated and sophisticated hacker implies that the risk is more difficult to identify and remains latent. From a risk perspective, the rule that smaller counterparts present less risk does not hold true in the cyber reality, as smaller vendors providing non-critical services may prove as risky as larger ones.

In the context of open banking, the question of cybercriminality becomes even more relevant. From a technical point of view, open banking is at least as safe as online banking. As noted earlier in this book, APIs are trusted programs and providers use strong customer authentication. APIs present a lower risk than the download of a static csv file. Data can flow to another bank or a third party with the explicit and specific consent of the user, without the need to download and upload data. Moreover, data can be refreshed on a regular basis and integrity is guaranteed with a direct access to the source. Nevertheless, a wider adoption of data sharing increases the opportunities for cyber criminality.

This has prompted regulators at the national and supranational levels to respond to this threat. Focusing on financial stability, the Committee on Payments and Market Infrastructures (CPMI) of the BIS and the International Organisation of Securities Commissions (IOSCO) published a report on "Cyber resilience in financial market infrastructures" in November 2014, followed by a guidance on cyber resilience for financial market infrastructures in June 2016.

In Europe, the Commission adopted the Directive on security of network and information systems (the NIS Directive) in July 2016. This Directive, which member States transposed into national law by May 2018, is the main legislative instrument supporting cyber resilience in the EU. It applies to operators of essential services, including banks and some financial market infrastructure (FMIs).

---

[15]BAE Systems (2021). The COVID Crime Index 202. Online, opportunistic and over-powering. BAE, April 2021.

The Directive ensures that all member states share the same level of development on their cyber strategy and that information flows between members. In March 2017, the Governing Council of the European Union approved the Eurosystem cyber resilience strategy for FMIs, based on the three pillars of FMI readiness, sector resilience and strategic regulatory-industry engagement. The ECB defines cyber resilience as "the ability to protect electronic data and systems from cyberattacks, as well as to resume business operations quickly in case of a successful attack." Regulators focus their attention on the ability to resume operations within two hours (2hRTO) following extreme cyberattacks.

Cybercriminality represents a threat to individual institutions, including banks, insurance companies and FMI such as payment and settlement systems. It also potentially poses a systemic risk to financial stability, considering the interconnectedness of institutions. In fact, FMIs can concentrate risk and propagate a shock. This is why "the level of operational resilience of FMIs, including cyber resilience, can be a decisive factor in the overall resilience of the financial system and the broader economy."[16] Along with its implications for systemic risk, cyberattacks can lead to losses for financial institutions, retailers and users. What data do we have to quantify those financial losses?

A large part of losses due to cybercrime relates to card frauds. Card fraud happens when credit or debit card numbers are given out to a fraudster by mistake, when cards are lost or stolen, when mail is diverted, or when a cyber criminal unduly gets access to the card information.

The European Central Bank has conducted six surveys on card frauds, with the latest report presenting data from 2018 for both the Eurozone and SEPA countries.[17] The total value of fraudulent transactions using cards issued within the Eurozone and acquired worldwide amounted to €0.94 billion in 2018. As a share of the total value

---

[16]Bank for International Settlements (2016). Guidance on cyber resilience for financial market infrastructures. Available at https://www.bis.org/cpmi/publ/d146.pdf. Last accessed October 6, 2021, p. 4.

[17]The Single Euro Payments Area (SEPA) was launched in 2008 and counts 36 member-states, including the EU, the UK, the European Free Trade Association (Norway, Iceland, Liechtenstein, Switzerland), as well as Monaco, San Marino, Andorra and the Vatican City State.

of card transactions, fraud increased by 0.002% points to 0.031% in 2018 compared with 2017 for the Euro area. In 2018, 79% of the value of card fraud resulted from card-not-present payments, i.e. payments via the internet, mail or phone, 15% from transactions at point-of-sale (POS) terminals, such as face-to-face payments at retailers or restaurants, and 6% from transactions at automated teller machines (ATMs), as seen in Figure 1. Frauds related to card-not-present transactions increased almost 18% in 2018 compared with 2017 — a meaningful increase that contrasts with the fall in card-present transactions possibly related to an increasing adoption of chip-and-pin transactions. From a geographical perspective, domestic transactions accounted for 89% of all card transactions by number but only 36% of fraudulent transactions. Cross-border transactions within SEPA represented 9% of all transactions but 49% of fraudulent transactions. Finally, although only 2% of all transactions were acquired outside SEPA, they accounted for 15% of all fraud. The euro area experienced slightly lower fraud levels from an issuing and acquiring perspective than SEPA as a whole. When cardholders are victims to fraud, they are only liable for the limited amount of € 50, or even less in some countries such as the Netherlands where a zero liability policy is pursued, while the rest of the amount has to be paid by their issuing bank, in accordance with PSD2 rules.[18]

In the US, the Federal Trade Commission (FTC) enforces federal consumer protection laws that prevent fraud, deception and unfair business practices. In the first half of 2021 alone, more than 800,000 identity thefts were reported to the agency, a large increase compared to the first semester of 2020, as seen in Table 1. This number has experienced a steady growth over the past few years, possibly because of increased awareness of customers but also no doubt because of an increase in frauds. There can be a delay in the reporting as it takes time for users to notice and report the fraud.

The 2019 Federal Reserve Payments Study is the seventh in a series of triennial studies conducted by the Federal Reserve System since 2001 to estimate aggregate trends in non-cash payments in the

---

[18]European Central Bank (2020). Sixth report on card fraud. Available at https://www.ecb.europa.eu/pub/pdf/cardfraud/ecb.cardfraudreport202008~521edb602b.en.pdf. Last accessed October 6, 2021.

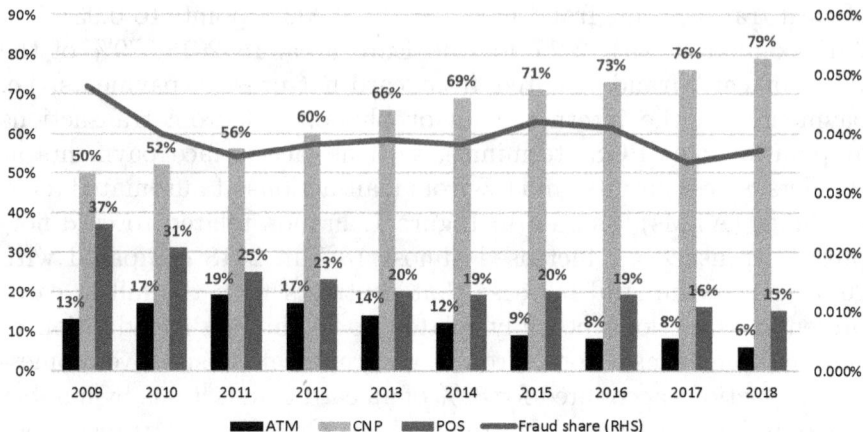

Figure 1: Evolution of the Total Value of Card Fraud Using Cards Issued Within SEPA

Notes: ATM: automated teller machine; CNP: card not present; POS: point of sale.

Source: European Central Bank (2020). Sixth report on card fraud. Available at https://www.ecb.europa.eu/pub/pdf/cardfraud/ecb.cardfraudreport202008~521edb602b.en.pdf. Last accessed October 6, 2021.

United States. Non-cash payments include Automated Clearinghouse Payments (ACH), checks and card payments.[19] Card payments represent a majority of transactions by number, but only a small portion of total non-cash payments in value. Total card payments (credit and debit) represented 7.3% of non-cash payments by value and 75.3% by number in 2018, growing at a rate of 8.9% per year by number between 2015 and 2018. ACH payments include regular transactions such as direct-deposit payroll payments, insurance or mortgage payment drawn from an individual's account on a prearranged basis. Most ACH payments pass between depository institutions over the ACH network and are reported by the network operators, but some are also processed internally by the institutions between accounts of different customers, called "on-us payments".

---

[19]Federal Reserve (2020). The 2019 federal reserve payments study. Available at https://www.federalreserve.gov/paymentsystems/2019-December-The-Federal-Reserve-Payments-Study.htm. Last accessed October 6, 2021.

Table 1:   Identity Theft Reports in the US

Theft Type	2017	2018	2019	2020	2021 (1H)
Government documents of benefits fraud	25,960	24,957	23,236	406,560	251,446
Other identity theft	65,457	122,666	215,897	353,388	203,187
Credit card fraud	133,104	157,743	271,937	393,327	190,642
Loan or lease fraud	30,099	51,940	104,775	205,064	104,689
Employment of tax-related fraud	82.050	67,290	45,580	113,590	80,792
Bank fraud	50,625	52,616	58,851	89,599	63,309
Phone or utilities fraud	55,144	63,658	83,641	99,571	47,035
Total identity theft reports	**370,915**	**444,339**	**650,323**	**1,387,597**	**803,817**

Source: US FTC Fraud Sentinel Network, data up to 1H2021.

For the first time in the time series, remote payments (card-not-present) represent the same value as card-present transactions (Figure 2). While remote transactions represented 28.0% of general-purpose card payments by number in 2018, the percentage represented 49.9% by value. No doubt the number that will be published in the next edition of this triennial survey will exceed 50%. This growth in remote transactions has been mostly driven by e-commerce, which accounted for 63% of remote card transactions in 2018.

Similar to trends seen in Europe, the Fed estimated, in its depository institutions survey of 2015, that fraud originated from card payments reached 97.8% by number and 77.5% by value, with the remainder coming from ACH and checks. Within card payments, card-not-present is the vehicle for the majority of frauds. The Fed flags that "remote card payments fraud is likely to be of increasing concern for the U.S. payments system going forward."[20] The Fed defines a payment fraud as a "cleared and settled transaction

---

[20]Federal Reserve (2018). *Changes in U.S. Payments Fraud from 2012 to 2016: Evidence from the Federal Reserve Payments Study*, October 2018. Washington D.C.: Board of Governors of the Federal Reserve System, p. 2.

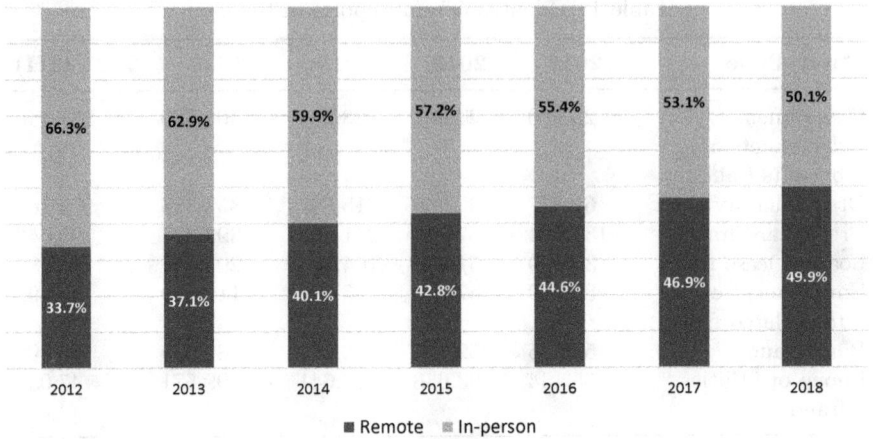

Figure 2: Growth in E-commerce: Trends of Remote and In-person General-purpose Card Payments (By Value in the US, 2012–2018)
Source: US Federal Reserve.

that a third party initiated without the authorization, agreement, or voluntary assistance of the authorized user (the accountholder or cardholder) with the intent to deceive for personal gain."[21]

The fraud rate, by value, rose from 0.38 basis points to 0.46 basis points for depository institutions between 2012 and 2015. The loss may be borne by the cardholder, her issuing bank, the bank of the retailer, or the retailer herself. Juniper Research calculates that retailers are set to lose $130 billion in digital card-not-present fraud between 2018 and 2023.

This explains the rising popularity of chip-and-pin authentication, which is known to be safer than payments via magnetic stripes for card-present transactions. In-person card payments increasingly involved chip authentication: more than half used chip authentication in 2018 compared with 2% in 2015. Data also suggest the need to improve cross-border payments, which give rise to a disproportionate amount of frauds, while retailers will be the main beneficiaries of a lower fraud occurrence.

---

[21] *Ibid.*, p. 6.

Chapter 8

How Can Regulators Foster Inclusion?

Responding to the COVID Crisis

Policymakers, regulators and supervisors dealt with the unique challenge of the COVID-19 crisis. The crisis and the ensuing Great Lockdown were triggered by a unique exogenous shock that resulted in a simultaneous collapse in supply and demand, which coincided with an oil price shock. How does the Great Lockdown compare and contrast with previous shocks and does it impact the focus of policymakers on financial inclusion?

There is a rich literature on the impact of crises on asset valuations and economic growth. Authors looked at warning signals or symptoms of an imminent currency crisis and found that declining exports, deviations of the foreign exchange from trend, ratio of broad money to gross international reserves, output, and equity prices were relevant signals that a currency crisis may take place in the coming 24 months.[1]

Research from 2009 explained the differences between countries in terms of the impact of the crisis. The IMF found that "a small set of variables explain a large share of the variation in growth revisions," in particular "countries with more leveraged domestic financial systems and more rapid credit growth tended to suffer larger downward

---

[1]Kaminsky, L. and Reinhart, C. (1998). Leading indicators of currency crises. IMF Staff Papers.

revisions to their growth outlooks." For emerging markets, the financial channel was more relevant than a collapse in trade to explain revisions in growth forecasts. The authors also find — weaker — evidence that countries with a stronger fiscal position before the crisis fared better, while exchange-rate flexibility buffered some of the impact of the shock.[2]

Reinhart and Rogoff note that "banking crises are associated with profound declines in output and employment."[3] Unemployment rises an average of 7% points over the down phase of the cycle, which lasts on average over four years, while output falls an average of over 9%. The authors also note that "government debt tends to explode, rising an average of 86% in the major post-World War II episodes." Importantly, the authors note that the main cause of debt explosion is not the widely cited bailing out and recapitalizing of the banking system, but rather a "collapse in tax revenues." They also analyzed the pace of recovery from financial crisis using evidence from 100 episodes. Examining the evolution of real per capita GDP around 100 systemic banking crises, they found that "it takes about eight years to reach the pre-crisis level of income," with a median at six and a half years. Considering the GFC of 2008, "only Germany and the US (out of 12 systemic cases) [had] reached their 2007–2008 peaks in real income" by 2014. They also found that 45% of episodes recorded double dips. While they acknowledge that every crisis has its specificities, postwar business cycles are not the relevant comparator for the recent crises in advanced economies. Their approach recognizes that policymaking and crisis management follows a pendulum, and that the "current phase of the official policy approach is predicated on the assumption that growth, financial stability and debt sustainability can be achieved through a mix of austerity and forbearance (and some reform)." Harsher policies, including debt restructurings,

---

[2]IMF (2009). The global financial crisis: Explaining cross-country differences in the output impact. Pelin Berkmen, Gaston Gelos, Robert Rennhack, and James P. Walsh, IMF Working Papers, WP/09/280.

[3]Reinhart, C. and Rogoff, K. (2009). The aftermath of financial crises. NBER Working Paper No. 14656, Issued in January.

higher inflation, capital controls and other forms of financial repression are typically observed in emerging markets alone.[4]

Looking at the financial sector, authors look at select features of the 2008 crisis, especially leverage, which is procyclical and increases during boom periods. They explain that bank lending and capital markets are intertwined, leading to a complementarity of micro and macro policies.[5] In the same vein, Tirole notes that the 2008 crisis was "characterized by massive illiquidity". He reviews "what we know and don't know about illiquidity and all its friends: market freezes, fire sales, contagion, and ultimately insolvencies and bailouts," and other types of market breakdowns. Tirole explains why liquidity cannot easily be apprehended through a single statistic. He emphasizes the need for macro-prudential policies, where liquidity should be regulated in conjunction with capital adequacy requirement.[6]

Evidence suggests that "banks in countries with stricter capital requirement regulations and with more independent supervisors performed better," and that differences in corporate governance did not have a statistically meaningful correlation with bank performance.[7] Importantly, "capital is effective to reduce systemic risk, and the type of capital matters," and increased regulatory focus after the 2008 crisis helped strengthen the capital base of banks.[8]. Proper regulation can reduce the duration of a crisis. This is what data suggest in the case of Indonesian banks. Research shows that "at the end of the 1997–2002 episode, the Bank of Indonesia had closed 70 banks and nationalized 13, out of a total of 237." The non-performing loans for the banking system were "estimated at 65–75% of total loans at the

---

[4]Reinhart, C. and Rogoff, K. (2014). Recovery from financial crises: Evidence from 100 episodes. NBER, January 2014.

[5]Adrian, T. and Shin, H. S. (2010). The changing nature of financial intermediation and the financial crisis of 2007–2009.

[6]Bank for International Settlements (2010). Illiquidity and all its friends. BIS Working Paper 303, 2010.

[7]Beltratti, A. and Stulz, R. (2012). The credit crisis around the globe: Why did some banks perform better? *Journal of Financial Economics*, *105*(1), 1–17.

[8]Anginer, D. and Demirgüç-Kunt, A. (2014). Bank capital and systemic stability. World Bank Policy Research Working Paper No. 6948.

peak of the crisis and fell to about 12% in February 2002," stressing the relevance of regulations such as capital adequacy, deposit insurance, reserve requirements to reduce the duration of the crisis.[9]

Moreover, a stream of the literature looks at the contagion effect of the crisis from one segment of the economy to another. There is evidence of only a small contagion from the U.S. and the global financial sector to domestic portfolios and valuations during the 2008 crisis.[10] By contrast, "there has been substantial contagion from domestic markets to individual domestic portfolios, with its severity inversely related to the quality of countries' economic fundamentals." This confirms that in the case of the 2008 crisis, markets focused more on country-specific characteristics. Contrary to 2008, the Great Lockdown is exogenous in nature, it was not caused by a credit crunch, a banking or an exchange crisis. Banking crises are always characterized by a cumulative stress on solvency and liquidity. But the combination of causes is unique to each.

The 2020 crisis did not present warning signals. Authors underline that the "damage in every systemic crisis in history is caused by endogenous risk amplification, even if the trigger can be an exogenous shock as it was in the 1914 systemic crisis." While the COVID-19 trigger is exogenous, they ask whether the financial system absorbs this shock, as it usually does for exogenous shocks, or "whether the shock interacts adversely with the latent feedback loops in the financial system and exposes existing vulnerabilities that culminate in a systemic financial crisis."[11] Banks were better prepared in 2020 than in 2008, with higher capital and liquidity levels. That said, a long period of historically low interest rates had led companies and households to increase debt levels, representing a risk for lenders, putting debt and loan repayments under stress.[12] In this context, "the appropriate

---

[9]Tchana, F. (2014). The empirics of banking regulation. *Emerging Markets Review, 19*(C), 49–76.

[10]Bekaert, G. *et al.* (2014). The global crisis and equity market contagion. *Journal of Finance, 69*(6), 2597–2649.

[11]Baldwin, R. and di Mauro, B. W. (2020). Economics in the time of COVID-19: A new eBook. *VOX CEPR Policy Portal*, 2–3.

[12]Bank for International Settlements (2019a). G7 working group on stablecoins. Investigating the impact of global stablecoins.

policy response cannot be limited to reducing interest rates or purchases of corporate or sovereign bonds on the open market but should also encompass forbearance and targeted help and similar policies."

While the uncertainty remains on the pace of economic recovery, most economic forecasts point to a full recovery by 2022,[13] more than two years after the beginning of the crisis, if we use March 11, 2020 as a starting date, which is when the WHO made the assessment that COVID-19 could be characterized as a pandemic.[14] The market response to the rising threat of COVID-19 anticipated the WHO announcement, starting in February as evidenced by a measure of asset valuation and risk such as S&P and VIX data. On February 24, the VIX exceeded its 30-day average of 15 and broke the level of 20 and did not decrease under this level for the rest of 2020. IMF Chief Economist Gita Gopinath noted that the Great Lockdown represented the worst recession since the Great Depression, with a "cumulative loss to global GDP over 2020 and 2021 from the pandemic crisis [...] around 9 trillion dollars, greater than the economies of Japan and Germany combined."[15]

By contrast, asset valuations and market expectations experienced a fast recovery already by May 2020, just two months after the beginning of the crisis, supported by unprecedented policy measures. Observers noted that the "speed of recovery surprised the markets," with "a bull market in the middle of the outbreak."[16] In fact, the S&P index reached a trough on March 23, 2020, and at the end of the first half of 2020, it was just 4% below its January 1 level. Similarly, VIX, a measure of market volatility, reached a peak of 82.7 on March 16,

---

[13]IMF (2020). The great lockdown: Worst economic downturn since the great depression, April 14. Available at https://blogs.imf.org/2020/04/14/the-great-lockdown-worst-economic-downturn-since-the-great-depression/. Last accessed July 5, 2020.

[14]World Health Organization (2020). WHO Director-General's opening remarks at the media briefing on COVID-19 — 11 March 2020.

[15]See footnote 13.

[16]Franco, G. (2020). Interview with Gustavo Franco during UBS Conference organized, 23 June 2020.

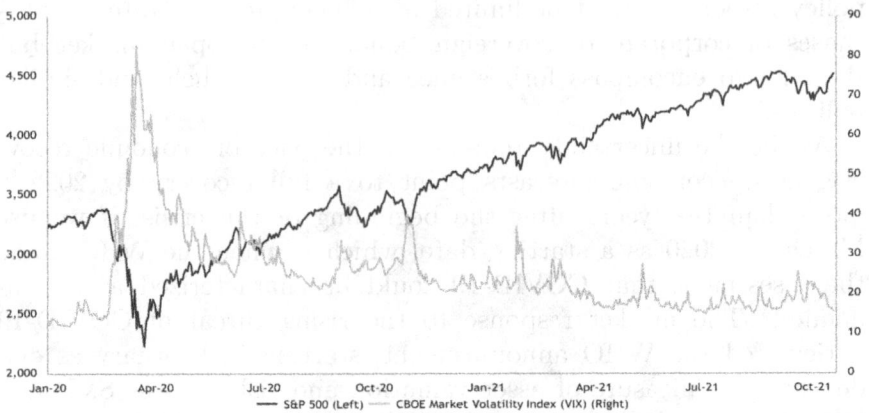

Figure 1:   Fast Recovery in Asset Prices Despite Volatility Post COVID (S&P 500, VIX)
Source: Bloomberg.

2020, and declined somewhat after that date, while not returning to its 2019 levels (Figure 1).

2020 policy responses were swift and aggressive, mostly using 2008 as a playbook. If the first-order impact was not unusual, the Great Lockdown stands out because of several unique characteristics. What is the role of the Financial Sector and FinTech in the context of the crisis?

In 2008, banks were to a large extent at the origin of the crisis, with rising defaults in select consumer segments, opaque accounting in off-balance sheet vehicles, loss of confidence and stress in interbank liquidity. The GFC led to banking bankruptcies and consolidation, favoring larger domestic deposit-taking institutions.[17] Unsurprisingly, the response to the 2008 crisis involved an increased focus on banking supervision and a crackdown on lax regulations with the definition of Basel III rules.

In 2020, financial institutions presented more robust balance sheets, with limited foreign exchange mismatch, stronger liquidity

---

[17]Claessens, S. (2006). Access to financial services: A review of the issues and public policy objectives. *The World Bank Research Observer*, *21*(2), 207–240.

and capital ratios. There is limited evidence of a "flight to quality" or "flight to size" in deposit-taking institutions or a preference for domestic institutions versus foreign-controlled banks, contrary to 2008. In 2008, financial institutions faced a perfect storm with a dual impact on their liquidity and capital positions. In 2020, the short-term impact on the financial sector included a shock to asset quality, leading to higher levels of loan loss provisions. Funding availability and cost were impacted, while interest rates decreased as a result of accommodating public policies, leading to margin compression. Banks acted as "shock absorber for the system, liquidity providers of second to last resort," as drawdowns on credit lines increased meaningfully, reaching a peak in May 2020, 29% above pre-COVID level, and subsequently normalizing (Figure 2).[18] From the perspective of capital markets, the shock to asset valuations and rating downgrades resulted in a first moment in a decrease in the value of collaterals and provisions, in particular for asset managers and insurance companies.

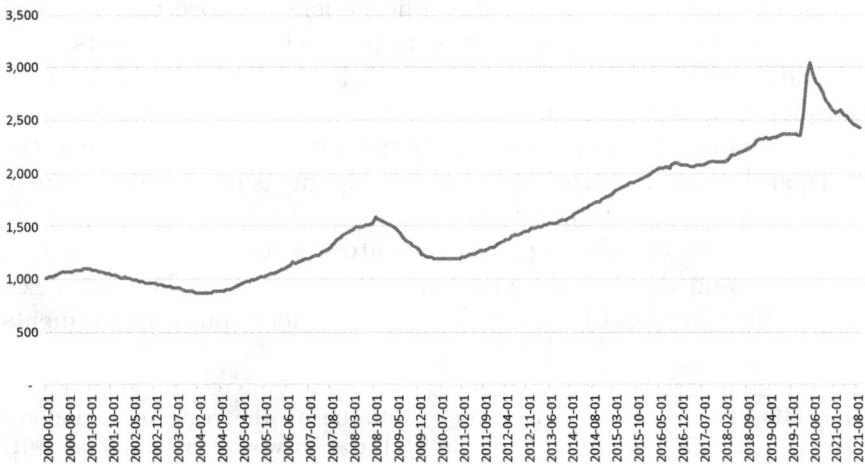

Figure 2:   Strong Increase in Drawdowns on Banks' Credit Lines (Billions of US$)

Source: Federal Reserve Economic Data, Federal Reserve Bank of St Louis. Commercial and industrial loans, all commercial banks, billions of U.S. dollars, monthly, seasonally adjusted.

---

[18]Oliver, W. (2020). Webinar: COVID-19 and the impact on the US financial system – Payments, June 3, 2020.

Outside of credit and insurance, payments experienced an acceleration in the adoption of contactless solutions, with COVID helping to "speed up the shift toward digital payments," with consumers massively mentioning for the first time hygiene as an important factor to prefer electronic means of payments over cash.[19] Lagarde highlights a European survey showing that "40% of respondents [. . .] say they have reduced their use of cash."[20] Brazilian FinTech company Ebanx noted in 2020 that "contactless payments grew fivefold in Brazil comparing with March 2019" citing data from the Brazilian Card Association ABECS, mostly driven by the near-field communication technology embarked on plastic cards.[21] Moreover, electronic payments are the financial backbone of e-commerce companies, which benefited from lockdowns and restrictions put in place during the pandemic.

In 2020, banks and payment companies were part of the solution of the crisis, offering innovative solutions to customers via digital channels, widening their service offering to support the resilience of businesses, becoming agents of public policies in government social programs, and renegotiating credit terms with their borrowers.

The first policy responses to the crisis focused on safeguarding the liquidity and capital base of banks, while allowing for flexibility in credit risk management. The BIS offered a very quick response to the crisis, and defined in April 2020 that "relief measures include a range of different payment moratoriums and government guarantees."[22] With a character of exception, regulators authorized that capital treatment and the definition of non-performing assets be more flexible. While "the Basel Framework applies higher capital requirements

---

[19]Bank for International Settlements (2020). Inside the regulatory sandbox: Effects on FinTech funding. Available at https://www.bis.org/publ/work901. htm. Last accessed October 6, 2021.

[20]Lagarde (2020). Keynote speech by Christine Lagarde, President of the ECB, at the European Banking Congress. Fostering sustainable growth in Europe. Available at https://www.ecb.europa.eu/press/key/date/2020/html/ecb.sp201120~e9 2d92352f.en.html. Last accessed October 6, 2021.

[21]Ebanx (2020). Beyond borders 2020–2021. A study on the state of cross-border e-commerce in Latin America.

[22]Bank for International Settlements (2020). FinTech and BigTech Credit: A new data base. BIS Working Paper no. 887. Available at https://www.bis.org/publ/ work887.htm. Last accessed October 6, 2021.

to loans that are categorised as past due or defaulted [...] the Committee has agreed that when jurisdictions apply this criterion, payment moratorium periods (public or granted by banks on a voluntary basis) relating to the COVID-19 outbreak can be excluded by banks from the counting of days past due." Accounting of loan loss provisions, based on IFRS 9 rule and expected loss considerations, was also made more flexible, acknowledging the high level of uncertainty surrounding future projections.

In Europe, the crisis reshaped policy priorities and the reaction to it was "sizeable and prompt".[23] State aid frameworks were made flexible; the European Central Bank offered fresh quantitative easing (QE), while strict clauses under the Stability and Growth Pact were suspended. Measures included a collaboration between the European Central Bank, the Commission, the European Banking Authority (EBA) and national governments. The IIF noted that "although the shock, by its very nature, is a symmetric one — hitting all countries in similar fashion — the ability of different nations has been hampered by differences in policy, with Italy and Spain doing relatively modest fiscal stimulus compared to Germany." The 2020 crisis therefore revived the debates over risk-sharing among countries and proposals to issue "Coronabonds, a special, one-time version of Eurobonds". In October 2020, the European Commission announced the issuance of EU SURE bonds of up to €100 billion as social bonds, being a "clear demonstration of the EU's long-term commitment to sustainable financing."[24] The first tranche issued on October 20 generated strong market demand and was close to 14 times oversubscribed. The funds "will be transferred to the beneficiary Member States in the form of loans to help them cover the costs directly related to the financing of national short-time work schemes and similar measures as a response to the pandemic."

As expected, policy responses included the traditional toolkit of lower policy rates, more flexible rules on loan loss provisioning

---

[23]IIF (2020). IIF European Conference, The EU, COVID-19 and the future of financial services. May 2020.

[24]European Commission (2020). European Commission announced the issuance of EU SURE bonds of up to €100 billion as social bonds. Press release. Available at h ttps://ec.europa.eu/commission/presscorner/detail/en/ip_20_1808. Last accessed October 6, 2021.

and capital rules, injection of liquidity through direct lending and asset repurchase, and expanding public balance sheets among others. Banks implemented their own responses to the crisis, by tapping into funding lines to increase their liquidity cushions, offering loan forbearance, renegotiating loans and serving as distribution agents for government subsidies. Capital markets, in turn, played their role, via record-high levels of debt issuance and convertibles. In the context of COVID-19, policymakers and banks globally have revived a series of measures and discussions, both old and new.

FinTech Brings New Challenges to Regulators

Adding to the challenge of COVID-19 crisis, regulators have had to face the growing challenge of digitization and FinTech. While the environment has been changing fast, regulators have been facing well-known dilemmas: how to ensure financial stability, guarantee customer protection, reduce informality, foster innovation and fair competition to create a financial environment that offers the best conditions to customers?

FinTech brings unique and specific challenges to both regulators and supervisors, be it because of the pace of innovation, its technicality, lower reliance on traditional sector and country borders, or new types of risks such as cybercriminality. FinTech, with its reliance on data, can bring new threats for customers, shedding a new light on customer protection. On the one hand, sandboxes are meant to foster a much welcome innovation. On the other hand, improperly designed innovation can put users at risk, as in the well-documented cases over indebtedness in microcredit. Regulators should not focus exclusively on access, which often brings the false impression of successful policies. To promote effective usage, quality is essential. In many cases, FinTech grows outside of the traditional banking sector, forcing regulators and supervisors to consider the essence of financial services and not just the form. Naturally, it should not be the role of regulators to single out winning solutions or technologies.

There are two perspectives to analyze financial intermediation: the institutional perspective focuses on the type of financial intermediaries, including their setup and legal status. The functional perspective looks at the financial products and services that are being offered. In a classic article, Merton adopts the functional perspective, since he notes that "functions of banks have been remarkably stable through time and geography." He writes that the "primary function of any financial system is to facilitate the allocation of economic resources, both spatially and temporally." Merton defines six core functions of financial systems, and underlines that the first function is to provide a "payments system for the exchange of goods and services."[25] A functional approach to regulation can be combined with a risk-based approach, where institutions whose potential failure constitutes a bigger fragility risk for the economy and society face more rigorous regulation and supervision.[26] This functional approach is essential to avoid regulatory arbitrage between entities supervised as banks, and new comers who may have to abide by a less strict set of rules to provide essentially similar services. In fact, this has become even more necessary considering the importance to avoid future banks' bailouts following the great financial crisis of 2008: "banks must be resilient because they can no longer rely on the support of the state."[27]

The regulatory challenges posed by payments are different from questions raised by credit or insurance, which are directly related to systemic risk. There is ample literature on regulations focused on capital, liquidity and banking risk,[28] supported by the relationship between market liberalization and banks vulnerability.[29] The regulatory challenges relating to payments include a focus on systemic risks,

---

[25]Merton, R. C. (1995). A functional perspective of financial intermediation. *Financial Management*, 23–41.

[26]Beck, T. (2015). Microfinance: A critical literature survey. IEG Working Paper, 2015/No.4. Washington, DC: Independent Evaluation Group, World Bank Group, p. 30.

[27]Bank for International Settlements (2015). Mark Carney: Introduction to the open forum. Available at https://www.bis.org/review/r151116c.htm. Last accessed October 6, 2021.

[28]Bank for International Settlements (2013). Literature review of factors relating to liquidity stress – extended version, Banking Committee on Banking Supervision. Working Paper No. 25; Klomp, J. and de Haan, J. (2012). Banking risk and regulation: Does one size fit all? *Journal of Banking & Finance, 36*(12), 3197–3212.

[29]Stiglitz, J. E. (1999). Reforming the global economic architecture: Lessons from recent crises. *The Journal of Finance, 54*(4), 1508–1521.

a reduction of informality, enabling innovation, and fostering inclusion. Brazil's financial regulation is among the strictest globally.[30] In 2013, the Central Bank of Brazil became the formal regulator of the payment sector in Brazil, including payment institutions and payment schemes.[31]

Reducing informality is a particularly important policy objective, allowing for a wider tax base in countries with sometimes fragile fiscal situations, while also being a first step to bringing public services and welfare coverage to vulnerable citizens. In Brazil, formal employment implies that the worker has a signed employment booklet. The absence of the booklet implies that the employment relationship is not covered by the Labor Code, leading to a lack of social protection. Informality is more prevalent for women than men, and particularly present in agriculture and construction. Informality is rarely a choice, but rather a necessity. According to ILO, 61% of the world's employment is informal. The self-employed are more exposed to informality, but still 40% of all employees are informal. 78% of older workers (aged 65 and above) are in informal employment. Ninety-four percent of workers with less than primary education are in informal employment.[32] The Gallup World Survey 2012 reports that only about 40% of adults globally have fixed employment in excess of 30 hours per week. These are averages across all countries and income groups. The share of informality is considerably higher for poorer countries and poorer income segments and can reach well over 80% in some developing countries.[33]

Avoiding policies that incentivize the use of cash is also desirable. The Brazilian government has permitted differentiated pricing based on payment type, allowing merchants to offer discounts for cash

---

[30]Giráldez-Puig, M. P. and Berenguer, E. (2013). Basel III: Impact on Latin America.

[31]Banco Central do Brasil (2015b). Relatorio de vigilencia do sistema de pagamentos brasileiros. Law n.12.865/2013.

[32]ILO (2019). 100 statistics on the ILO and the labour market to celebrate the ILO centenary. Available at https://ilostat.ilo.org/100-statistics-on-the-ilo-and-the-labour-market/. Last accessed October 6, 2021.

[33]ILO (2013). Statistics. Available at https://www.ilo.org/shinyapps/bulkexplorer22/?lang=en&segment=indicator&id=SDG_0831_SEX_ECO_RT_A. Quoted by CGAP (2014). Financial inclusion and development: Recent impact evidence. No. 92 April 2014.

and debit card payers, as opposed to credit card. Countries, such as Colombia and Argentina, do the opposite, offering discounts for sales paid with electronic payments. Argentine retailers that accept card payment can claim a tax discount for the cost of the terminal. Similar policies in Korea have led card payments to increase from 5% of personal consumption expenditures to more than 50% in 2009.[34] Reducing the reliance on cash and levels of informality can provide a powerful boost to the effectiveness of government policies, as they reach more users.

Innovation is another decisive challenge for regulators, as they try to strike the right balance between risk and innovation. Innovation, such as mobile payments or payments by crypto-currency, increased competition and can be tools for inclusion. With those innovations, the "end game is to make grids safer, more convenient, more contestable, and cheaper, especially for small transactions."[35] Regulators acknowledge that "the Digital Finance Revolution is the greatest technological change that has happened to payments systems since the invention of paper money."[36]

In some cases, they have developed simplified regulatory requirements to allow smaller or emerging financial institutions and users to adopt financial services while complying with a minimum set of rules. Essentially, select categories of institutions may be regulated "differently from banks as long as they do not hold, collectively, a significant proportion of deposits in a financial system."[37] A critical question is the identity requirements to be imposed on payments and simplified accounts, with the standard recommendation being a risk-based approach. In Brazil, the simplified bank account is tailored to low-income individuals or micro-entrepreneurs, with monthly balance

---

[34]Guedes Filho, E. M. *et al.* (2011). Analise economica dos beneficios advindos do uso de cartoes de credito e debito, Tendencias Consultoria Integrada.

[35]Mas, I. (2016). Strains of digital money. *Capco Journal of Financial Transformation*, No. 44, November 2016.

[36]Schydlowsky, D. M. (2015). Commentary on Basel Committee guidance on financial inclusion, CFI: Boston.

[37]Bank for International Settlements (2016). Guidance on the application of the core principles for effective banking supervision to the regulation and supervision of institutions relevant to financial inclusion. Available at https://www.bis.org/bcbs/publ/d383.htm. Last accessed October 6, 2021.

below 5,000 reais (approximately 1,000 US$). The account does not entail opening or maintenance charges and the customer can only use a debit card, being an entry product into financial formality. Users can use the simplified account with just a card proving they are a recipient of one of the government redistribution programs, such as Bolsa Familia, and can be opened at banking correspondents such as lotteries in the case of the simplified Caixa accounts known as "Poupança Caixa Facil". There are approximately eight million simplified checking accounts and three million simplified savings accounts in Brazil. All savings accounts, simplified or not, are exempt from income tax on interest and can be withdrawn at any time. The regulator not only created the simplified accounts but also standardized the number of services included for free, such as cash withdrawals, transfers and account statements.[38]

The growth of simplified accounts and distribution of government programs via banks suggests new government–bank relationships, with a mix of collaboration and intervention. On the one hand, governments may prefer to use banks as a part of the solution, supporting funding and emergency programs for enterprises and people, be it via the credit channel, or more simply as a distribution agent for subsidies. In the case of Caixa Tem in Brazil, the program launched by the government-owned bank Caixa added more than 40 million new customers to its client base during the Great Lockdown in order to receive government emergency benefits. Caixa became the exclusive distribution agent of a specific emergency subsidy, nicknamed "coronavoucher". Strikingly, the program allowed the government in collaboration with Caixa to identify 40 million citizens who were excluded from the banking system and whose needs may be better identified in future social policies. Another focus of policymakers and supervisors has been to ensure that liquidity is not frozen at some large banking institutions, preventing "money to flow to the edges of the system," but that the credit channel is well functioning and performs its mission to reach consumers and corporates, both large and small.[39] On the other hand, the government may be tempted

---

[38] https://www.bcb.gov.br/estabilidadefinanceira/tarifas3594.

[39] Franco, G. (2020). Interview with Gustavo Franco during UBS Conference organized, 23 June 2020.

to resort to unorthodox policies. Legislative proposals in Brazil in April and May 2020 included proposed caps on credit card lending rates, a removal of negative data from credit bureaus, or an increase in corporate taxes for banks. These proposals were eventually dismissed.

While COVID-19 was certainly not the direct cause of some policies that were years in the making, it has proven to be a formidable catalyst for digitization of the delivery of public services. Brazil launched a policy agenda focused on micro reforms whereby the "Brazilian federal government launched a two-year strategic initiative, which establishes the objectives and goals for the digitalization of public services."[40] The goal of this strategy is "to improve service quality, by promoting transparency in interactions between the Brazilian public and the Brazilian federal government," using technology to "reduce bureaucracy and corruption, prevent fraudulent activity, protect information and regain the confidence of Brazilians and companies involved in government processes, in addition to reducing overall costs to Brazilians and to the Brazilian government". The government also planned to cut on the number of websites (with 1,500 government websites currently) to one single portal "gov.br" by the end of 2020, and to integrate all of the Brazilian State governments onto the portal by the end of 2022. Only one login will be necessary for Brazilian citizens to access all federal and state public services and as well as broad access to government information. Business creation and closure, and work permits will also be facilitated. As a result of the digital government strategy, the Brazilian federal government predicts a saving of BRL 37.9 billion in the next five years (approximately US$7.3 billion). Furthermore, Brazilian citizens will save 147 million hours collectively through the digitization of governmental services, which is equivalent to one full workday per capita.

FinTech and the Great Lockdown enhance the challenge for regulators to innovate and reassess their relationship with banks. One of the greatest challenges related to the rise of FinTechs consists in consumer protection. Consumer protection in financial services revolves around four main aspects: (1) disclosure of rates and fees charged in

---

[40]Hogan, L. (2020). Brazil's digital government strategy takes effect.

a transparent, accurate, comparable and clear way, (2) prohibition of unfair business practices, (3) possibility to action recourse mechanisms, (4) emphasis on financial education.[41] Select countries impose caps on lending rates or floors on deposit rates. However, the effectiveness of those policies has often been criticized, as they provide an incentive for banks to simply stop serving segments of customers.

One important consideration related to consumer protection is the focus on antitrust or anticompetitive practices. Protecting the consumer also means that regulators create a level playing field where users can switch providers if they wish to. Meanwhile, some have argued that the new economy, based on data and knowledge, was leading to increasing rates of returns, providing an advantage to larger companies and first movers.[42] This goes against the classical law of diminishing marginal returns, articulated by Ricardo. If in fact, FinTech experiences rising instead of diminishing returns, then we may face the formation of monopolies with meaningful barriers of entry for newcomers. Platform effects create economies of scale and network effects, in a self-reinforcing logic. Setting up a FinTech platform requires large upfront costs, with diminishing unit costs. Network effects appear when users chose a platform because it is compatible with their other apps or software, reinforcing switching costs, which can be monetary or not. FinTechs have found a way of offering the same financial services as traditional providers, leveraging technology for data analysis and treatment, regulatory support and the ubiquity of cell phones. This leap in efficiency is not only a huge challenge for incumbents, they may also represent a barrier to entry for newcomers and reinforce a monopoly or oligopoly of large financial providers. The winner-takes-all dynamic should be a concern for regulators. Is tech leading to more competition or more monopoly?

For Aghion, innovation is likely to meet with the resistance of incumbent firms, who will defend their rents at all cost, often with

---

[41]Rutledge, S. L. (2010). Consumer protection and financial literacy: Lessons from Nine country studies. Policy Research Working Paper; No. WPS 5326. World Bank.

[42]Arthur, B. (1996). Increasing returns and the new world of business. Harvard Business Review. Available at https://hbr.org/1996/07/increasing-returns-and-the-new-world-of-business. Last accessed October 6, 2021.

the support of their employees, who fear losing their jobs. Innovation is a "source of income and wealth inequality between those at the top and the rest of society, but it enhances productivity growth and social mobility." Innovation is therefore desirable for the common prosperity and policymakers should design rules that protect property rights and allocate capital to innovative ideas. The risk is that today's innovators become tomorrow's incumbents, entrenched in rent-seeking behaviors and deterring further innovation by new entrants. Aghion explains that capitalism needs to be regulated and "we need to protect capitalism from the capitalists" and "rethink competition policy in light of the IT and digital revolutions and the emergence of the new superstar firms."[43]

Aghion notes that on average, competition stimulates innovation and growth and is "positive for firms close to the technological frontier, whereas it is negative for firms far from the technological frontier."[44] He illustrates his hypothesis by giving the example of a class of students. The students at the top of the class have good grades (equivalent to the profits of firms at the technological frontier) while others are at the bottom of the class with low grades. Aghion describes the potential reaction of students if a brilliant new student would join the class (external shock). He concludes that most likely, the arrival of the brilliant new student will incite the best students to work even harder in order to beat competition, but "it will discourage the weaker students, for whom it becomes even more difficult to catch up."

For Nubank's founder David Velez, the main challenge for incumbents will be to maintain relevance with customers, which requires not just building new products, but more fundamentally adapting the culture and the use of data and technology. Velez notes that select incumbents have been able to adjust successfully, as in the case of Walmart, vis-à-vis the rising pressure of Amazon. Other incumbents may not be able to adapt successfully. In between those two categories, a third category of players will adjust their business model,

---

[43] Aghion, P. (2021). Innovation and inequality. Chapter 18 included in Rodrik D., Blanchard, O. (ed.). *Combating Inequality: Rethinking Government's Role.* Cambridge, MA: MIT Press, pp. 171–176.

[44] Aghion, P. *et al.* (2021). *The Power of Creative Destruction.* Belknap Harvard, pages 58 and 73.

focus on the niche where they have a competitive advantage, such as mortgages or lending to large corporates, which require large balance sheets.

The three founders of Nubank, David Velez, Christina Junqueira and Edward Wible, explain that the entire experience of opening a bank account in Brazil was "incredibly frustrating". Linked to the "immense profitability of Brazilian banks and the low penetration of banking in the country," the founders spotted a unique "entrepreneurship challenge." The decade-long journey led the founders to define and implement what a "company in the 21st century looks like," empowering people and making an impact. While Latin America counts more than 650 million people, market structures, and in particular oligopolies, had often been a "barrier for access and innovation." The three founders saw a "massive opportunity, using technology, data and truly thoughtful service" and aimed at creating a "new experience, not a digital copy." The company developed a cloud-based technology platform. Nubank's founder David Velez explains that "great brands drive love and engagement" and wants customers to "love [Nubank] as loyal and enthusiastic fans," with "approximately 80%–90%" of clients acquired organically, without marketing, via word-of-mouth, leading to an acquisition cost below $5.

Regulators have been open to innovation, as a way to spur contestability in the financial market. Velez explains that Brazilian financial services are among the most regulated globally, and obtaining a financial license is a lengthy and complex process. Velez notes that "technology is creating a window of opportunity for more competition" and regulators are embracing those changes while also respecting prudent regulations. Open banking is a key component of the regulatory agenda of increasing competition. Velez notes that the financial market presents a high degree of inertia and friction. Open banking bears the promise to reduce that friction, create a level playing field for financial institutions, and allow that the best products win. This is the "best scenario for consumers" and a "great opportunity of innovation."[45]

---

[45]Interview with Nubank's founder and CEO David Velez, November 17, 2021, and SEC F-1.

When Regulators Innovate

Regulators have responded to the combined challenge and opportunity of technology with regulatory innovation. Regtech, or the regulatory framework applied to tech companies and in particular FinTech, has expanded its toolkit. One of the most popular approaches involves regulatory sandboxes, which are meant to foster innovation while allowing regulators to follow closely emerging risks.

The UK Financial Conduct Authority (FCA) launched the first regulatory sandbox in 2015. The UK sandbox operates on a cohort basis with two six-month test periods per year, and "five cohorts of firms have been accepted into the sandbox on the following dates: 7 November 2016, 15 June 2017, 5 December 2017, 3 July 2018, and 29 April 2019." Each cohort counts 25 firms on average. A total of 118 firms had been accepted into the UK sandbox as of 2020. Most participants are startups in retail banking, payments, wholesale markets, investment and insurance.[46]

Evidence from the UK suggests that entry into the sandbox is associated with "significant increase of 15% in capital raised post-entry, relative to firms that did not enter; and their probability of raising capital increases by 50%." The most likely explanation is that sandboxes reduce information asymmetries for investors and regulatory cost for entrepreneurs. This is particularly true for smaller and younger firms, which are usually subject to more severe informational frictions. Firms with a CEO without prior experience in financial regulation benefit more from participating in the sandbox, as they learn from guidance provided by supervisors.[47]

Since 2015, more than 50 countries have adopted sandboxes. In Europe alone, seven countries followed suit and set up sandboxes, while an additional eight countries are in advanced preparatory stage

---

[46]Bank for International Settlements (2020). Inside the regulatory sandbox: Effects on FinTech funding. Available at https://www.bis.org/publ/work901.htm. Last accessed October 6, 2021, p. 10.

[47]Bank for International Settlements (2020). Inside the regulatory sandbox: Effects on FinTech funding. Available at https://www.bis.org/publ/work901.htm. Last accessed October 6, 2021.

or announced their intentions to set up a sandbox.[48] The sandbox allows testing new models in a controlled environment where risks to the system are limited — a concept that was borrowed from the IT sector. Eligibility criteria across European sandboxes and innovation hubs include five main elements: they present a genuine innovation, benefit consumers and the financial system, providers understand the regulatory framework, the project has reached a sufficiently mature stage, and the project needs regulatory support to grow.[49]

In Brazil, the sandbox was created by a resolution of the National Monetary Council on October 26, 2020 and received 52 proposals, more than three times the expected number of approved projects.[50] Businesses are set to launch at the end of 2021 or beginning of 2022. The selection of 10 to 15 projects was based on four criteria: the adherence with one or several of the Central Bank's nine priority objectives (40%), the level of maturity of the project (30%), the nature and magnitude of risks carried in the project (20%), the technical capabilities and governance of the entity (10%). The Central Bank of Brazil defined its nine priorities for the first cycle of the sandbox as follows:

- Projects that offer solutions for the FX market
- Development of capital markets using mechanisms that create synergies with credit markets
- Development of credit to micro and SMEs
- Solutions for open banking
- Solutions for PIX (Central Bank of Brazil peer-to-peer payment system)
- Solutions for rural credit
- Solutions that increase competition in the national financial system and Brazilian payment system

---

[48] European Parliament (2020). Regulatory Sandboxes and Innovation Hubs for FinTech. Impact on innovation, financial stability and supervisory convergence. Radostina Parenti, Policy Department for Economic, Scientific and Quality of Life Policies. Luxembourg: Policy Department Edition, p. 21.
[49] *Ibid.*, p. 32.
[50] Resolution CMN 4.865/2020, complemented by Resolutions of the Central Bank BCB29/2020 and BCB 50/2020.

- Financial and payment solutions that enhance financial inclusion
- Development of sustainable finance

Sandboxes allow participants to test their products during a limited period of time. In Brazil, that period spans one year, renewable once. Time to market is quick. Singapore implemented "Sandbox Express," where companies can launch their products 21 days only after applying to participate. Testing their services with real clients and with lower regulatory risk is a meaningful support to nascent companies, which helps their fundraising efforts. From the viewpoint of regulators, sandboxes allow to analyze the impact of regulations in real time and the potential of new financial services. Ultimately, they are useful to improve the functioning of the sector, enhance supervision and increase financial inclusion.

Sandboxes also trigger controversies, as some consider that they could create an unlevel playing field between companies who have been accepted into the sandbox and others. This fear can be mitigated by knowledge-sharing mechanisms with the broader market. Moreover, there could be a regulatory arbitrage for companies and a "race to the bottom" if regulators allow companies to disregard proper market rules in the name of innovation and to raise their attractiveness as a FinTech hub. In the case of the European Single Market, the emergence of several hubs and sandboxes can create a risk of market fragmentation, if they lead to divergent market practices and prevent or slow down the scaling up of innovations across the EU market. While they can have a positive signaling effect, sandboxes are also expensive to operate and require significant time from supervisors. As highlighted in a report commissioned by the United Nations Secretary-General's Special Advocate for Inclusive Finance for Development, sandboxes are "not always the answer for regulating inclusive FinTech".[51]

While sandboxes have captured a lot of attention, there are several other ways regulators and policymakers can make their jurisdiction attractive and promote innovation, including simplified and lighter regulations or horizontal exemptions for nascent companies, specific regulatory licenses for FinTechs, or innovation hubs. Innovation hubs

---

[51]UNSGSA (2019). Early lessons on regulatory innovations to enable inclusive FinTech: Innovation offices, regulatory sandboxes, and regtech.Technical report. New York, NY and Cambridge, UK: Office of the UNSGSA and CCAF.

provide a "scheme, via which firms can engage with the supervisory authority to raise questions and seek clarifications or non-binding guidance about FinTech related issues."[52]

Horizontal exemptions or simplified criteria applied to FinTechs remove the discretionarity of sandboxes as they apply to all potential candidates. The Swiss "sandbox" regime involves a horizontal exemption from the obligation to obtain a banking license, conditioned upon pre-defined volume threshold and disclosure requirements. A company may "accept clients' deposits up a total amount of 1,000 CHF," and it must inform its clients in advance that it is not a supervised entity and does not benefit from deposits insurance. It may also not engage in interest margin activities. Once the company reaches the threshold, it must either obtain a banking license or the specific FinTech license.[53]

Some countries have also developed the issuance of specific licenses for digital banks or for specific activities related to FinTechs. Those countries include, for example, Taiwan, Hong Kong, South Korea, Malaysia, and the United Arab Emirates and the specific rules of those licenses vary from one country to another. In Brazil, the National Monetary Council allowed in 2016 for deposit account to be opened, maintained and closed via digital channels, with no obligation for the physical presence of the customer.[54] Furthermore, a resolution from 2018 regulated FinTechs activity, creating two types of licenses for credit FinTechs and for peer-to-peer FinTechs (Figure 3).[55]

---

[52]European Parliament (2020). Regulatory Sandboxes and Innovation Hubs for FinTech. Impact on innovation, financial stability and supervisory convergence. Radostina Parenti, Policy Department for Economic, Scientific and Quality of Life Policies. Luxembourg: Policy Department Edition, p. 9.

[53]Confédération Suisse (2018). Swiss Federal Department of Finance, Revision der Bankenverordnung (BankV) "FinTech-Bewilligung", Erläuterungen.

[54]Resolutions CMN 4.480/ 2016 and 4.753/2019 permit a simpler process, under a risk-based approach.

[55]Resolution CMN 4.656/2018 regulated credit FinTechs, categorized as SCDs and peer-to-peer players SEPs.

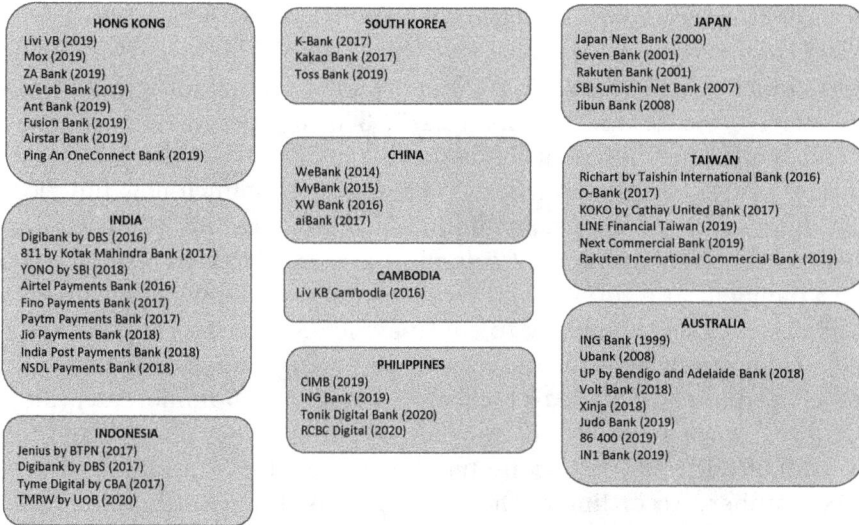

Figure 3: New Banking Licenses in Asia
Source: Adapted from Asian Banker (2019).

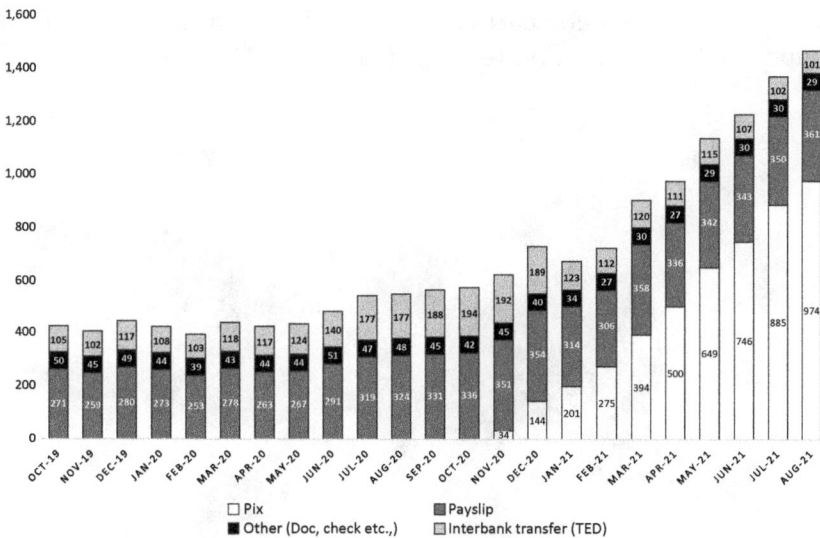

Figure 4: Growth in Peer-to-Peer Payments in Brazil
Source: Central Bank of Brazil.

In a rare move, a regulator can also create and operate the infrastructure that disrupts the financial market. This is the case of peer-to-peer payment platform known as Pix, which was developed, launched and operated by the Central Bank of Brazil. Pix was launched in November 2020 and allows for instantaneous peer-to-peer payments and transfers 24/7, 365 day per year. More than 1,000 banks and financial institutions participate in the infrastructure. The Central Bank of Brazil is planning to launch new functionalities beyond payments, including cash withdrawals (to withdraw cash at ATMs and points of sale via Pix), and "Pix change" (to top up a payment at a retailer and receive an extra cash withdrawal). Pix will also include the ability to split payments in several installments. Less than one year after its launch, 59% of the adult population in Brazil had already made or received a Pix, and 316 million identifiers or "keys" were recorded. Keys comprise unique identifiers like a tax ID, email address, cell phone number or can be a randomly generated number. According to the Central Bank, tax identification numbers (CPF) represent 35% of identification keys, with phone numbers representing an additional 22% and personal emails 16%. The huge success of Pix is driving a reduction of the use of cash and other payment methodologies, such as TEDs and DOCs, which are slower and more expensive for participants. Pix brings a more convenient, cheaper and safer solution to users (Figure 4).[56]

---

[56]More details and data available at www.bcb.gov.br/estabilidadefinanceira/Pix.

Chapter 9

Finance Without Banks?

BigTech versus Banks

With the use of financial services from non-traditional providers set to rise sharply, banks have responded to threats from FinTech competitors via partnerships. In many cases, FinTech ventures are not disrupting existing players but searching for opportunities to collaborate, as incumbents bring the benefits of deeper pockets and proximity with the regulators. FinTech firms benefit from low client acquisition cost and can offer niche solutions and a simpler customer experience.

BigTech firms are different: they have special characteristics that distinguish them from FinTech firms. The FSB provides an indicative list of BigTech firms, including Alibaba, Amazon, Apple, Baidu, eBay, Facebook, Google, Microsoft. While FinTech firms offer financial services with digital technology, BigTech firms approach it from the other direction: their primary business can be in e-commerce, transportation or online entertainment, and they aim to add financial services. Those financial services often start with payments, to offer convenience to their clients, and can extend to credit, insurance, or investment products such as money market funds. Asset management is a natural extension for FinTech activity, as payments often imply that users leave some cash balance and asset management can become an appropriate tool to better manage cash positions and extract a yield from existing balances.

Data give BigTech firms an edge over competitors. To policymakers, this aspect represents one of the greatest challenges.[1] The business model of BigTechs leverages three factors: the data they already have on consumers, aiding BigTechs to understand customer needs better; the advanced analytics they use to deepen this understanding further; and the reliance on strong networks effects. Their presence in banking is currently limited but their expansion into financial services could happen quickly, as network effects drive interaction, user activity and the generation of ever greater amounts of data. The well-known "flywheel" effect is often mentioned by BigTech and FinTechs alike, describing how new customers drive new data, data drive better analytics and a better product market fit, which in turn attracts more clients.

Based on their large global user base of non-financial products, they benefit from cross-subsidization and economies of scale and scope. That makes them well-positioned to capture a significant market share of financial services once they start providing them. Network effects lead to positive externalities as they gain additional customers: the benefits users incur from participating in the platform increase with the number of users. Network effect is not the privilege of BigTechs, but generally common for two-sided platforms.

BigTechs firms have gained particular relevance in emerging markets, where financial penetration was lower and access to smartphones is widespread. In China, 82% of the unbanked population owns a smartphone. BigTechs have a built-in advantage to screen and monitor clients at a lower cost than traditional banks. Giambacorta gives the example of a retail platform, where a BigTech can monitor transaction processed volumes to assess the financial health and credit risk of a merchant, and deduct loan repayments directly from merchant receivables. In China, the share of transactions processed by non-bank payment institutions has increased from 59% of the total number of payments made in 2013 to 76% in 2017, even though these account for a much lower share of payments value.[2]

---

[1] Bank for International Settlements (2018). Big tech in finance and new challenges for public policy. Keynote address by Agustín Carstens. General Manager, Bank for International Settlements. FT Banking Summit London, 4 December 2018.
[2] Gambacorta, L. and Marques-Ibanez, D. (2011). The bank lending channel: Lessons from the crisis. *Economic Policy*, *26*(66), 135–182.

Growth in BigTech firms' provision of payment services has been most pronounced in China, where mobile payments are now equivalent to 16% of GDP, far more than in any other market, including the US where it reaches 0.7% of GDP. Since PSD2 entered into force in 2018 in Europe, the number of BigTech firms with a licensed payment subsidiary in the EEA has grown significantly. Facebook, Alipay, Airbnb and Google Payments all acquired an EEA payment-related license in 2018, followed by Uber in 2019.[3] BigTechs could quickly become systemically important — or "too big to fail," stressing the importance of cross-sectoral and cross-border cooperative regulatory arrangements.[4]

BigTech firms raise the question of the applicable regulation and supervision. Their large size, global nature and complexity may be a problem for regulators. According to the FSB, BigTech could "potentially affect financial stability in three ways: (1) even if their isolated financial activities might not be systemic, they could cumulatively generate significant financial risk, especially because these could be scaled-up very rapidly, (2) risks could be magnified by their interlinkages with regulated financial entities, such as partnerships to originate and distribute financial products, and (3) they could generate risks as they carry out a systemically important activity ancillary to financial services, such as cloud services."[5] In fact, most FinTechs and BigTechs already evidence a strong dependence on a small number of technology providers such as cloud. The Bank of England, in a 2020 survey, estimated that more than 70% of banks and 80% of insurers rely on just two cloud providers for IaaS (Infrastructure as a service). Globally, 52% of cloud services are provided by just two BigTech entities, while more than

---

[3]Financial Stability Board (2019). BigTech in finance: Market developments and potential financial stability implications. Available at https://www.fsb.org/2019/12/bigtech-in-finance-market-developments-and-potential-financial-stability-implications/. Last accessed October 6, 2021.

[4]Bank for International Settlements (2021). Big techs in finance: Regulatory approaches and policy options. Juan Carlos Crisanto, Johannes Ehrentraud and Marcos Fabian, March 2021, FSI Briefs No. 12. Available at https://www.bis.org/fsi/fsibriefs12.htm. Last accessed October 6, 2021, p. 1.

[5]See footnote 3.

two-thirds of services are provided by four BigTechs.[6] BigTech firms could potentially pose a threat to financial stability. The BIS also lists the three types of risks arising with BigTechs, including traditional financial risks (such as credit exposure), the interconnectedness between non-financial and financial activities (contagion) and operational risks (such as BigTech operating as third-party cloud service providers for financial services). This is not to say that BigTech completely escapes any form of regulations. The current regulatory framework includes activity-based rules as well as cross-sectional regulations applied to all activities, such as consumer protection.

Antitrust is another meaningful risk, if BigTechs were to become dominant in financial services.[7] However, competition authorities estimate that competition law is flexible enough and can adapt to the challenges of the digital economy, including financial innovation and the entrance of BigTech firms into financial services.[8]

Moreover, BigTech, because of their international nature and because they do not operate banking licenses, raise the question of regulatory arbitrage. Supervisors regularly question whether the additional efficiency of BigTechs stems from superior efficiency or from relaxed regulatory requirements vis-à-vis banks. It is true that most BigTech firms are already subject to activity-based regulations such as anti-money laundering and consumer protection rules. Policymakers debate whether one should favor regulation of entities (in which case BigTech would not be supervised) or regulation of activities (in which case the type of legal entity adopted by the

---

[6]Bank of England (2020). How reliant are banks and insurers on cloud outsourcing? Available at https://www.bankofengland.co.uk/bank-overground/2020/how-reliant-are-banks-and-insurers-on-cloud-outsourcing. Last accessed October 6, 2021.

[7]See the US investigation of competition in digital markets (2020) at https://judiciary.house.gov/uploadedfiles/competition_in_digital_markets.pdf?utm_campaign=4493--519; for the European Union, see the Digital Markets Act and Digital Services Act (2020).

[8]G7 (2019). Common understanding of G7 competition authorities on "Competition and the Digital Economy". Paris, June 2019.

company is irrelevant). In China, regulators have gradually adopted the approach to analyze financial conglomerates, bringing BigTech firms under their perimeter. Potential monopolistic behavior and microlending practices by Alipay and WeChat Pay drew the attention of the Central Bank, triggering notices by the China Banking and Insurance Regulatory Commission and leading for example to the postponement of Ant Financials' IPO in 2020 and the definition of new policies.

Is China representative of a risk present in all jurisdictions or rather a point outside of the curve? Outside of China, BigTechs have made only a small dent into lending, focusing mostly on payments for now. The volume of credit extended by BigTech firms varies considerably by geography. In China, new credit extended by BigTech firms in 2017 amounted to around 1.5% of the stock of total non-bank credit. Globally, according to BIS, the stock of credit conceded by FinTech and BigTech was just 0.3% of total credit at the end of 2018.[9] Moreover, in some jurisdictions such as the US, there are regulatory requirements that separate banking and commerce. Specifically, the US legal framework prohibits deposit-taking banks, or their corporate affiliates, from engaging in commercial activities, albeit with limited exceptions. Amazon, for example, has launched its payments offering (Amazing Pay), credit (Amazon Lending) and insurance (Amazon Protect) under new legal entities.

The chart shows the breakdown of alternative credit. Within the category of alternative credit, BigTech market share is higher in South Korea, Argentina and Brazil, being above 40% (Figure 1). In 2018, BigTechs' core businesses accounted for around 46% of their revenues, while financial services represented about 11%.[10] At present, financial services represent a relatively small part of

---

[9]Bank for International Settlements (2020). FinTech and BigTech Credit: A new data base. BIS Working Paper No. 887. Available at https://www.bis.org/publ/work887.htm. Last accessed October 6, 2021.

[10]Bank for International Settlements (2021). Big techs in finance: Regulatory approaches and policy options. Juan Carlos Crisanto, Johannes Ehrentraud and Marcos Fabian, March 2021, FSI Briefs No. 12. Available at https://www.bis.org/fsi/fsibriefs12.htm. Last accessed October 6, 2021, p. 5.

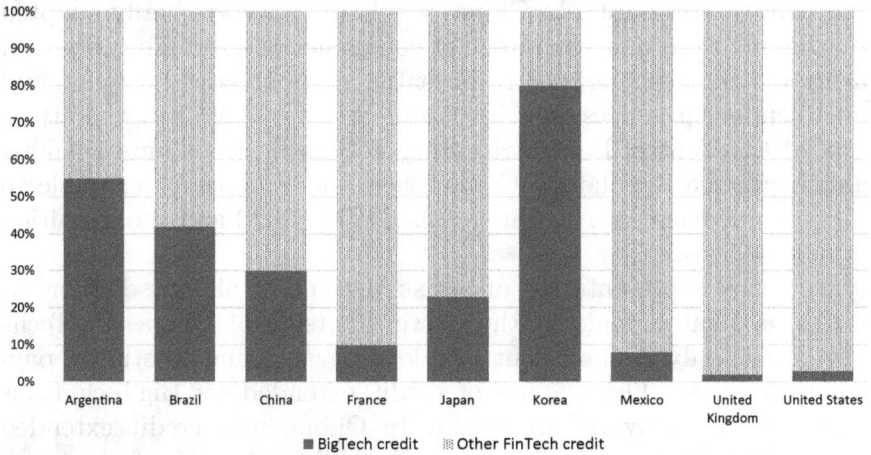

Figure 1: Credit Extension by BigTech and FinTech Firms
Source: BIS (2020a) based on Cambridge Centre for Alternative Finance, 2017 data.

BigTechs' overall activities, though this could change rapidly. The often quoted statement by Bill Gates in the 90s that we will always need banking but we will not need banks has not become reality.

So far, BigTechs have used existing rails and partnered with banks rather than trying to create new autonomous architecture. Partnerships take numerous forms: BigTech firms provide technology services and infrastructure (e.g. cloud computing and data analytics) to financial institutions; and vice versa, i.e. incumbent financial institutions provide their infrastructure and funding to operationalize BigTech firms' offering of financial services. Such partnerships can also take the form of 'interfacing', where BigTech firms act as intermediaries between financial institutions and their customers. BigTechs can favor collaboration, as in the example of Amazon and JPMorgan to offer credit cards, where Amazon provides the customer-facing layer.

The emergence of BigTech and FinTech firms and their oscillation between competition and collaboration with incumbents illustrate the principle of creative destruction. Creative destruction creates a "contradiction at the very heart of the growth process". While on the one hand, "rents are necessary to reward innovation and thereby motivate innovators; on the other hand, yesterday's innovators must not use their rents to impede new innovations." In his book on the power of creative destruction, Aghion analyzes the mechanisms of innovation and explains that it is possible to overcome this contradiction by regulating capitalism or "saving capitalism from the capitalists."[11]

Sotelino highlights the tension between incumbents and challengers, and the need to constantly strive for agility, even as the organization grows. As challengers gain market share and relevance, and incumbents adjust their processes, products and workforce, he sees a convergence process. For challengers, he described the "asymptotic growth" of firms, which can only be changed with the launch of new products and new geographies.

All banks follow a three-pronged strategy of large product scope, diversified geography, and leadership in each of those products and locations, according to Sotelino.[12] Innovation can stem from incumbents. In his view, three factors explain the success of Marcus, the digital retail arm launched by Goldman Sachs in 2016, namely the availability and stability of funding, the access to capital, and the favorable market structure, both in terms of the addressable market and competitive forces. He highlights the strategic choice to make visible the affiliation with the controlling group through its brand "Marcus, by Goldman Sachs".[13]

Why are BigTechs still relatively shy in the provision of financial services, outside of China? It may be just a matter of time. It may be that financial services are not that profitable, as credit requires accurate pricing models and access to ample funding. Returns of financial activities tend to be meaningfully lower than the core business of BigTechs. BigTechs may want to focus on their core strengths and

---

[11] Aghion, P. *et al.* (2021). *The Power of Creative Destruction.* Belknap Harvard, p. 5.

[12] Finel-Honigman, I. and Sotelino, F. B. (2015). *International Banking for a New Century.* Routledge.

[13] Interview with Fernando B. Sotelino, Adjunct Professor of international banking and business strategy for financial institutions at Columbia University's School of International and Public Affairs (SIPA), former President of Unibanco (Brazil's third largest private sector bank), November 10, 2021.

value added, which is to serve the end customers, and manufacturing financial products may sometimes be less effective than simply distributing those. However, adding financial capabilities has been driven by the desire to diversify revenue streams, further monetize their client base, potentially increase client loyalty and raise switching cost, and acquire a new source of data on their clients.

Moreover, BigTech may not be able to tap enough funding and capital to grow credit. There are limitations to the originate-to-distribute business models, whereby BigTechs (and FinTechs) originate credit and resell it immediately in the form of securitized vehicles, so as not to consume their balance sheets and scarce access to funding. Carstens asks "how much skin in the game do BigTech firms keep," when a new originate-to-distribute model creates incentive problems and financial instability.[14]

To summarize, BigTech can potentially disintermediate traditional banks and make the financial sector more efficient, lead to improved customer outcomes and boost financial inclusion. However, it may create or increase risks for financial stability and consumer protection, and comes with challenges for competition, data privacy and cyber security. So far, BigTechs have been mostly present in payments while their share in credit is small but rising. Several voices have stressed that "relevant risks are not fully captured by the regulatory approach up to now"[15] and that current policy does not recognize "the potential systemic impact of incidents in BigTech operations" (Table 1).[16]

---

[14]Bank for International Settlements (2018). Big tech in finance and new challenges for public policy. Keynote address by Agustín Carstens. General Manager, Bank for International Settlements. FT Banking Summit London, 4 December 2018, p. 6.

[15]Bank for International Settlements (2020). FinTech and BigTech Credit: A new data base. BIS Working Paper No. 887. Available at https://www.bis.org/publ/work887.htm. Last accessed October 6, 2021, p. 12.

[16]Bank for International Settlements (2021). "Public policy for BigTechs in finance", introductory remarks by Mr Agustin Carstens at the Asia School of Business Conversations on Central Banking webinar, "Finance as information", Basel, 21 January. Available at https://www.bis.org/speeches/sp210121.htm. Last accessed October 6, 2021.

Table 1: Services Offered by BigTechs

BigTech	Main Business	Banking	Credit	Payments	Crowd-Funding	Asset Management	Insurance
Google	Internet search/advertising	Yes		Yes			
Apple	Tech/producing hardware			Yes			
Facebook	Social media/advertising			Yes			
Amazon	E-commerce/online retail		Yes	Yes	Yes		Yes
Alibaba (Ant Group)	E-commerce/online retail	Yes	Yes	Yes	Yes	Yes	Yes
Baidu (Du Xiaoman)	Internet search/advertising	Yes	Yes	Yes	Yes	Yes	Yes
JD.com (JD Digits)	E-commerce/online retail	Yes	Yes	Yes	Yes	Yes	Yes
Tencent	Tech/gaming and messaging	Yes	Yes	Yes	Yes	Yes	Yes
NTT Docomo	Mobile communications	Yes	Yes	Yes	Yes		
Rakuten	E-commerce/online retail	Yes	Yes	Yes		Yes	Yes
Mercado Libre	E-commerce/online retail		Yes	Yes		Yes	

Source: BIS (2021). Big techs in finance: Regulatory approaches and policy options, p. 3. Juan Carlos Crisanto, Johannes Ehrentraud and Marcos Fabian, March 2021, FSI Briefs No. 12, p. 1. Available at https://www.bis.org/fsi/fsibriefs12.htm. Last accessed October 6, 2021.

Crowd Funding and Peer to Peer Lending: What Potential?

When customers have a hard time finding capital via banks, what if they could go directly to sources of funding? Could technology enable models where the supply and demand of capital meet without the need for financial intermediaries? Will it be possible to fund the next successful entrepreneur with this type of mechanism and fulfill the promise that crowdfunding "makes it possible for an entrepreneur in Kenya to more easily engage investors and customers anywhere; whether that be locally, the diaspora, or with others anywhere in the world," so that "the developing world has the potential to leapfrog developed countries."[17]

infoDev defines crowdfunding as "an internet-enabled way for businesses or other organizations to raise money in the form of either donations or investments from multiple individuals."[18] Crowdfunding is essentially a digital version of the traditional funding via family and friends, allowing entrepreneurs to potentially reach a much wider net of contacts. It pools a large number of savers together with the goal to fulfill a project or business. This is akin to what banks do (grouping savers and connecting them with the demand for capital), but the nature of this intermediation differs.

Crowdfunding, either for debt or equity, builds on the success of crowdsourcing platforms such as Kickstarter. Kickstarter lists projects that receive donations, while charging a fee of 5% on the amounts raised. As of July 2021, 38.9% of Kickstarter's projects were successfully funded, a precondition for backers to be debited. Since its launch in 2009 and up to July 2021, it helped raise $59 billion. From the viewpoint of entrepreneurs, crowdfunding may be a link between minimum viable projects and venture capital. FinTech blurs the border between banking services and capital markets, creating frameworks for early-stage finance that facilitate entrepreneurship,

---

[17]World Bank (2013). Crowdfunding's potential for the developing world. Washington, DC. Available at https://openknowledge.worldbank.org/handle/10986/1 7626. Last accessed on October 6, 2021, pp. 4–9.

[18]World Bank (2013). Crowdfunding's potential for the developing world. Washington, DC.

fostering innovative technology enterprises and the emergence of new competitive industries.

Fundraising for young companies has become a focus of policy-making. In April 2012, President Obama signed into law the Jumpstart Our Business Startups (JOBS) Act with the goal of reducing regulatory restrictions on raising capital for young and small businesses. The move legalized equity investments by non-accredited investors, even considering that a total loss of investment is possible in those types of early-stage investments.

In Brazil, the CVM (Securities Commission) published its initial guideline for the sector of equity crowdfunding on August 8, 2016.[19] The 68-page long document deals with small issuances of public securities with no prior approval by the CVM and that raise funds via crowdfunding on electronic platforms. In this document, the CVM attempted to strike a balance between the need to provide more sources of funding for small companies and provide adequate protection for investors and crowdfunding platforms. Crowdfunding was born as a marginal source of funding for companies, with 43 offerings in 2015 and roughly $10 million raised. It soon showed its limitations.

The CVM proposed two relevant regulatory changes to relax requirements for companies that are looking to list. Brazilian Corporate Law required registration and approval of issuances by the CVM as well as the participation of a financial intermediary to distribute those securities. The CVM, however, can waive those two requirements in select cases. Those issuances need to be below R$2.4 million (a cap that could be increased to R$5 million or roughly US$1 million) and apply to limited partnerships (this rule could be relaxed to apply crowdfunding to all companies with annual revenues below R$10 million). The new regulation would also clarify the role of crowdfunding platforms and require their registration with the CVM, a key element to strengthen the sector.

Improving the existing platforms is also key to the growth of the segment. Importantly for companies, investors and other market

---

[19]Comissão de Valores Mobiliários (2016). Edital de audiência pública SDM No 06/2016, on "Investment-Based Crowdfunding", August 2016. Available at http://conteudo.cvm.gov.br/export/sites/cvm/audiencias_publicas/ap_sdm/a nexos/2016/sdm0616edital.pdf. Last accessed on October 6, 2021.

participants, the CVM document highlights the following: (1) the importance of isonomy of the platform, which should be open to all companies that meet some clear predefined requirements; (2) the focus on disclosure and equal access to information; (3) rules to reduce risks to investors; and (4) the need to reduce the risk for conflicts of interests. In fact, some existing platforms adopted mixed characteristics of private equity fund managers, market analysts and exchanges. The document also clarifies the concept of a Brazilian syndicate, where retail investors follow a lead investor, self-defined as an expert in private investments; an imprecise translation of the US concept of a syndicate. Risks for investors include the limited level of information available, the absence of liquidity of those investments and potential dilution on future rounds of capital raise.

In Peru, the Peruvian Securities Market Superintendency (SMV) gave the green light to crowdfunding and crowdequity regulations in 2021.[20] With the regulation, platforms will be allowed to mediate investments in those two instruments. The SMV published in November 2020 the draft regulation and offered to gather comments from the industry and included several points of feedback. One of the alterations was the reduction of the minimum required capital to platforms to PEN 300k or roughly US$75,000 (from 400,000 in the initial proposal). Also, the crowdfunding agent now has 24 months (up from 12 months initially) to achieve the minimal capital required. In the second year of operations, capital may be no less than 80% of the requirement, ending the second year at 100%. The platform's responsibility was also one of the key points that evolved. In the initial draft, the platform was deemed responsible for evaluating the risks of every venture that would receive the financing, so that investors would know the level of risk they were exposed to. The revised version of the regulation demanded that the platform confirms that all information is disclosed to investors, so that they can make their own evaluation. The regulation was meant to facilitate access to funds for small and medium-sized companies. Peru also

---

[20]Superintendencia de Mercado e Valores (2021). Reglamento de la actividad de financiamento participativo financiero y sus sociedades administradas. Available at https://elperuano.pe/NormasElperuano/2021/05/20/1954665-1/1954665-1.ht m. Last accessed October 6, 2021.

announced its intention to launch its own sandbox, a move that is aligned with other countries in the region, most notably Brazil and Colombia.

Crowdequity and crowdfunding can play a role for incipient, smaller-sized projects, or projects that have a specific appeal to a community or group of like-minded people. While crowdfunding sounded promising a decade ago, the success of crowdfunding platforms has been limited. Raised amounts pale in comparison with transactions on capital markets or banking loan books. Peer-to-peer platforms have experienced mixed success, highlighting the classical functions of screening and monitoring performed by financial intermediaries. Overall, peer-to-peer lending and crowdequity are based on the misunderstanding that banks' primary role is only to source funding. Finance is not a product like the others, it suffers from asymmetries of information.

Start-ups' high-failure rate presents a risk of loss of capital for investors and securities law typically tries to protect retail investors against excessive risk-taking. Moreover, platforms have a key responsibility by presenting the opportunities to investors but stop short of performing due diligence or taking responsibility for the poor performance of select investments, raising the question of their role as intermediary and the ability of investors to perform in-depth financial analysis. Platforms may also suffer from adverse selection, as best-in-class start-ups may have direct access to venture capital and private equity, leaving other less successful start-ups to rely on platforms.

Disintermediation of Banks by Capital Markets and Venture Capital

FinTechs will displace incumbents in some of their functions and force them to rethink their strengths. On the flip side, from a regulatory standpoint, FinTechs will adapt and incorporate the same rules as regulated players. Financial services will remain essentially the same: economic actors will continue to require credit, savings and protection, but the delivery and features of those products will evolve. Technology will be the backbone of financial services delivery in the short term. Select incumbents may not adapt fast enough to changes, and will be replaced by new players with digital characteristics.

That being said, in some instances, disintermediation may come from a different type of player, namely capital markets and private capital. This will depend on the best vehicles to finance innovation. Do banks present the characteristics to source, select, finance and nurture the types of business models that will support tomorrow's economy or should we look elsewhere for sources of capital?

Banks may not be the best vehicle to finance innovative ventures. As noted by Banerjee and Duflo in the context of microentrepreneurs accessing loans, "this problem stems from the structure of banks," as large organizations, which find it hard to screen and monitor small projects. If banks decide to "punish loan officers for default (which, to a point, they must), loan officers start looking for the absolutely safest projects, which are unlikely to be small, unknown firms."[21] Research underscores the importance of venture capital in funding young, innovative firms. Aghion notes that in 2005, startups — defined as firms that have existed less than one year — generated 142% of net new jobs in the United States.[22]

While emphasizing the importance of rising entrepreneurs, Patton Power explains that for a majority of them, venture capital does not offer the appropriate source of funds. Small firms may not present the growth profile expected by venture capitalists, nor may the traditional funding instruments be adequate for them. The author explains that, alongside equity, debt, loans and grants, those entrepreneurs may need or prefer other vehicles, including quasi-equity, mezzanine financing or trade finance. This will eventually depend on their business characteristics, future funding needs and the desire of founders to potentially lose control in the future.[23]

Similarly, debt or loans may not be the best financial instrument to finance innovative unproven business ventures. Debt can be an excellent instrument for more mature businesses, which can commit to a regular repayment of principal and interest, and for banks, which benefit from the frequent and predefined dates to monitor the health

---

[21]Banerjee, A. V. and Duflo, E. (2011). *Poor Economics*. New York: Perseus Books, p. 180.

[22]Aghion, P. *et al.* (2021). *The Power of Creative Destruction*. Belknap Harvard, pages 5 and 237.

[23]Patton Power, A. (2021). *Adventure Finance, How to Create a Funding Journey That Blends Profit and Purpose*. London: Palgrave Macmillan.

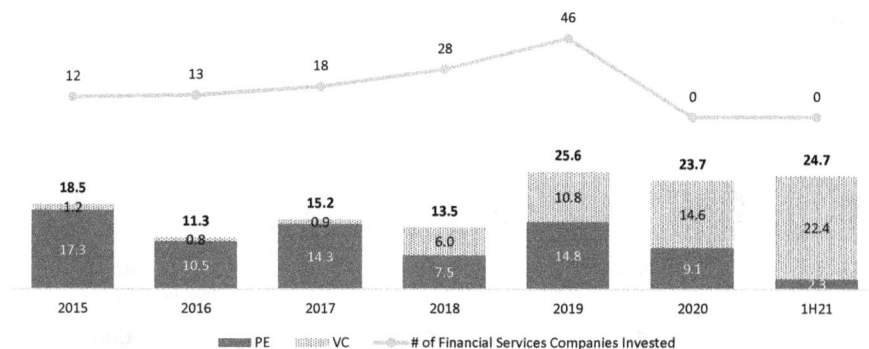

Figure 2: Rapid Growth in Private Equity Funding: Investments in Private Equity and Venture Capital in Brazil (R$, bn)
Source: ABVCAP, Brazilian Association for Venture Capital and Private Equity. Data available at https://www.abvcap.com.br/pesquisas/estudos.aspx?c=en-us.

of their borrowers. Debt may not be the right fit to finance high-risk early ventures, where failure or uncertain cash flows may not match the required regular repayments. We should not expect microcredit or larger credit lines to fill this gap.

Venture capital and private equity funds have experienced strong growth in the recent past, especially to fund innovative businesses such as FinTech and BigTech business models (Figure 2).

Research on adequate public policies to foster innovation emphasizes the existence of market failures and the role that accelerators and incubators can play to identify and nurture high-potential entrepreneurs and business ideas.[24] Policymakers can also incentivize innovation with the tool of regulatory sandboxes, as discussed in a previous chapter.

In some instances, innovative companies also forego the services of banking intermediaries and access investors directly on an exchange. Banks and broker-dealers act as underwriters of transactions, either in equities or fixed income, and broker-dealers perform trading services to provide liquidity for buyers and sellers of securities. Cases occur where banking intermediaries are removed from the equation,

---

[24]Gonzalez-Uribe, J. and Reyes, S. (2019). Identifying and boosting 'Gazelles': Evidence from business accelerators. Available at SSRN: https://ssrn.com/abstract=3478290 or http://dx.doi.org/10.2139/ssrn.3478290.

foregoing investment banking fees. Direct listing is one such instance where a company follows listing rules on its own without the intervention of an investment bank and lists directly on a stock exchange, as in the case of Coinbase, which listed on Nasdaq in April 2021.

Yunus identified this issue in his work with microentrepreneurs and proposed to connect investors with social businesses in a new type of social stock market where only the shares of social businesses will be traded. This type of stock market would attract a special type of like-minded investors, developing a new sector of rating agencies, standardized terminology and reporting, and impact measurement tools. This type of exchange has not yet materialized in any relevant size.

While it is too soon in our view to call a "Kodak moment" for banks, it is clear that threats have increased, coming from FinTechs, BigTechs and from the disintermediation of capital markets, putting at risk banks' business models and requiring banks to rethink their purpose.

Conclusion: The Way Forward

The financial system is inherently based on innovation, and recent years have shown an acceleration in this trend. Technology bears the promise of a radical transformation in financial services. This revolution is currently taking place. Inclusion has made considerable progress and sometimes led to excesses. Examples in China, Brazil, Mexico, and Kenya show the untapped social and financial opportunity of financial inclusion.

Technology jumps enabled innovation with the rise of the internet, better connectivity and mobile networks, or the growth of new models with the blockchain. Importantly, our understanding of those trends benefited vastly from considerable progress made in the fields of economy and social sciences, with novel ideas and debates including information asymmetries and two-sided platforms, and innovative research methodologies such as randomized controlled trials, financial diaries or the creation of longer econometric time series.

Innovation requires regulation so that today's disruptors do not become the incumbents of tomorrow and try to secure monopolistic rents. While the role of policy is essential, policymakers should not substitute the private sector, providing payment systems, public credit or picking champions. Regulators have been more successful innovating with adapted rules, sandboxes and a functional "same risk, same rule" approach to supervision.

Beyond the business aspect, this is a unique opportunity for societies to build a more open and inclusive financial system, which can foster development and alleviate poverty, provide safety nets, and allow citizens and businesses to deploy their full potential thanks to quality, affordable and tailored finance. Similar to the advent of the internet 25 years ago, financial technology may reinforce the existing divide in our societies, or — if we are successful — bear the promise of a more inclusive society. FinTech is not the latest silver bullet, nor is it the latest fad. It can have a significant positive impact if designed, regulated, supervised and supported the right way.

In lieu of a sweeping conclusion, we raise an open question for regulators, entrepreneurs and researchers of the ideal delivery of financial services in the future. Will banks be displaced by FinTech and BigTech firms, or absorb them? How should forces eventually combine for the most efficient and inclusive financial intermediation process? This is a topic of first-order importance for theoretical and empirical research as banking services experience a historic transition.

List of Figures

Chapter 4

Chapter 5

Chapter 6

Chapter 7

Chapter 8

Chapter 9

List of Tables

Index

www.ingramcontent.com/pod-product-compliance
Lightning Source LLC
Chambersburg PA
CBHW052111230326
41599CB00055B/5579